Tithing Practices Among Seventh-day Adventists

A Study of Tithe Demographics and Motives in
Australia, Brazil, England, Kenya and the United States

Revised Edition

by Robert K. McIver

ASTR Research Monographs

D. J. B. Trim, General Editor

Number 1

Tithing Practices Among Seventh-day Adventists

Tithing Practices Among Seventh-day Adventists

A Study of Tithe Demographics and Motives in Australia, Brazil, England, Kenya and the United States

Revised Edition

by Robert K. McIver

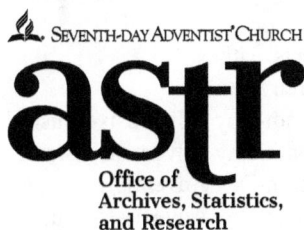

Avondale
ACADEMIC PRESS

SEVENTH-DAY ADVENTIST CHURCH
astr
Office of
Archives, Statistics,
and Research

Co-published by:
Avondale Academic Press
PO Box 19
Cooranbong NSW 2265
Australia

and

Office of Archives, Statistics, and Research
General Conference of Seventh-day Adventists
12501 Old Columbia Pike
Silver Spring MD 20904
United States of America

Copy editor: Howard Fisher
Cover Design: Ann Stafford

National Library of Australia Cataloguing-in-Publication entry

Creator: McIver, Robert K., author.

Title: Tithing practices among Seventh-Day Adventists: a study of tithe demographics
  and motives in Australia, Brazil, England, Kenya and the United States / Robert
  K. McIver.

ISBN: 9780959933703 (paperback)
ISBN: 9780958159197 (ebook)

Subjects: Tithes.
  Church finance.
  Seventh-Day Adventists--Australia.
  Seventh-Day Adventists--Brazil.
  Seventh-Day Adventists--England.
  Seventh-Day Adventists--United States.

Dewey Number: 248.6

Table of Contents

List of Tables

List of Figures

Preface

It is a great pleasure to contribute a preface to this book and to the series of monographs it inaugurates. Dr. Rob McIver's study of tithing practices among Seventh-day Adventists in Africa, Australia, Europe, North America, and South America, is the by-product of a multi-year research project funded by the General Conference of Seventh-day Adventists through its Office of Archives, Statistics, and Research—or ASTR (based at the Seventh-day Adventist Church's world headquarters in Silver Spring, Maryland). Research in Brazil, England, Kenya and the United States was financed and supervised by ASTR, and much of this book is drawn from Dr. McIver's report. This book additionally, however, draws on research McIver carried out some years earlier in Australia. The result is an excellent example of social-science research: highly professional human-subject research (both quantitative and qualitative) is integrated with financial research, and with adept and insightful statistical analysis. We in ASTR are delighted to be able to co-publish, with Avondale Academic Press, the fruit of Rob McIver's research—it makes a splendid first volume in our new ASTR Research Monographs Series.

In Seventh-day Adventist thought, tithe is not something church members give. Rather, Adventists "return" tithe, reflecting a biblical understanding that 10 per cent of one's income is already God's. In consequence, while offerings are considered to be a measure of generosity, tithing is considered to be a measure of faithfulness. What Rob McIver's research reveals, however, is that consistently returning a 10 per cent tithe is very frequently an indication of feeling close to God, even of feeling that one is in dialogue with God. I strongly suspect the same is true for offerings. While tithe is a measure of faithfulness, then, faithful tithing is caused not by a sense of obligation, but by a sense of being in relationship with our heavenly Father. That is a powerful spiritual point and has theological implications. Dr. McIver's data-laden study will repay the attention of academic specialists in philanthropy and ecclesiastical finance, practitioners of human-subject research, and sociologists and statisticians. But it also deserves the attention of theologians and other scholars of religious studies, church leaders of denominations that encourage tithing, and indeed any Christians who want to reflect on what it means to give; all would find it amply repays their reading. This is testimony to McIver's deep research and penetrating analysis, as well as to his personal understanding of the lived experience of Seventh-day Adventist Christians.

D. J. B. Trim
Director of Archives, Statistics, and Research
General Conference of Seventh-day Adventists
Silver Spring, MD, 2016

Foreword

Where it all Started

This book provides an analysis of the results of a large research project that eventually took 15 years and spanned five countries in five different continents, yet its origins can be traced back to an almost off-hand remark made in a committee in 1999. It was during the discussion of the conference financial reports by the Executive Committee of the North New South Wales Conference of Seventh-day Adventists that the youngest member of the Committee made a short speech to the effect that, "My generation is not tithing as they should. Somebody should study that because if we are not careful the future of the conference is at risk."

The Committee agreed that the question, "Who is tithing and why?", is something that should be studied, and it transpired that I and Steve Currow were those tasked to undertake the research in North New South Wales. The research that started in one region of Australia eventually evolved to encompass a project that gathered data from five different countries scattered across the globe and which was conducted at the behest of the General Conference of Seventh-day Adventists (details of the progress of the research may be found in Appendix A, "The Development of the Survey Instrument and Progress of the Research Project"). At each stage, the research has concentrated on two main questions. The first was raised back in 1999 – "What is the tithing behavior of the different age-groups that make up the congregations found in Seventh-day Adventist churches?" The second question was, "What is motivating Seventh-day Adventists to tithe?"

Who Are the Expected Readers of this Book?

This book is written in a manner that makes it suited to at least four general groups of readers:
1. Academics and Researchers who are interested in the demographics of and motivations for giving behaviour;
2. Professionals such as church pastors, church administrators, Conference Union and Division Stewardship Directors, local church stewardship secretaries, Conference and local church treasurers, and other professionals who are interested in what is motivating church

members to tithe and other factors that influence giving;

3.   PhD students and early career researchers who would welcome the ability to access details of survey design, tested scales (with a report on the Cronbach's Alpha for each scale), adaptation of surveys to various cultures in a manner that retains the statistical reliability of the results of using the adapted survey instrument, and other considerations which might assist them;

4.   Other individuals who are interested in patterns of and motives for giving.

How to Use this Book

The book is designed so that the main findings of the research may be found in the very first chapter (Headline Results), and the details of the evidence on which these findings are based are progressively revealed in the subsequent chapters. Thus, readers have easy access to the most important results and are able to determine for themselves how deeply they wish to be acquainted with the details of the research.

Those looking for the fastest way to find the main outcomes of the research should read Chapter 1 (Headline results), Chapter 10 (Conclusions), and perhaps the chapter detailing the results for their country of residence. These are the very chapters that professionals such as church pastors, stewardship directors and stewardship secretaries would probably be most interested to read. Some of the results given in the tables in Appendices D and E may also be of interest to such professionals.

Academics and researchers will be interested in Chapter 2 (Methodological Considerations), and the detailed analysis of results found in the body of the book. They will be able to use the material in the appendices in a manner that suits their research needs and professional interest. For some the listing of the various items that make up the scales will be of interest (Appendix B), and others will welcome the extra detail of responses to various items in the survey provided by the tables in Appendices D, E and F.

PhD students and other early career researchers may find the details regarding of the development of the survey instrument in Appendix A of interest and value. They may be very interested in the scales in Appendix B, and in the actual surveys that were used in Appendix C.

In sum the book is written in a manner than allows all readers to choose the level at which they wish to interact with the analysis of the data gathered in this research and its analysis.

My Thanks to ...

At every stage of this research I have been repeatedly struck by the reserves of good will within the Seventh-day Adventist Church from which I have been able to draw. This is evidenced by the responses of the conference leadership teams who had very little warning of the project before my arrival (especially in Central Kenya and São Paulo), by the willingness of those working at the local conference offices and the field ministers to fit this very large project into their already intolerably heavy workloads and, most of all, by the literally thousands of church attenders who took time out to fill in a survey. To all church administrators, departmental directors, secretaries and personal assistants, field ministers, and the many church-attenders who have been involved in the research project I give my heartfelt thanks. I would also like to thank my research assistants who have contributed to various parts of the project, including data entry, data manipulation, scanning, and translation. I thank David Trim for recruiting me to do this research and for providing sage advice and support during the project, the Future Plans Working Group for funding the research, Emeritus Professor Paul Bierne (Dean and CEO of Melbourne College of Divinity/MCD University of Divinity 2001 to 2012 and currently Director Heart of Life Spirituality Centre) and Dr Brad Kemp (President New Zealand Pacific Union Conference of Seventh-day Adventists) for their insightful and helpful academic referee's reports. For all of this and more, I give thanks to everybody who has been involved. Thank you!

Rob McIver
Cooranbong September 2016.

1. Headline Results

1.1 Overview of Research

This book reports the results of research into tithing practices and motivations among Seventh-day Adventists in five different countries located in five different continents.[1] Two distinct data sets were employed to form an accurate picture of both self-reported and actual tithing practices. The first data stream derived from a survey instrument designed to reveal tithing behavior and what motivates Seventh-day Adventists to return tithe. The second was derived from an analysis of receipts of actual tithe donations.

The survey was conducted in four countries: in the year 2012 in the Northern California Conference (NCC) in the United States, in the South England Conference (SEC) in the United Kingdom, in the São Paulo Conference (SPC) in Brazil; and in 2006 in the Western Australia Conference (WAC) in Australia. This report is based in part on 8,058 surveys collected during that period (3,370 from NCC, 1,055 from SEC, 1,973 from SPC and 1,660 from WAC).

The tithe receipts from Conferences in five countries were analyzed. The resultant data set is based on an analysis of 118,230 separate tithe receipts (38,038 receipts representing a total value of $10,670,311 from NCC; 34,358 receipts representing £3,574,998 from SEC; 22,417 representing R$6,656,649 from SPC; 22,219 receipts representing $3,072,308 from WAC; and 1,195 receipts representing KSh4,891,486 from Central Kenya Conference (CKC). Several matters stand out as of importance from the analysis of these two data sets.

1.2 Majority of Tithers Report "God HAS blessed me"

The overwhelming majority of those who tithe 8% or more of their income believe that "God has blessed them because they tithe." Of the

1 The research reported here was supported by a grant from the Future Plans Working Group of the General Conference of Seventh-day Adventists. The contract was signed in October 2011 by Juan Prestol (then under-treasurer) and D. J. B. Trim (Archives, Statistics and Research) of the General Conference of Seventh-day Adventists, and Paul Hattingh (vice-president, finance) and Robert K. McIver (principal investigator) of Avondale College of Higher Education.

3,138 responses to this question, fully 1,846 (or 59%) strongly agreed, and a further 712 (23%) agreed more than disagreed. For such individuals, it is in their tithing that they can see the hand of God in their lives, and in a most practical manner. Figure 1.1 shows the responses from those that tithed 8% or more of their income for the four conferences studied.

Fig. 1.1: "God HAS blessed me because I tithe" (%)

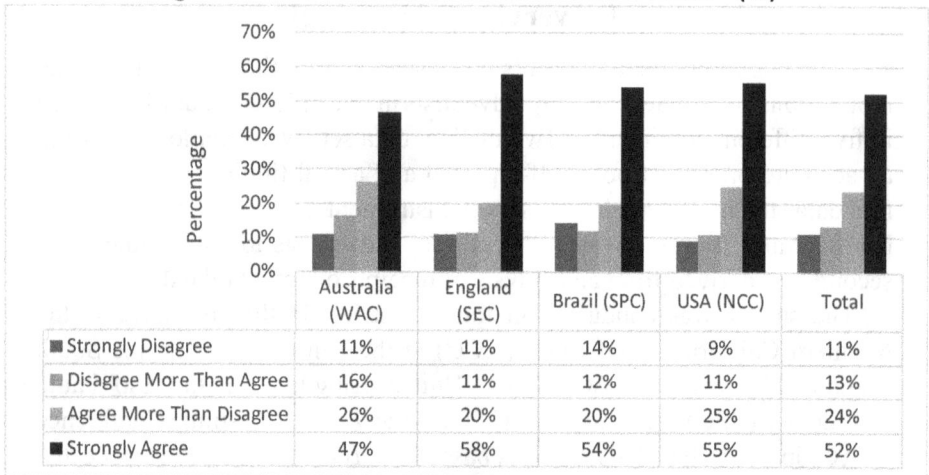

	Australia (WAC)	England (SEC)	Brazil (SPC)	USA (NCC)	Total
■ Strongly Disagree	11%	11%	14%	9%	11%
■ Disagree More Than Agree	16%	11%	12%	11%	13%
▨ Agree More Than Disagree	26%	20%	20%	25%	24%
■ Strongly Agree	47%	58%	54%	55%	52%

Curiously enough, while there was a small positive correlation between the motive for tithing, "Because God will bless," and tithing practice in Western Australia Conference, there was a small negative correlation in Northern California Conference, South England Conference and São Paulo Conference. In other words, the more the respondents thought they tithed "Because God will bless" them, the [marginally] less likely they were to tithe. On the other hand, in all the conferences studied (except São Paulo Conference) there was a strong correlation between the motive for tithing because of "Gratitude to God" and returning tithe. Thus it appears that in most places, tithing promotion that emphasizes the motive of gratitude to God would be much more effective than promotion that emphasizes the blessings of God to those that tithe, real though those blessings are. Stories about God's blessing to tithers should continue to be told, but they should be shared as evidence of God's presence in the lives of believers, not as a motive for tithing.

1.3 Proportion of Income Returned as Tithed Has Steadily Decreased for at Least the Last 40 Years

That Seventh-day Adventists return so much of their income to the church as tithe is a truly remarkable testament to their commitment to the church and its mission. Almost every year the amount of tithe received by the church increases in terms of the local currency in which it is given, and positive reports are presented to church-members thanking them for their contributions to the church. Yet this apparently healthy trend in the tithe received by the church hides an underlying problem. While the amount of tithe is increasing, so is the income of church-members and at a faster rate than tithe. When income and tithe are compared in Northern California, Southern England and Western Australia, the long term trend reveals that for at least the last 40 years the church has been receiving a smaller percentage of the income of its members as tithe. Figure 1.2 shows tithe against potential tithe (10% of average income) in the South England Conference since 1955. It may be observed that since 1975 at least, there has been an increasing gap between tithe and 10% of income (percentage figures may be found in Table 7.5 in Chapter 7; graphs and tables showing similar divergence between tithe and income for Northern California and Western Australia may be found in Table 5.8 and Figures 5.5 and 5.6 in Chapter 5, and Table 4.7 and Figures 4.5 and 4.6 in Chapter 4, respectively).

**Fig. 1.2: Per-capita Tithe (SEC) Compared
to 10% Average Income (Britain)**

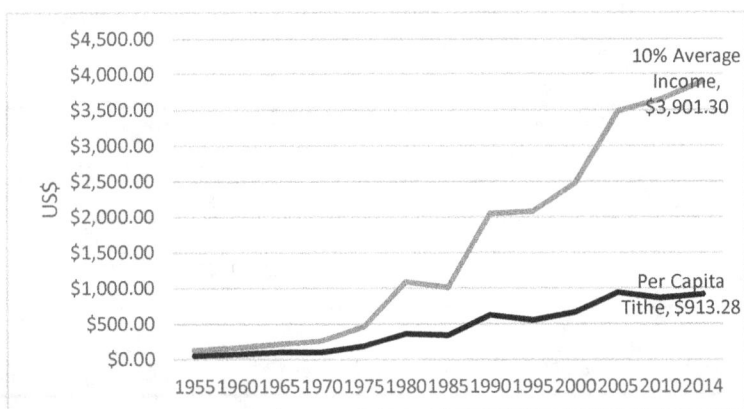

That church-members are returning a smaller proportion of their income as tithe has a significant impact on the ability of the church to sustain its mission. The research reported in this book provides an explanation of why a progressively smaller proportion of Adventist income is being returned as tithe, and points to several results which reveal that the trend of a decreasing proportion of income being returned as tithe is something that may be reversed.

1.4 There is a Willingness to Tithe Even Among Those who Tithe Sporadically or Not at All.

There is a significant willingness to tithe, even amongst those who are not currently tithing, or who tithe less than 10% of their income. Many respondents agreed that "I think I should tithe, I just need to get into the habit." This outcome emerged from an analysis of that part of the survey which begins by asking for a yes/no response to "I tithe a full 10% of my income." Those that responded "No" were asked the additional response option, "I do not currently give a full tithe, or do not give tithe. The following changes would need to happen before I would consider returning a full tithe." The response given most frequently to this additional option was, "I think I should tithe, but need to get into the habit."

In an effort to understand this phenomenon a little better, a statement, "Sometimes I forget to return tithe," was placed elsewhere in the survey and respondents were offered the opportunity to answer "Yes" or "No." An analysis of the responses revealed that there was a striking age-related difference in the responses to this option. In a cumulative tally from all of the surveys from the different countries, 782 of 1,686 (or 46%) of 20–39-yr-old respondents admitted, "Sometimes I forget to return tithe." As may be observed in Table 1.1, the proportion dropped to 32% for the 40–59-yr age-group; and to 23% for those aged 60 or older.

Table 1.1: Age-group vs "Sometimes I forget to tithe" (NCC, SEC, SPC, WAC)					
Age-group	No		Yes		Total
20-39	904	54%	782	46%	1,686
40-59	1,676	68%	785	32%	2,461
≥ 60	1,472	77%	446	23%	1,918
Total	4,052	67%	2,013	33%	6,065

Figure 1.3 (below) shows this trend very clearly.

Fig. 1.3: Age-group vs "Sometimes I forget to tithe" (%, NCC, SEC, SPC, WAC)

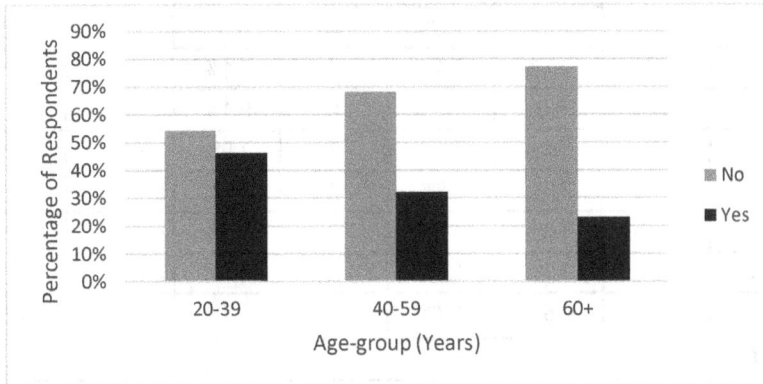

Differences in frequency of giving across the various age-groups, as reported in the survey, were also found in the analysis of tithe receipts from those churches whose members took part in the survey. While not a phenomenon unique to them, the younger age-groups are characterized by sporadic tithing. The differences in giving patterns were found to be statistically significant. Table 1.2 gives the breakdown of frequency of giving from the various age-groups that were found in the tithe receipts of Northern California Conference and São Paulo Conference (for SEC see Table 7.5 in Chapter 7, and for WAC see Tables 4.4 in Chapter 4). Wages are usually paid Monthly in Brazil (see Table 3.1 in Chapter 3), and thus a member who returned tithe each pay period would contribute at the maximum frequency of giving (12 times per year). The figures in the table represent the percentages from a particular age-group that gave tithe with the indicated frequency (once per annum, twice per annum, etc). In Northern California, the majority are paid semi-monthly (see Table 3.7). Thus if they returned tithe at every pay period, they would tithe at a frequency of 24 times per year. If those who were paid weekly (a smaller group) they would tithe at a frequency of 52 times per year. Table 1.2 reveals the percentages from the various age-groups that returned tithe at each particular frequency.

Table 1.2: Age vs Frequency of Returning Tithe (%; NCC & SPC)							
Northern California Conference, USA				São Paulo Conference, Brazil			
Freq	20-29 yr	40-49	60-69	Freq	20-29 yr	40-49	≥ 60
2	34.3%	13.4%	12.8%	1	14.8%	6.9%	5.3%
4	17.6%	9.5%	7.3%	2	11.6%	7.3%	4.6%

Table 1.2: Age vs Frequency of Returning Tithe (%; NCC & SPC)							
6	11.1%	8.9%	8.0%	3	8.4%	6.4%	5.0%
8	3.7%	5.0%	7.6%	4	11.1%	6.0%	4.0%
10	5.6%	9.7%	8.1%	5	7.1%	8.6%	3.8%
12	10.2%	15.6%	15.1%	6	9.1%	5.8%	5.2%
14	2.8%	6.4%	8.1%	7	7.9%	6.0%	5.6%
16	1.9%	3.3%	5.8%	8	8.1%	9.1%	7.1%
18	2.8%	5.0%	4.7%	9	7.6%	8.6%	9.2%
20	0.9%	4.2%	1.7%	10	4.7%	8.9%	9.9%
22	0.9%	2.5%	1.7%	11	3.7%	10.2%	14.5%
24	2.8%	4.5%	5.3%	12	5.9%	16.1%	25.8%
26	1.9%	3.9%	3.0%				
52	3.7%	8.1%	10.8%				

The contrast in the tithing behaviour of those aged from 20–29 years when compared to those aged 60 years or older is revealed in Figures 1.4 and 1.5, which show the frequency of giving for these two age-groups in Brazil (similar graphs for NCC may be found in Chapter 5, Figures 5.3 and 5.4).

Fig. 1.4: Frequency of Tithing 20–29-yr Age-group (SPC)

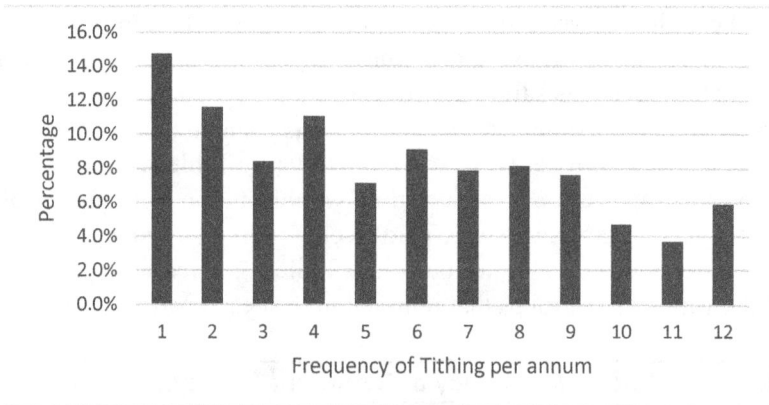

Fig. 1.5: Frequency of Tithing by those Aged ≥ 60 (SPC)

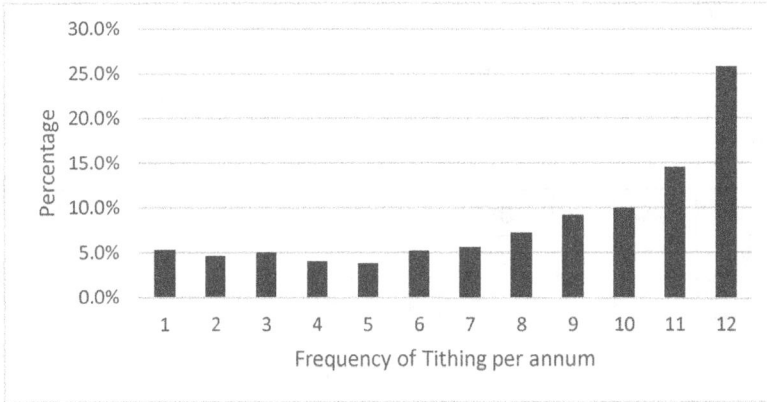

That the willingness to tithe on the part of those who "just need to get into the habit" has important practical implications for how the church manages its tithing processes is self-evident. This response from 623 of those who indicated that they do not tithe a full 10% of their income (55% of those in this category) indicates that these are members who are already convinced that they should tithe, but need to be provided with a means to do so regularly. In parts of the world where it is legal, automatic wage deductions are seen by some church-members as an ideal way to ensure that this takes place. Furthermore, giving culturally appropriate reminders about tithing as part of each regular worship service seems to be a practice that should be encouraged as an effective way to promote tithing.

1.5 Challenge Caused by Observation that Cash Not Used by 50% of Some Congregations

In some parts of the world church, less than 50% of the church-members use cash for purchases costing between $10 and $49. This is true of all age-groups. The church offering system during the worship service is suited to giving by cash or check, and tithe is also largely received by cash or check. Thus the church is facing challenges because the way individuals manage money is rapidly changing. Many church-members are moving to a cashless economy in which credit and debit cards are used for all financial transactions. Table 1.3 reveals the responses to a question in the Northern California surveys that asked what payment-method respondents typically used for purchases costing between $10 and $49 (more than one option could be chosen; the Table reports the reponses of 2,363 individuals). These results are shown as percentages. Credit cards and cash are used by about the same percentage of all age-groups. Younger respondents tended to use debit cards more frequently, and older respondents tended to write checks more frequently.

Table 1.3: "For purchases between $10 and $49, I would usually use" (NCC)					
	Percentages				
Age-group)	Cash	Debit Card	Credit Card	Check	Other
20-29	47	53	34	5	1
30-39	43	54	34	9	2
40-49	45	51	35	11	1
50-59	49	48	32	12	1
60-69	46	41	35	15	2
70-79	49	38	32	17	1
≥ 80	49	36	28	21	1

Published data confirm the conclusions reached from conversations I had with a variety of individuals in Kenya and Brazil that credit and debit cards are not used as widely in those countries as in Northern California. There is ample evidence to show that the use of credit and debit cards in England and Australia is very similar to that in North American. In the North American Division and the South Pacific Division, where the change to a cashless society is well under way, there is substantial thought being given within the church's financial administration at all levels as to how to meet this challenge. For example, the South Pacific Division is in the process of rolling out a mobile-phone-app accross Australia that can be used at any time to give tithes and oferings, including the time in the worship service when offerings are collected. The North American Division is close to having a cell-phone-app ready, and web-based e-giving has long been available in both divisions. Nevertheless, in all the conferences studied it is still a significant challenge to provide effective ways for the less-organized individual to contribute offerings and tithes via credit and debit cards.

1.6 Motives, Beliefs and Attitudes which Correlate to Tithing Behaviour

The statistical analysis showed several of the scales tested to be significantly correlated to tithing behavior in all countries, others in some countries, and yet others in none. The correlations are tabulated in Table 1.4.

Table 1.4: Scales that are Statistically Correlated to Tithing Behavior					
	Combined Data (WAC, SPC, SEC, NCC)	Australia (WAC)	Brazil (SPC)	England (SEC)	USA (NCC)
M1 Bible requirement	Yes	Yes	Yes	No	Yes
M2 God will bless	Yes	No	Yes	No	Yes
M3 Church as family	No	No	Yes	Yes	No
M4 Gratitude	Yes	Yes	No	Yes	Yes
M5 Pay your way	No	No	No	No	No
B1 Bible rule of faith	Yes	Yes	No	No	Yes
B3 Global mission	Yes	No		Yes	No
B4 Pooling tithe	No	Yes	Yes	No	Yes
B5 Church not needy	Yes	Yes	Yes	Yes	Yes
A1 Good Admin	No	Yes	No	Yes	No
A3 Comfort as SDA	No	Yes	No	No?	Yes
A4 Pastor	Yes	Yes	No	Yes	Yes
A5 God is Lord of life	No	No	No	No	No
A6 OK to divert tithe	Yes	Yes	Yes	Yes	Yes
P1a No smoke alcohol	Yes	No	Yes	No	No
P1b No tea meat	Yes	No	Yes	Yes	No
P2 Spiritual practice	Yes	Yes	Yes	Yes	Yes

Scales that were correlated to tithing behavior in all countries:

- P2 Spiritual practice (e.g. study Sabbath School lesson; attend prayer meeting) (positive correlation—in other words, the more things on the list that a respondent indicated they did regularly, the more likely they were to tithe).
- B5 The belief that the church has enough money to carry on without my help (negative correlation—in other words, the more the respondent thought that the church had enough money to carry on without their help, the less likely they were to tithe)
- A6 the attitude that it is OK to divert tithe (negative correlation)

Scales that were not correlated to tithing behavior in any country:

- M5 Pay your way
- A5 God is Lord of my life

Scales that were significant in some countries and not in others:
- M1 The belief that tithing is a biblical requirement
- M2 The motive that God will bless the tither (positively correlated in WAC; negatively correlated in SPC and USA; not correlated in SPC)
- M3 The Church feels like my family
- M4 Tithing out of gratitude for God's goodness
- B1 Bible is a rule of faith
- B3 Belief in the global mission of the Seventh-day Adventist Church
- B4 Belief that pooling tithe between churches is strategically valuable
- A1 Confidence in financial administration of the Church
- A3 Comfort as a Seventh-day Adventist
- A4 Attitude to local pastor
- P1a & P1b Beliefs regarding Adventist lifestyle (P1a relating to not smoking, no alcohol; P1b relating to vegetarian diet, no coffee, etc.)

1.7 Tithing Correlates Strongly to Practices such as Prayer and Bible Study

Amongst Seventh-day Adventists, tithing behavior is very closely related to a range of other practices relating to their religion, such as whether they attend Sabbath School, open and close Sabbath, study the Sabbath School Quarterly, read and reflect on the Bible each day, and pray often during the day. It would seem that a natural strategy to increase the practice of tithing is to encourage more Bible study, more prayer, more study of the Sabbath School Quarterly and tithing, as part of the practices that make up personal piety for Seventh-day Adventists.

1.8 Tithe "Diversion" Negatively Correlated to any Tithing

The more that respondents felt that it was appropriate to direct tithe to places other than the tithe envelope or other official ways to return tithe, the less they self-reported on the survey that they tithed. One might expect, then, that much more effort needs to be given to educating the church-members about where it is appropriate to direct tithe. This report also traced where tithe was being directed. Within officially approved channels, the tithe envelope is still the most commonly used method used to return tithe, although a number of respondents are using electronic methods of giving where donations were possible by using the internet.

1.9 The Best Methods to Promote Tithing

The motive or belief that had the strongest effect on tithing behavior proved to be the belief that tithing is a biblical requirement. Whether they tithe or not, the overwhelming majority of respondents strongly agree that tithing is indeed a biblical requirement. Thus, while tithe promotion to church-members should continue to contain an element of education about the biblical principle of tithing, it should not be overly stressed, as most who hear will be already convinced that such is the case. What is more likely to shift tithing behavior is to make the habit of tithing natural and to ensure that the means of giving tithe to the Church are convenient, straightforward, and transparent. Furthermore, continuing to promote tithing in the wider context of bible study, regular prayer, attending Sabbath school, etc., is also likely to be highly effective. Promotion of tithing should emphasize tithing as being a response of gratitude to God.

1.10 Tithing Is Not Only About Money; It's About Mission and Working in Partnership with God

Many stories have been shared with me during the course of visiting churches and conferences throughout the world. While such stories fall into the category of anecdotal evidence, they often served to reinforce aspects of the research, the significance of which might not have been seen with such clarity. I would like to share two of these stories, both about visitors who had come to a Seventh-day Adventist church for the first or second time, and where they heard a sermon on stewardship and tithing.

One person reported indignantly to me that after some months of urging, they had finally persuaded a friend to attend their local Seventh-day Adventist Church with them. That day the topic of the sermon happened to be stewardship. Their friend's response: "I won't ever be coming back to an Adventist Church, they are only looking for your money." Here is the problem with anecdotal evidence. It could be that nine other people hearing about tithe on their first visit to a church might conclude they would like to belong to a group of people who took their religion seriously. Indeed, the visitor in question may have just been looking for an excuse not to come back. Without a larger sample it is hard to know the significance of this one event. Yet the story does illustrate an important point: it is all too easy to give the false impression that stewardship and tithing is all about money. But the church isn't about money. It's about mission, it's about sharing the good news that Jesus has saved us from our sins, it's about representing the love of God to lost humanity. Money is important in that it enables mission, but the link of stewardship to mission needs to be kept to the fore in any conversation about tithe.

The experience of a second visitor strongly contrasts to that of the first. The story was told to me as I was visiting a church in Sydney while collecting surveys. As was my usual practice on such occasions, after the survey had been completed, I had preached on tithing, and during the sermon had mentioned in passing some of the results of the research, including the fact that most people thought that they had been blessed because they tithed. Between the service and the church luncheon that followed, I happened to get into conversation with somebody who, to my personal alarm, informed me that this was the second time he had ever attended a Seventh-day Adventist Church. I said to him that the sermon he had heard was directed more at regular attenders than at visitors, and asked him what he thought about it. He replied that he thinks he understood what tithing was about. It was probably rather like what he had already experienced with regard to Sabbath observance. He ran a small business, and most of the activity associated with that business took place on a Saturday. He had explained this to the pastor who was having Bible studies with him. The pastor had suggested that he test God by closing his business on Sabbath and waiting to see what happened. He reported to me that he had done just that, and discovered that his business as a whole improved, and that he was doing better now that he was closed Sabbaths than he had done before when he was open Saturdays when most of his business has taken place. He thought tithe was going to be a bit like that. He would test God by tithing, because God had promised to bless him because he tithed. I got the good feeling from that conversation that this person was well on his way to changing his status from visitor to member. This story has a particularly Seventh-day Adventist flavor to it, but illustrates what the research has shown: it is in their tithing that the vast majority of Seventh-day Adventists see the hand of God directly in their lives. There is a research context to this anecdote!

To sum up, for church-members tithing is not just about money, or even mainly about money. For them it is about working in partnership with God and furthering the mission of the church. *It is in their tithing, and the material blessing that they see flowing from it, that most church-members see the hand of God in their lives in a tangible way.*

2. Methodological Considerations

2.1 Approach Used to Research Tithing Behavior

The tithing behavior of Seventh-day Adventists in five countries has been investigated using two main research tools: (1) an analysis of tithe receipts from a sample of 5,000 to 10,000 church-members in each of 4 countries, segregated into age-groups; (2) surveys conducted in churches that make up the sample used in the analysis of tithe receipts [3 countries] or a set of churches that has a large overlap with the wider sample of churches used in the tithe-receipt analysis [SEC]. The analysis of tithe receipts reveals patterns of actual giving to the Adventist church. The surveys provide information on where people report they direct their tithe, their intentions regarding tithing, and their motivation for tithing. Together, the two sets of data enable a wide range of informed conclusions to be drawn concerning tithing behavior of Seventh-day Adventists in different age-groups and their motivation for tithing.

This chapter is divided into several sections as follows: the reasons why specific conferences were chosen for study (2.2); something about each of the conferences that participated (2.3); country-specific features of how tithe receipts are written and processed that could potentially influence the accuracy of the results reported (2.4); and the hypothetical model of tithing behavior that is tested by the survey (2.5).

2.2 Rationale for Choosing Conferences

Groups of Seventh-day Adventist churches in a particular region are clustered in administrative units termed Conferences. Groups of conferences are organized into Unions, and the Unions are organized into the thirteen Divisions of the General Conference of the Seventh-day Adventist Church. The research was conducted at the Conference level of church organization. In two of the conferences (Southern England and Western Australia) every church in the conference participated in some way in the study; in the other three (Central Kenya, Northern California, and São Paulo) there was a sample of churches from the conference. Working with conference administrators and departmental directors enabled access to the leadership of the individual churches in the sample.

The conferences asked to participate in this study were selected to provide wide geographic representation. They were selected from the continents of Europe, Africa, South and North America and Australia. The conferences chosen are based in countries that make the greatest contributions to the budget of the Seventh-day Adventist Church world-wide. In other words, while there are social, economic and demographic differences between the conferences, the differences are not of such an extent as to prevent useful comparisons between them.

2.3 Overview of Conferences:

Each of the conferences visited had its own unique characteristics. Three conferences represented different stages of church development and financial circumstances.

2.3.1 Central Kenya Conference

The Central Kenya Conference administers a vital church that is flourishing in a country undergoing rapid economic growth. The workforce of the country includes many expatriates and locals that have internationally recognized professional qualifications, many of whom are remunerated at rates comparable with those received in Europe and America. Wages for most of the population, however, are much less. In 2012, the Conference had a membership of approximately 100,000, scattered amongst approximately 1,000 churches and 1,000 companies. The ministers working for the Conference are professionally trained, and each usually looks after at least 5,000 members. This often translates to 10 or more churches per minister in Central Kenya Conference, so elders also provide an important leadership role. For example, one minister interviewed as part of this research was responsible for more than 5,000 members spread across 12 churches. Of these, 9 churches had purchased their land for the church building (a process that takes about 10 years) and were in the process of building a church and school on the property. Funds are desperately short and the needs very pressing. The Seventh-day Adventist Church in Kenya, though large in membership, is in the process of building the basic infrastructure of the church and its institutions with very limited resources.

2.3.2 São Paulo Conference

By way of contrast to Kenya, the São Paulo Conference—and the church as a whole in Brazil—is in a strong growth stage. It has a critical mass of membership, infrastructure and funding that allows the whole church to work together in the process of building new churches and developing those that exist. Expectations of large numbers joining the church through baptism are met over and over, and each of the institutions of the church is focused on their contribution to the overall church goal of spreading the expectation of the soon return of Jesus. In partnership with local church communities, the conference plays a large role in the establishment of new churches and physical renewal and upgrading of existing churches (it employs a full-time building team, and the conference has a group of architects working as one of its departments).

2.3.3 Northern California Conference:

Northern California Conference is reaping the benefit of over 100 years of well-funded church development. It has extraordinary financial and human resources, is associated with very large church-related institutions, and has a large number of well-built and well-funded churches in all of the major population centers. The conference is well-governed and resourced, and the professional talent associated with the church in its varied activities is very impressive indeed. The Northern California Conference represents a mature Seventh-day Adventist church functioning well in a sophisticated first-world environment.

2.3.4 South England Conference:

South England Conference has a unique social heritage. While England itself has a very strong Christian heritage, and while there is a resurgence in involvement in the activities of the Church of England, taken as a whole, England is a strongly secular society. It is also characterized by large groups of immigrants from various racial and religious backgrounds. The Seventh-day Adventist Church in South England has absorbed within its churches Seventh-day Adventist members from all across the globe and who arrived in England from families who were already Seventh-day Adventists before they arrived in England. It is not easy to document the variety of immigrants into the English Adventist Churches, but some of the larger trends are clear. The English church first absorbed large numbers of West Indians, and people having West Indian heritage form the majority of many congregations, especially in the churches in central London. Many members are second- or third-generation UK citizens who have been educated in the English school system and grown up in England. More recent waves of Adventist immigrants have come from many countries, including countries in the former Eastern Bloc in Europe. For example, many Ghanaian Adventist doctors serve in the English public health system, and there are several large and very well-financed Ghanaian churches. It is interesting that South England Conference was the only conference that asked for data to be collected about the cultural background with which those filling in the surveys identified in order to determine whether there were different motivations for contributing tithe differed between the different heritages. Heritage is important also in Kenya and in the United States, but in Central Kenya Conference and Northern California Conference the conference administration did not wish to have attention drawn to the matter of heritage, given its sensitive nature.

2.3.5 Western Australia Conference:

At the time of the survey, Western Australia was experiencing an unprecedentedly long mining-led economic boom that was supercharging the Western Australian economy right up to the time of the global financial crisis (2008) and kept it buoyant for several years thereafter. This unprecedented long boom was lifting the Western Australian economy to ever-greater heights. Given their refusal to take paid employment that involved Sabbath work, Seventh-day Adventists in Western Australia participated only tangentially in the boom—they experienced the increases in the value of their homes, they were living in a full-employment economy, and while farming commodity prices did not prosper in the same manner as the mining economy, during much of this period the farm prices were less depressed than they had been before and since. The Adventist Church in Western Australia is scattered through this vast and sparsely populated state. Physical isolation from the rest of Australia means that the Western Australian Church, like the whole state, perceives itself as operating with a little more independence than some of the other conferences in Australia. The conference has a relatively small membership which is conducive to many close ties between Adventists. It is a warm, well-led conference. It is also relatively homogeneous from a heritage perspective. By way of contrast, Adventist churches in Sydney and Melbourne are very multi-ethnic. While there is immigration from outside of Australia into Western Australia, and hence into the Adventist church there, non Anglo-Australian cultures are just beginning to form a significant visible presence in the church.[1]

---

1 In a personal communication, Glenn Townend comments, "Although WA does not have long-established Polish, Spanish-language, Samoan, Tongan or former Yugoslavic churches, during the period of the survey there was an increase in immigration and new churches for Sudanese, Burundis, Karen (from the Thai—Burmese border), Filipino and Samoan churches were formed. Perhaps it is better to say that immigration was just beginning to have a visible presence in the church" [rather than it has yet to form a significant visible presence in the church].

2.4 Country-specific Features of how Tithe Receipts Are Written and Processed

While there is a general pattern of how tithe is collected and receipts generated across all of the five conferences that took part in this research, each conference used technology in different ways, and had different levels of centralization. The following account of these common and different processes will alert the reader to the various factors that could potentially influence the accuracy and completeness of the data presented in the following chapters.

The elements of common practice are as follows. Each local Seventh-day Adventist church provides envelopes which allow donors to direct some or all of the money contained in the envelope for specific purposes. These envelopes are usually termed tithe envelopes because the first item listed on them is usually "Tithe." Other entries varied by country, and in some cases by the initiative of the local church. For example, a church involved in a building program will have a separate line entry for "Church Building Fund," an item not found on tithe envelopes from larger established churches with sound buildings. Money received in a tithe envelope is receipted by the local church treasurer or treasury team, and the receipt is returned to the donor, often in a new tithe envelope for future use. The bulk of tithe donated to the Seventh-day Adventist church is donated through such tithe envelopes, although there are several other routes by which tithe makes its way to the church. In some countries (including Australia, England and the United States), individual donors can use the internet to donate tithe. Other donors direct their tithe to various administrative units of the Adventist Church.

The Seventh-day Adventist church groups churches in a given region into administrative units termed Conferences if they are self-sufficient financially and administratively, or Missions if they receive funds and administrative support from "higher" organizations of the Church structure. It has been the practice of the Adventist Church to pool tithe from the various churches at conference level, and then to use the tithe strategically to support the mission of the church. The bulk of tithe is used to support ministers in local churches, although some is used to support conference-level activities such as youth events, and other functions of the church, including, in some countries, church schools. A percentage of tithe is directed "upwards" in the organizational structure, to fund Unions, Divisions and the General Conference.

These procedures are common to the churches that took part in this study, but there were important differences in the way that the various conferences managed their receipts. In Southern England, Central Kenya and Western Australia, tithe receipts were paper-based in 2012, although there were plans in both Australia and England to move to an electronic receipting system. Where paper-based receipts are used, the top copy is given to the donor, the next copy is sent to the conference, and the final copy is kept in the local church. In Brazil, almost all church treasurers have moved to a centralized accounting system that tracks tithing and other donations. There are plans to combine these data with church membership data, currently held in a separate database accessed through the internet. It is expected that eventually church-members in Brazil will be able to log on and see the record of their giving, as well as obtain information about what the church is doing with the tithe it has received. In the Northern California Conference almost all tithe receipts are prepared and managed using computers. While some local churches in Northern California Conference have developed their own receipting software from commercial accounting packages, most treasurers use the church-developed package. Since tithing is tax deductible in California, these packages were designed to provide summary data, and care is taken to ensure that there is accurate linking of individual donations to the correct donor. In Southern England many churches participate in a program that provides accurate data for "Gift Aid," a program that provides government funds to entities equivalent to a certain percentage of donations that have been reported appropriately. Donors are given a Gift Aid identity number, and a certain percentage of tithers in each church are registered with the Gift Aid program. This percentage varies from church to church, with some churches having the great majority of members registered, and other churches having a small minority of members registered. Those registered with Gift Aid provide their identification number on the tithe envelope, and the number is noted on the tithe receipt. At the end of the financial year, the conference gathers into one database all the records of the donations that come from registered Gift Aid participants. These data are gathered carefully, and represent a high quality source of data on giving behavior. The fact that the data are consolidated means that it is only possible to track giving over the 6 separate reporting periods, rather than weekly as is the case with the tithe receipts. This consolidation tends to hide differences in giving behavior, particularly the frequency of giving. As frequency of giving is one of the primary features of interest revealed by the research reported here, this is a matter of some concern. Comparative data were collected by analyzing the tithe receipts of selected churches. These data were of significantly lower quality than those obtained from the Gift Aid records. As will be apparent from the Australian and Kenyan data, one of the challenges in tracking giving behavior of individuals from written tithe receipts is that consistent identification of an individual may be difficult. Variations that can occur in the naming of one individual, and distinguishing between members of the same family can be difficult from viewing the receipts without knowing the family. Reading handwriting faintly reproduced by carbon copies also represents a challenge. Thus it is the Gift Aid data that will be reported for England, as well as the analysis of the tithe receipts.

By way of contrast, in Western Australia and Kenya, as well as for some donors in England, there is no occasion where there is a yearly report written on tithe and other offerings received by the local church. As a result, because of variations occurring in the naming of individuals on tithe receipts (e.g. without knowing something about the individuals attending a local church, one would ask whether Dr McIver, Robert McIver, and RK McIver are the same person), frequency of giving may be under-reported for Western Australia and Central Kenya. While undesirable, this is also unavoidable owing to the constraints necessary in the protection of privacy. Nevertheless, the variation brought about by multiple versions of the same name is constant across the whole sample, and will not affect adversely the accuracy of comparisons of giving patterns across the various age-groups.

Tithe receipts include the name of the donor, but not the age, which is essential information for any demographically-based analysis. Reports were provided to the researchers without the names attached, which meant that it was necessary to develop a method by which the amount given by individual donors over a 12-month period was totaled, and by which age estimates could be made for those donors. These data were collated by those who already were processing tithe receipts. The personnel who accumulated and linked the data to an age-group varied by conference: in Western Australia, South England, Central Kenya and São Paulo the data was totaled and linked at the Conference level, by someone within or appointed by treasury who was already in the small trusted circle of those who had access to tithe receipts. Because information about individual donations is not reported to the conference in Northern California, but stays within the local church, in that conference the process was carried out by local church treasurers.

The ways by which ages were estimated for individual donors also varied by conference. Exact birth-dates were used to work out the age-group for Brazilian donors,[2] and for about one third of donors in Southern England.

---

2   The church member database in Brazil has exact birth dates. These were used to generate the age-group for members by somebody who was already working with the data base, and the aggregated summary of the numbers in each age-group was reported to the researchers without names and without exact birth-dates.

Everywhere else, the age of an individual church-attender was estimated by the local church pastor or elder. This might seem open to error, but in practice it generally proved possible to give estimates of the age of regular attenders within a few years, even in very large congregations. Church rolls were provided to whoever was analyzing the tithe receipts which were annotated with information about church attendance—whether a member or non-member attends 3 or more times per month—and their estimated age. At the suggestion of several pastors and church treasurers, in Northern California attendance was provided in three categories: those who attended 3 or more times per month, those who attend once or twice per month, those who attend once per month or less. These lists were provided to whoever was doing the analysis of tithe receipts, and after the report was generated, the following data were given to the researchers for each individual donor who attended church 3 or more times per month for the twelve-month period of the most recent financial year :

- Randomized ID number (to replace name)
- Age
- Total amount of tithe donated
- Number of tithe donations
- Total amount of other donations

Table 2.1 lists the financial years for with tithe receipts [and Gift Aid donations for SEC] were analysed by country:

Table 2.1: Financial Year Analyzed for Each Country,		
Conference	Financial Year	Period Analyzed
Central Kenya	July to June	1 Jul 2011 to 30 Jun 2012
Northern California	January to December	1 Jan 2011 to 31 Dec 2011
São Paulo	January to December	1 Jan 2011 to 31 Dec 2011
S. England Gift Aid	April to March	1 Apr 2011 to 31 Mar 2012
S. England Tithe	April to March	1 Apr 2013 to 31 Mar 2014
Western Australia	July to June	1 Jul 2004 to 31 Jun 2005

2.5 Hypothetical Model of Tithing Behavior that Is Tested by the Survey

In the process of developing the survey instrument used in this research, it was hypothesized that tithing behavior is the result of a complex interaction of motives, beliefs and attitudes, each of which in turn is influenced by demographic factors such as age and education. The process by which these factors were identified and scales developed is reported in Appendix A, "The Development of the Survey Instrument." Information regarding the reliability of the scales and the items that make up each scale is provided in Appendix B, while Appendix C provides reproductions of the survey instrument as it was used in each country. The scales were developed to measure the following motives, beliefs, attitudes and commitment to the Adventist "Package":

Motives:
Tithe a biblical requirement
God will bless
Church as family
Gratitude
Pay your way

Beliefs:
Bible a rule of faith and practice
Biblical directive to use only tithe to support ministers
In global mission of SDA Church
It's strategically valuable to pool tithe between churches
Church not needy
In salvation and goodness of God

Attitudes:
Confidence in financial probity and competence of church administration
Attitude to SDA church (comfort as Adventist)
Think well of local pastor
Lordship of Jesus over money
OK to divert tithe
Sectarian view of SDA Church

Commitment to Adventist "Package":
Full adoption of Adventist lifestyle (e.g. no alcohol and no meat in diet)
Personal religious practices (e.g. study the Sabbath
    School Quarterly, attend prayer meeting)
Commitment to SDA Church

One might visualize the research model tested by the survey instrument as follows:

Fig. 2.1: Theoretical Model of SDA Tithing Behavior

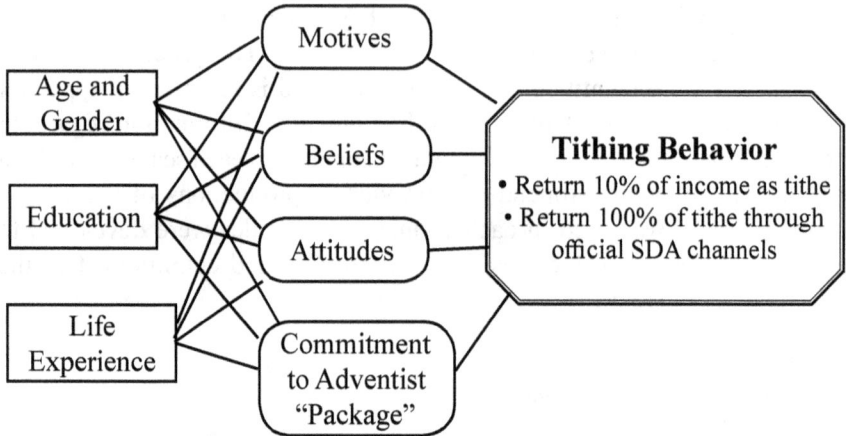

A more detailed representation of the theoretical model may be found in Figure 2.2, which includes lists of the various scales used to measure motives, beliefs, attitudes and the commitment to the Adventist "Package." To avoid overcomplicating the figure, the relationships between age and gender, education, and life experiences and each of the motives, beliefs, attitudes and commitment have not been represented as they are in Figure 2.1.

Fig. 2.2: Theoretical Model of SDA Tithing Behavior (Detailed)

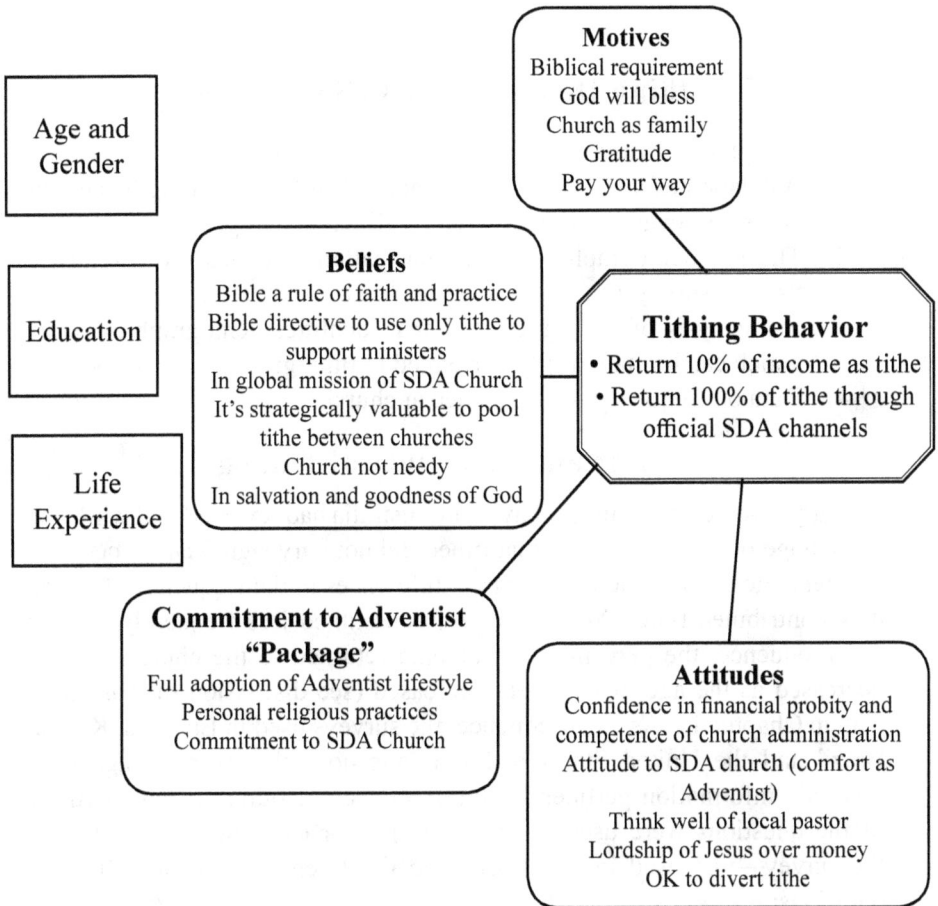

Age and Gender

Education

Life Experience

Motives
Biblical requirement
God will bless
Church as family
Gratitude
Pay your way

Beliefs
Bible a rule of faith and practice
Bible directive to use only tithe to support ministers
In global mission of SDA Church
It's strategically valuable to pool tithe between churches
Church not needy
In salvation and goodness of God

Tithing Behavior
• Return 10% of income as tithe
• Return 100% of tithe through official SDA channels

Commitment to Adventist "Package"
Full adoption of Adventist lifestyle
Personal religious practices
Commitment to SDA Church

Attitudes
Confidence in financial probity and competence of church administration
Attitude to SDA church (comfort as Adventist)
Think well of local pastor
Lordship of Jesus over money
OK to divert tithe

3. Tithing Demographics (Survey Data)

This chapter includes:
1. A detailed examination of differences identified in tithing behaviour amongst Seventh-day Adventists in different age-groups;
2. The age demographics and giving patterns of those who returned useable surveys;
3. An analysis of the survey data that identifies demographic factors which can be statistically correlated to tithing;
4. Data on frequency of attendance at church.

3.1 Age and Frequency of Tithing

Early research on tithing behavior in Australia had revealed that while the percentage of each age-group that tithed did not vary significantly between different age-groups, there were large differences in the frequency at which they contributed tithe. Younger age-groups tithed less frequently and, as a consequence, the percentage of income returned to the church as tithe decreased as the age of members decreased (see discussion of Australian data in Chapter 4). As a consequence, the surveys used in England, Kenya, Brazil and the United States had four questions that were designed to ascertain information pertinent to the frequency of tithing behavior (three of the questions were used in the WAC[1]). For example, version 9.4 of the survey—that used in South England Conference—had the following questions:

A7. I am:
○ Self-Employed
○ Wage/Salary-earner paid monthly
○ Wage/Salary-earner paid fortnightly
○ Wage/Salary-earner paid weekly

B18. I try to return tithe:
○ Weekly
○ Fortnightly

---

1 The version of the survey used in WAC did not have a question equivalent to A7.

- ○ Monthly
- ○ Quarterly
- ○ Yearly

B19. Sometimes I forget to return tithe
- ○ No (I never forget, or only rarely) — Go to question C1
- ○ Yes — Go to question B20

B20. Because I sometimes forget, I estimate that the number times each year I actually contribute tithe is about
- ○ 1–3 times
- ○ 4–6 times
- ○ 7–11 times
- ○ 12–17 times
- ○ 18–24 times
- ○ 25–29 times
- ○ more than 30 times

Almost the same questions were asked in other versions of the survey used in Kenya, Brazil, the United States[2] and Western Australia, although numbered differently.[3] Question A7 was designed to elicit information about the frequency with which wage-earners were paid, with the underlying assumption that the highest frequency of tithing would be likely to be once each pay-period. As may be observed in Table 3.1, the majority of participants from England and Brazil (73% and 56% resp.) were wage-earners paid monthly, while in Northern California the largest group of wage-earners were paid semi-monthly (58%). While question A7 or its equivalent was not asked on version 7.1 of the survey (the version used in Western Australia), by far the most common wage-payment interval in Australia is fortnightly (every two weeks) and most respondents indicated they intend to tithe fortnightly (745 respondends indicated fortnightly; vs. 395 who intended to tithe weekly, 69 monthly, 147 quarterly, and 175 yearly).

---

2 One small adjustment was made in Northern California, where "semi-month-ly" was used rather than "fortnightly" (a term which is appropriate in Australia and England, but little used in the United States).

3 For example, B18, B19 and B20 were numbered B46, B47a and B47b resp. in the Western Australian version of the survey. Because they were embedded in the coding used in the SPSS database, anytime these quesitons are referenced by specific question numbers in the appendices, they will be referred to by the numbers used in version 7.1 of the survey—the version used in Western Australia..

Table 3.1: Country vs. Self-employed or Wage-earner (%; NCC, SEC, SPC)				
Country	Self-employed	Wage/Salary earner paid monthly	Wage/Salary earner paid fortnightly/ semi-monthly	Wage/Salary earner paid weekly
Brazil (SPC)	32%	56%	10%	2%
England (SEC)	12%	73%	3%	12%
USA (NCC)	21%	17%	58%	4%
Total	21%	47%	26%	6%

As might be expected, these employment patterns are reflected in the intentions that participants said they had regarding their tithing frequency, at least in Australia, Brazil and England. Table 3.2 shows that the most common frequency of intended tithing in Brazil, England and the United States was monthly (83%, 67% and 50% resp.), while 49% of Western Australian participants intended to tithe fortnightly.

Table 3.2: Country vs "I try to return tithe" (%; NCC, SEC, SPC, WAC)					
Country	Weekly	Semi-Monthly / Fortnightly	Monthly	Quarterly	Yearly
Australia (WAC)	26%	49%	5%	10%	11%
Brazil (SPC)	7%	7%	83%	2%	0%
England (SEC)	23%	4%	67%	4%	2%
USA (NCC)	9%	23%	50%	12%	5%

Table 3.3 shows that the proportion of those who intend to tithe weekly, semi-monthly, monthly, quarterly and yearly is relatively constant accross those aged between 20 and 69 years.

Table 3.3: Age vs "I try to return tithe" (%; NCC, SEC, SPC, WAC)					
Age-group (Years)	Weekly	Semi-Monthly / bi-weekly / fortnightly	Monthly	Quarterly	Yearly
20-29	15%	23%	49%	7%	6%
30-39	14%	22%	53%	5%	6%
40-49	14%	23%	51%	8%	5%
50-59	16%	22%	48%	8%	6%

Table 3.3: Age vs "I try to return tithe" (%; NCC, SEC, SPC, WAC)					
Age-group (Years)	Weekly	Semi-Monthly / bi-weekly / fortnightly	Monthly	Quarterly	Yearly
60-69	15%	24%	48%	7%	5%
70-79	13%	22%	51%	10%	4%
≥ 80	12%	12%	63%	10%	3%

While participants may have definite intentions of tithing at a set interval, when they reflected about their actual practice, 43% of participants in São Paulo, 20% in South England, 29% in Northern California and 33% of participants in Western Australia admitted, "Sometimes I forget to return tithe" (see Table "Country * b47a Sometimes I forget to tithe" in Appendix D).

Table 3.4: Age-group vs "Sometimes I forget to tithe" (NCC, SEC, SPC, WAC)					
Age-group (Years)	No		Yes		Total
20-39	904	54%	782	46%	1,686
40-59	1,676	68%	785	32%	2,461
≥ 60	1,472	77%	446	23%	1,918
Total	4,052	67%	2,013	33%	6,065

Table 3.4 reveals that there is an age-related trend. Only 23% of those aged 60 years or older admit that "Sometimes I forget to tithe," while 46% of those between 20 and 39 years of age admit that they do forget. Later analysis of tithe receipts will reveal that every age-group over-estimates their frequency of tithing (see chapters 4 through 7), but even so, younger age-groups self-report that they tithe more sporadically than older age-groups. This trend is all the more striking when viewed on a graph (Figure 3.1).

Fig. 3.1: "Sometimes I forget to tithe" by Age-group

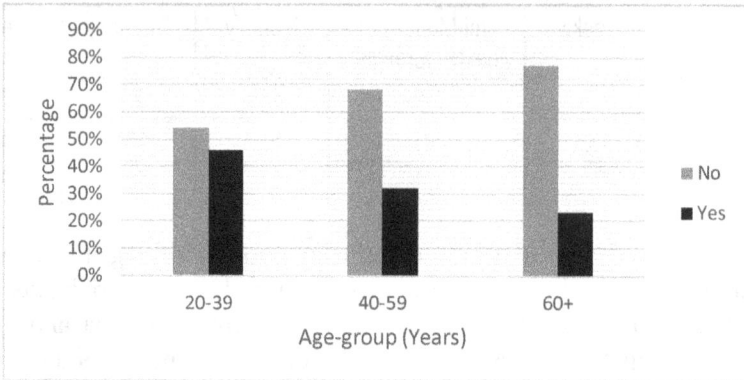

The responses from the surveys in all conferences indicated that of the several possible intervals between tithing (weekly, bi-weekly, monthly, quarterly, yearly), the largest number of respondents indicated an intention to tithe monthly. So that tithing frequency is not confused with the number of those who intend to tithe at other intervals (e.g. fortnightly), the statistical package used to analyze the data, SPSS, was programmed so that only responses from those who intended to tithe monthly were selected. A cross-tabulation was then made between age and the participants' estimate of the number of times they contribute tithe each year. The results are shown in Table 3.5, which reveals that tithers sometimes forget to tithe, and many who intend to tithe monthly do not tithe the 12 times per year that would be expected if they contributed once per month. It is also noteworthy that 108 (7%) of those who intend to tithe monthly (or 12 times per year) estimate that they actually tithe 18 to 29 times per year; and 85 (or nearly 6%) tithe in excess of 30 times per year.

Table 3.5 Age-group vs Number of Times Estimate Contribute Tithe each Year (%; NCC, SEC, SPC, WAC) [Including only those 1,508 respondents who intend to tithe monthly]								
Age-group	1-3 times	4-6 times	7-11 times	12-17 times	18-24 times	25-29 times	> 30 times	n =
20-39	27%	18%	25%	20%	3%	2%	4%	518
40-59	20%	15%	22%	29%	5%	3%	6%	578
≥ 60	18%	12%	25%	31%	5%	3%	7%	412

Note: In Table 3.5, the column labelled "n =" refers to the number of respondents in that row. The rest of the data consist of percentages within the age-group. There was a total of 1,508 respondents who indicated they intended to tithe monthly, and who had also answered both the question asking about their age and the question asking their tithe practice.

From Figure 3.2 (below) it is evident that the biggest percentage of respondents aged 60 or more who intend to tithe monthly consider themselves to have actually done so. By way of contrast, while a number of those that are between 20 and 39 years of age also report that in line with their intentions they tithe 12 times per year, the greatest percentage from this age-group report that though they intend to tithe 12 times per year, in practice they tithe only between 1 and 3 times per year. Figure 3.2 also reveals that a substantial number in the older age-groups are aware that they tithe with a much smaller frequency than they intend. The attitudes of the group who tithe sporadically are explored further in Chapter 8 "I think I should tithe, but I need to get into the habit of tithing regularly." The majority of them agree that, "I need to get into the habit of tithing regularly."

Fig. 3.2: Age-group vs Number of times estimate contribute tithe each year (%; NCC, SEC, SPC, WAC) [Including only those 1508 respondents who intend to tithe monthly – survey data]

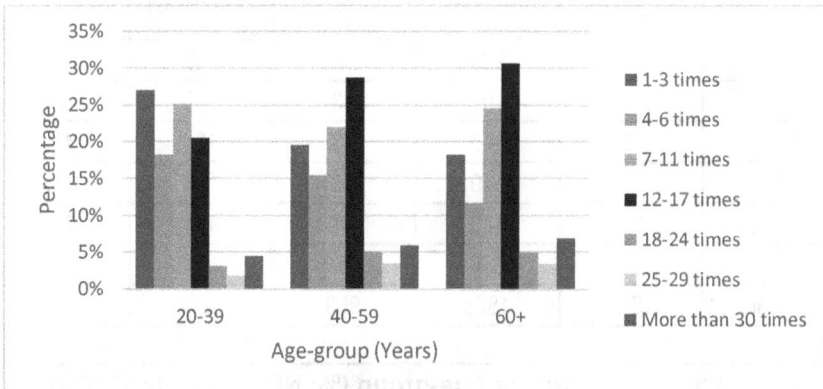

3.2 Age Demographics and Giving Patterns of those who Returned Usable Surveys

A total of 8,058 usable surveys was collected from respondents aged 20 years or more in four conferences: the Northern California Conference (3,370 surveys), the São Paulo Conference (1,973), the Southern England Conference (1,055), and the Western Australia Conference (1,660). The age-groups represented in these surveys are show in Table 3.6 below.

Table 3.6: Age-Group vs Country (NCC, SEC, SPC, WAC)					
Age-group (Years)	Australia (WAC)	Brazil (SPC)	England (SEC)	USA (NCC)	Total
20-29	231	353	66	216	866
30-39	256	496	119	338	1,209
40-49	293	440	216	483	1,432
50-59	322	344	278	698	1,642
60-69	271	198	178	748	1,395
70-79	210	119	103	503	935
≥ 80	77	23	95	384	579
Total	1,660	1,973	1,055	3,370	8,058

Tables 3.7 and 3.8 show the amount of tithe returned as a percentage of income, first by country, and then by age-group.

Table 3.7: Tithe Status vs Country (NCC, SEC, SPC, WAC)					
Tithe Status	Australia (WAC)	Brazil (SPC)	England (SEC)	USA (NCC)	Total
0%	127	220	103	190	640
<2%	90	0	93	200	383
2-4%	75	142	73	186	476
5-7%	84	140	72	256	552
8-9%	84	443	67	161	755
10%	1061	930	551	2280	4822
Total	1521	1875	959	3273	7628

Table 3.8: Tithe Status vs Age-group (%; NCC, SEC, SPC, WAC)								
Tithe Status	20-29	30-39	40-49	50-59	60-69	70-79	≥ 80	Total
0%	16%	13%	10%	7%	5%	4%	1%	640
<2%	8%	7%	5%	5%	4%	3%	1%	383
2-4%	10%	8%	7%	7%	5%	3%	2%	476
5-7%	8%	8%	10%	7%	7%	5%	3%	552
8-9%	13%	13%	12%	9%	9%	7%	3%	755
10%	46%	52%	56%	64%	70%	78%	89%	4,822
Total	823	1,157	1,365	1,552	1,325	873	533	7,628

Note: In Table 3.8, the column and row labelled "Total" refer to the number of respondents in that row/column. The rest of the data consists of percentages within the age-group. There was a total of 7,628 respondents who answered both the question asking for their age, and the question asking their tithe status. A more-detailed analysis of age demographics and giving patterns may be found below in "3.5 Age and Tithing; Age and Frequency of Tithing by Country."

3.3 Key Demographics that Relate to Tithing Behavior According to Survey Data

In their substantial study of 625 church congregations variously having allegiances to the Assemblies of God, Baptist, Catholic, Lutheran and Presbyterian Churches, Hoge *et al.* showed that giving was positively correlated to the level of income, education, being married, whether both partners attended the same congregation, and age—at least for those younger than 66 years of age.[1] Working mainly with evangelical congregations,[2] George Barna reported that age, education, income, female gender were all positively correlated with increased levels of giving.[3]

The responses to the tithe survey conducted in 2012 in the Northern California Conference (n=3,572), the São Paulo Conference (n=2,410), and the South England Conference (n=1,170), as well as the 2006 survey conducted in Western Australia (n=1,851) reveal one similar demographic

---

1 "Past research has consistently found that religious giving varies by age, with the highest giving done by the people fifty to sixty-five years old. After age 65, giving decreases because household income often decreases" (so say Dean R. Hoge, Charles Zech, Patrick McNamara, and Michael J. Donahue, *Money Matters: Personal Giving in American Churches* [Louisville: Westminster John Knox, 1996], 62). Reports regarding the relationship between income, education, and age may be found in Hoge *et al. Money Matters,* 58–62 (cf. Dean R. Hoge, Charles Zech, Patrick McNamara, and Michael J. Donahue, "Research Report of the American Congregational Giving Study," Life Cycle Institution, The Catholic University of America, Washington DC 20064, 1995, pp. 101–11), and marital states in Hoge *et al. Money Matters,* 65–66 (c.f. Hoge *et al.* 1995: 112–13). The questionnaires used by Hoge *et al.* were sent by mail to 30 members selected by the researchers in each of the congregations in the study (or 18,750 surveys), and there was an overall return rate of 61% (approx. 11,440 participants).

2 George Barna, *How to Increase Giving in Your Church* (Ventura, CA: Regal, 1997), 161–79 reports sample sizes of various studies that have 1,015, 1,202, 1,204, 1,164 ,527, and 2,022 participants each. For two of the surveys for which he can report affiliation (n=2,022), 85% of his respondents are classified as Evangelical Christians (p. 178).

3 Barna, *How to Increase Giving,* 38–39 (age), 39 (education), 29, 41–42 (income), 42 (female gender).

influence on giving behavior, as well as several significant differences. Consistent with the research reported by Hoge *et al.* and Barna, the proportion of income given as tithe and the frequency of returning tithe was positively correlated with age of the members in all conferences except São Paulo. But by way of contrast, education, income levels, gender, marital status, and whether or not a partner attends the same church were *not* significantly related to tithing amongst those Seventh-day Adventists who participated in the study. The survey data reported here also reveal four other major demographic influences on tithing behavior of Seventh-day Adventists: whether the participant is a baptized member of the Church; whether they tithe consistently at regular intervals; how frequently the participant attends church; and—with the exception of South England—the number of times they contribute over a year. While not true of the other countries in which surveys were conducted, in São Paulo the number of years a participant has been a member of the church, and being an employee of the Adventist Church also significantly relates to tithing behavior. In three of the conferences in which surveys were done, there was no difference in tithing behavior between long-term and short-term members or between members who were church employees and members who were not church employees.

The survey instrument was constructed in such a way that several other possible demographic items were available for testing against tithing behavior. It is therefore possible to report that there was no statistically significant relationship between tithing behavior and level of education, whether employed or not, whether self-employed or employed on wages, how frequently one intends to tithe, gender, income, marital status, whether parents were Seventh-day Adventists or worked for the Adventist Church, whether partners attend the same congregation, and how many sermons on tithing had been heard in the last 2 years. In the USA, having a personal budget, and using a credit card for purchases of between $10 and $49 were *not* found to be significantly related to tithing behavior.[4]

The significance levels applying to demographic factors for the whole data set and the results for each individual country are reported in Tables 3.9 and 3.10, together with notes of explanation.

---

4 The Northern Californian surveys included questions about whether or not the participant had and followed a personal budget, and whether they used cash, debit card, credit card, check or other for purchases between $10 and $49, and purchases between $50 and $150. When only these variables are correlated against percentage of income given as tithe, whether a credit card was used for purchases between $10 and $49 was found to be statically significant at a 5% level (Sig. = 0.045). When considered along with a wider range of demographic factors, these two items ceased to show statistical significance.

Table 3.9: Demographic Factors that are Positively Correlated to Tithing in SDAs (NCC, SEC, SPC, WAC)									
	All data	Sig.	Northern California	Sig.	São Paulo	Sig.	South England	Sig.	Western Australia	Sig.
Significant Correlations Most Countries										
Baptized Member	Yes	0.000	Y at 5%	0.027	Yes	0.000	Del		Yes	0.000
Never forgets to tithe	Yes	0.000	Yes	0.000	No	0.183	Yes	0.000	Yes	0.000
No of times contributes / year	Yes	0.000	Yes	0.000	Yes	0.000	No	0.222	Yes	0.000
Age	Yes	0.001	Y at 5%	0.026	No	0.288	Yes	0.002	Yes	0.001
Significant Correlations Some Countries										
Attendance frequency	No	0.178	Yes	0.011	Yes	0.000	Y at 5%	0.045	No	0.069
Works for SDA church	No	0.066	No	0.376	Y at 5%	0.048	Del		No	0.461
No. of years a member	No	0.228	Del		Y at 5%	0.011	Del		No	0.479

Notes

1. The correlations listed in Tables 3.9 and 3.10 are calculated against the variable representing the question, "In the last 12 months, as a percentage of my income, I estimate that I have given as tithe: ..."

2. The column labeled "Sig." represents the probability of the result obtained on the assumption (or null-hypothesis) that there was no difference in tithing behavior associated with the indicated variable (e.g. age). In working out the correlation of each variable to the tithing percentage variable, SPSS takes into account all the possible ways of arranging the variables, and then estimates the probability of the outcome so obtained. In social science research, such as is reported here, it is usual to choose a significance of 5% (i.e. 0.05), or 1% (i.e. 0.01). Unless otherwise stated, this chapter uses a significance level of 0.01. Thus if the outcome observed is likely to occur by chance less than 1% of the time, the null hypothesis that there is no relationships between two variables is rejected; or, to put it another way, it is concluded that there is, in fact, a statistically valid relationship between the two variables. It may be observed that many of the

probabilities in the correlation tables are much less than 1%. A table entry of 0.000 probability means a probability of ≤ 0.0005, and indicates that an event is unlikely to happen 5 or more times out of 10,000 occasions (or 1 out of 2,000 times).

3. Where no significant correlations were found in the various models used by SPSS, the "Sig." level shown in both Tables 3.9 and 3.10 is the lowest of either (i) the significance shown on the last three iterations of the significance tables or (ii) the significance in the first iteration of the significance tables.

4. Del. indicates variables that were removed by SPSS from the correlation analysis, usually on the grounds that they are constants, or that they have missing correlations.

Table 3.10: Demographic Factors that are NOT Correlated to Tithing in SDAs (NCC, SEC, SPC, WAC)									
	All data (NCC, SEC, SPC, WAC)		Northern California		São Paulo		South England		Western Australia
		Sig.		Sig.		Sig.		Sig.		Sig.
Credit Card used for $10 to $49 purchases	N/A		No	0.427	N/A		N/A		N/A	
Education	No	0.487	No	0.309	No	0.645	No	0.991	No	0.991
Employed	No	0.926	No	0.565	No	0.916	No	0.188	No	0.191
Employed by self / wage-earner ft/pt	No	0.873	No	0.512	No	0.818	No	0.659	No	0.669
Follow personal budget	N/A		No	0.274	N/A		N/A		N/A	
Frequency of tithing intended	No	0.809	No	0.477	No	0.676	No	0.584	No	0.563
Gender	No	0.692	No	0.818	N/A		No	0.38	No	0.380
Income	No	0.344	No	0.332	No	0.118	Del		No	0.384

Table 3.10: Demographic Factors that are NOT Correlated to Tithing in SDAs (NCC, SEC, SPC, WAC)									
	All data (NCC, SEC, SPC, WAC)		Northern California		São Paulo		South England		Western Australia
		Sig.		Sig.		Sig.		Sig.		Sig.
Married	No	0.599	Del		N/A		No	0.854	No	0.869
Parents SDAs	No	0.485	Del		N/A		No	0.982	No	0.953
Parents worked for SDA Church	No	0.864	No	0.921	N/A		No	0.502	No	0.505
Partner attends same congregation	No	0.463	Del		N/A		No	0.771	No	0.334
Sermons on tithe last 2yrs	No	0.197	Del		Del		No	0.607	No	0.609

3.4 Frequency of Attendance at an Adventist Church

Frequency of attendance at a Seventh-day Adventist church is significantly ($p<0.05$) related to percentage of income returned as tithe in Northern California, São Paulo, and England. It is to be expected that those who attend church rarely would be under-represented in an unpredictable manner in the statistics in Table 3.11. However it is anticipated that while those who report attending 2 or 3 times per month would also be under-represented, at most their numbers would only be double those recorded here. Respondents are likely to over-report their attendance, just as they have over-reported their tithing behavior when compared to actual money received by the conferences, but even so it appears that the great majority of respondents attended church every week or most weeks. As may be observed in Table 3.11, 86% of those completing surveys from Northern California, 84% from São Paulo, 89% from Southern England, 92% from Western Australia, and 92% from Central Kenya report that they attend an Adventist church every week or most weeks.

Table 3.11: Country vs "I attend an Adventist church" (%)						
Country	Rarely / never	1 to 9 times per year	About once a month	2 to 3 times per month	Every week / most weeks	n =
Australia (WAC)	0.3%	1.3%	2.3%	4.4%	91.7%	1,621
England (SEC)	0.6%	0.7%	1.9%	7.0%	89.8%	1,001
Kenya (CKC)	0.0%	0.0%	2.1%	5.7%	92.2%	141
Brazil (SPC)	0.9%	0.7%	2.3%	12.3%	83.7%	1,080
USA (NCC)	0.5%	1.0%	1.8%	10.9%	85.9%	2,220
Combined	0.5%	1.0%	2.0%	8.5%	85.7%	6,063

Note: In Table 3.11, the column labelled "n =" refer to the number of respondents in that row. The rest of the data consists of percentages within the Conference. There were a total of 6,063 respondents who answered the question asking about their pattern of attendance at church.

4. Western Australia Conference (Tithe Receipts, Survey Data, Census Data)

The analysis of the surveys has revealed the importance of both age and frequency of giving in the tithing behavior of Seventh-day Adventists in selected churches in America, Australia, Brazil, and England. This is reflected in the larger amount of tithe as a percentage of income that is contributed by the older age-groups when compared to those who are younger. In this chapter a new perspective will be introduced. This was made possible by an analysis of tithe receipts in the light of some of the demographic and income data provided through the survey responses.

Each of the five conferences studied will be considered in turn. It is helpful to begin with the Western Australian data, because it is possible in that state to include a third way to evaluate tithing behavior, which is to compare data published by the Australian Bureau of Statistics (ABS) concerning income reported in the Australian Census by Adventists living in Western Australia with the amount of tithe received by the Western Australian Conference of Seventh-day Adventists. The survey and tithe analysis allowed a short-term evaluation to be made of tithing behavior. Consideraition of the Australian Bureau of Statistics' data allowed a long-term analysis of the percentage of income that members of the Adventist Church in Western Australia donated to the church as tithe.

4.1 Each Year Tithe Increased in Terms of AU$ Received, but this Hides the Reality that Each Year a Smaller Proportion of Member Income Is Received by Church in Western Australia

Like their fellow-Adventists around the world, Seventh-day Adventists living in Western Australia demonstrate their commitment to the mission of the Adventist Church in a most tangible manner when they donate up to 10% of their income to the Church as tithe. Year by year in the Western Australian Conference, church-members have contributed increasing amounts of tithe. This is reported widely in church circles as a good news story, and indeed it is. That so many give so willingly to the church is remarkable. Yet, as will emerge below from a comparison of census data with official Adventist tithe statistics, these apparently good results conceal an underlying trend which has the potential to have a significant negative impact on the ability of the church to fulfill its mission. While the dollar values of tithe are increasing year by year, tithe income is falling behind the cost of operating the church. Most costs in operating the Church are wages expenses, and evidence will be presented (see Table 4.7 and Figures 4.5 & 4.6) that between 1976 and 2001 tithe fell from 6.7% to 4.4% of total SDA income in Western Australia. This downward trend has already had an impact on the church, and if it continues, the negative impact on church supportive structures will be significant. Tithing is about more than money, it is about the ability of the church to fulfill its mission.

Compared to rising income levels, there has been a significant relative decrease in tithe given as a proportion of total income. This research reveals the likely explanation of that reduction, and by so doing, also reveals strategies by which the trend may be addressed and potentially reduced.

4.2 Age-profile of Church-attenders Compared with Population of Western Australia

Part of the protocol for distributing and collecting surveys in Western Australian churches was for the minister to designate someone to estimate the number of those who were in attendance who were qualified to fill in the survey and return it (i.e. all those aged at least 20 years). According to these reports, 2,292 individuals aged at least 20 years were in attendance at church in the Western Australian Conference on the Sabbath on which the churches participated in the survey.[1] They returned 1,822 usable surveys, which corresponds to an 80% participation rate.[2] Given that the survey asks

1 Official church statistics record the membership of Western Australia Conference as 5,402 on the 31st December 2006 ("144th Annual Statistical Report – 2006," General Conference of Seventh-day Adventists, p. 19). This number is considerably in excess of the 2,059 reported to be in attendance in the churches in the conference when the tithe surveys were conducted. Several factors would explain the difference between the official figures and those actually in attendance. First, children are usually between the ages of 9 and 13 when they are baptized and become members as a consequence. Thus many members would not have met the age qualification (≥ 20 yrs of age) to be counted among those attending. Second, the churches have many active programs that take numbers of their members away from attending on a particular Sabbath (e.g. Pathfinder expeditions). Others may have been on holiday. Third, Australian churches are often reluctant to remove from church rolls the names of those who no longer attend church, including some whose attendance has long ceased.

2 Participation rates in individual churches ranged from a low of 11% in one church, to a high of 100% in 8 churches.

for the age of the respondent, and that all the churches in the conference who usually have more than 20 attenders at their worship hour participated, the survey results can act as a proxy census of the Seventh-day Adventists who attend church in Western Australia. The numbers of respondents in the various age-groups are reported in Table 4.1 in the column headed "Survey Data (WAC)."

These data may be compared to data available from the Australian Bureau of Statistics. A question about religious affiliation has long been part of the Australian census. The question provides options such as "Anglican," "Catholic," and "Other" as potential answers. An individual who wished to identify themselves as a Seventh-day Adventist has the opportunity to write "Seventh-day Adventist" next to "Other." The Australian Bureau of Statistics is able to provide anonymized data regarding the age and income of those who specifically identified themselves as Seventh-day Adventists on a census form since 1976.

Not all of those who identified themselves as a Seventh-day Adventist on a census form would be in regular attendance at an Adventist Church, nor would all those who regularly attend an Adventist Church identify themselves as Seventh-day Adventist on the census. For this reason, the demographic profile of church-attenders from the survey is likely to be more accurate than that derived from the census data, although it is instructive to compare the numbers of those who declare themselves Adventists on a census to those who were attending church. This information may be found in Table 4.1, in the column headed "2001 Census (SDA)." It is enlightening to compare the age-demographics of the church with that of the general population of the state. This information is provided in the column labelled "2001 Census (WA)."

Table 4.1: Age-profile of Western Australia Population (Census), Western Australia Conference (Census, Survey) of those aged ≥ 20-Years						
	2001 Census (WA)		2001 Census (SDAs)		Survey Data (WAC)	
Age-group	Number	%	Number	%	Number	%
20-29	326,954	20%	754	17%	219	13%
30-39	317,678	19%	746	17%	247	14%
40-49	326,590	20%	705	16%	281	16%
50-59	284,263	17%	613	14%	313	18%
60-69	206,855	13%	442	10%	261	15%
70+	188,552	11%	642	15%	277	16%
Total	1,650,892		4,314		1,717	

It is easier to visualise the relationships between the three groups of numbers by viewing Figure 4.1

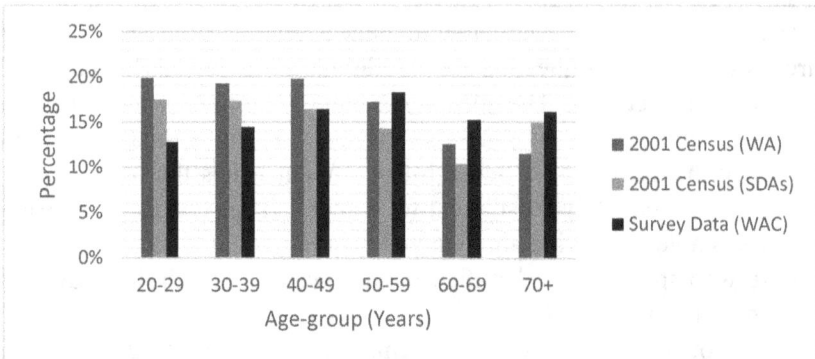

Fig. 4.1: Age-Profile from Census and Survey Compared (≥20 years, %, WAC)

The graph in Figure 4.1 highlights that compared to the general population, the 20-29 year old age-group is under-represented in the Adventist Church in Western Australia, and those aged 60 or more are over represented compared to the general population. The 30-49 year olds are also underrepresented when compared to the general population. This is true of both those who attend (i.e. the Survey data), and those who consider themselves to be Adventist (the Census data on SDAs).

4.3 Approximately Same Proportion of Each Age-group Tithes in Western Australia Conference

Previous research had indicated that age was a strong predictor of percentage of income contributed as tithe to the Seventh-day Adventist Church in Australia.[1] Older age-groups were more likely to provide a greater percentage of their income as tithe. Similar trends were also observed in the age-related patterns of tithing amongst Western Australian Seventh-day Adventists (see Table 4.3). It was thus surprising that this study revealed that about the same proportion of each age-group tithed at least once per year. This is the conclusion that grows out of the observation that the demographic pattern amongst tithers revealed by the analysis of conference tithe receipts is very close to the demographic pattern of attenders revealed by the survey (compare the number of respondents in Table 4.2 for both the

---

1   Robert K. McIver and Stephen J. Currow, "A Demographic Analysis of the Tithing Behavior of 2562 Seventh-day Adventists in Northern New South Wales, Australia," *Australian Religion Studies Review* 15 (2002): 115–25.

surveys and the tithe receipts), at least for those aged 20 to 59 years. In fact, both the number and proportion in each age-group that returned surveys is within 2% of the numbers who tithed at least once per year. This does not mean that everybody who returned a survey tithed at least once per year (not everybody that attends an Adventist Church in Western Australia was present on the day of the survey), but it does strongly indicate that a similar proportion of people in each age-group donates tithe at least once per year.

Table 4.2 Age-profiles of Survey Respondents and those who Contributed Tithe at Least Once in the Year Compared (≥ 20 yrs; WAC)					
	Survey Data (WAC)		Tithe Receipt Data (WAC)		
Age-group (Years)	Number	%	Number	%	Diff to Survey (%)
20-29	219	12.8%	214	11.4%	-1.4%
30-39	247	14.4%	236	12.6%	-1.8%
40-49	281	16.4%	334	17.8%	1.4%
50-59	313	18.2%	310	16.5%	-1.7%
60-69	261	15.2%	274	14.6%	-0.6%
70+	277	16.1%	406	21.6%	5.5%
Total	1717		1879		

4.4 Per-capita Tithe as a Proportion of Income Decreases Progressively from the Oldest to the Youngest Age-group

The 2006 West Australian Conference Tithe Survey was conducted in almost all of the churches in the conference (the exceptions all had fewer than 20 members in regular attendance). The survey asked questions regarding age and income. It was possible to determine from these surveys the demographic profile of those in attendance, and to estimate total income from each age-group. Dividing the total income by the numbers in the age-group gave an estimate of the average per-capita income for that age-group. Similar calculations were used to derive the average per-capita yearly tithe for each age-group, and the proportion of tithe to 10% of income. These statistics may be found in Table 4.3. When the proportion from each age-group is graphed, a clear age-related pattern emerges.

Table 4.3: Tithe Receipts vs.Income Estimated from Survey by Age (WAC)										
	Tithe Receipts Data				Survey Data				Comparison	
Age-group (Years)	Number of Tithers	Total Tithe (Receipts; Aus$)	Proportion of Total Tithe (%)	Per-capita Tithe (Aus$)	No of respondents	Estimated Total Income (Aus$)	Proportion. of Total Survey Income (%)	Per-capita Income (Aus$)	%Diff Survey Income vs Receipts	Per-capita Tithe as % of Potential Tithe
20-29	214	$49,035	5.6	$229	206	$4,897,500	11.8	$23,774	-6.2	9.6
30-39	236	$91,213	10.4	$386	219	$7,484,500	18.1	$34,176	-7.6	11.3
40-49	334	$166,373	19.0	$498	253	$9,687,500	23.4	$38,291	-4.4	13
50-59	310	$179,152	20.5	$578	279	$9,516,000	22.9	$34,108	-2.5	16.9
60-69	274	$171,196	19.6	$625	231	$5,525,500	13.3	$23,920	6.2	26.1
70+	406	$210,374	24.0	$518	240	$3,434,000	8.3	$14,308	15.7	36.2
Totals	1,879	$875,456			1,527	$41,465,000				

Definitions for columns in Table 4.3

Tithe Receipts Data: The four columns under the heading "Tithe Receipts Data" report on the results of an analysis of tithe receipts from the Western Australian Conference of Seventh-day Adventists

Survey Data: The figures in the four columns under the heading "Survey Data" were derived from an analysis of the surveys conducted in the Western Australian Conference

Comparison: The two columns under this heading report on comparisons made between the data derived from the analysis of tithe receipts and the analysis of survey responses

Number of Tithers: The number in each age bracket of discrete individuals for whom at least one tithe receipts had been written in the time period considered.

Total Tithe (Receipts; Aus$): Total tithe captured in tithe receipts for each age bracket, expressed in Australian dollars

Proportion of Total Tithe (%): The figures in this column were calculated by dividing the amount of tithe for each age-group by the total amount of tithe, expressed as a percentage

Per-capita Tithe (Aus$): The total amount of tithe divided by the number of tithers for each age bracket, expressed in Australian dollars

No. of Respondents: The number of individuals of each age-group who completed and returned a survey

Estimated Tot Income (Aus$): The estimate of income in Australian dollars was calculated by multiplying the number of respondents to the survey in a particular age-group that chose each income range by the mid-point of that income range; the result is an estimate of the total income received by a particular age-group

Proportion of Total Survey Income (%): The percentage of total income (all age-groups) that is earned by a particular age-group

Per-capita Income (Aus$): The number in this column was calculated by dividing the survey income by the number of individuals in the age-group

%Dif survey income vs. tithe receipts: The difference between the proportion of total survey income and the proportion of total tithe contributed by that age-group

Per-capita Tithe as % of Potential Tithe: Actual tithe as a percentage of potential tithe (potential tithe =10% of total income). In other words, the amount of tithe divided by the number of those who tithe at least once per year, expressed as a percentage of 0.1 (or 10%) of total income for the age-group estimated from the survey divided by the number of that age-group

The trend in the ratio of per-capita tithe receipts versus potential tithe (or one tenth of per-capita income) is already clear in Table 4.3 but becomes unmistakable when presented in graphical form (Figure 4.2).

Fig. 4.2: Per-capita Tithe as % of Potential Tithe (i.e. 10% of income; WAC)

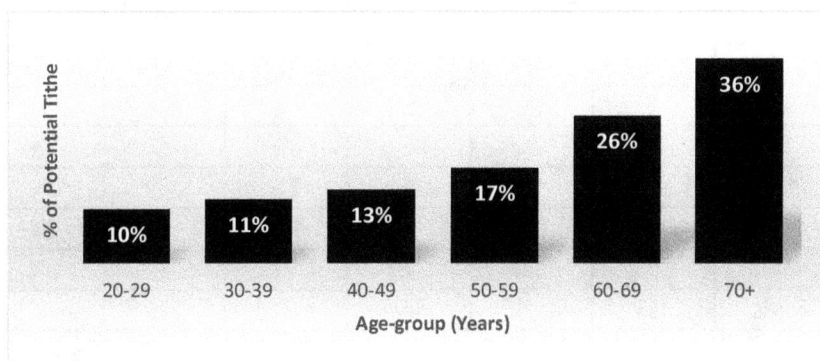

In sum, in Western Australian Seventh-day Adventist Churches, each progressively younger age-group is contributing a smaller proportion of income as tithe than the age-group immediately above it.

4.5 Frequency of Giving: Data from Tithe Receipts

It is clear from Table 4.3 and Figure 4.2 that the proportion of income given as tithe diminishes with each younger age-group. This is in spite of the fact, revealed in Table 4.2, that at least between the ages of 20 and 59, the proportion of those who are tithing in each age-group appears to be very similar. An explanation is found in an examination of the frequency of giving in the tithe receipts. Table 4.4 records the frequency of giving for each age-group, together with a percentage of the tithers that contribute that frequently. Since the numbers of non-tithers was very large compared to numbers in other frequency classes, it was decided not to include frequency 0 in either the percentage calculations or the graph. Two additional factors led to the conclusion that this was in fact a better way to approach the data: (i) it highlighted the behavior of those who were giving; (ii) it discounted any variation that might have occurred in how church pastors dealt with those who attended church less than 3 times per month.

Table 4.4: Frequency of Giving by Age-group (WAC Tithe Receipts)						
	20-39 yrs		40-49 yrs		≥ 60 yrs	
Freq	Count	as% of tithers	Count	as% of tithers	Count	as% of tithers
0	343		459		447	
1-5	58	53%	63	34%	52	19%
6-10	22	20%	34	18%	51	18%
11-15	10	9%	39	21%	36	13%
16-20	8	7%	16	9%	29	10%
21-25	10	9%	15	8%	41	15%
26-30	1	1%	8	4%	43	15%
31-35	0	0%	5	3%	6	2%
36-40	1	1%	3	2%	7	3%
41-45	0	0%	3	2%	6	2%
46-50	0	0%	2	1%	7	3%
Totals	453	n=110	647	n=188	725	n=278

The analysis of giving patterns in the tithe receipts provided in Table 4.4 provides evidence that frequency of tithe-giving increases with age of the member. For example, most wage-earners are paid fortnightly and if they tithed after every pay period they would do so 26 times per year, and certainly more than 21 times per year. Yet tithe receipts reveal that only 11% of the 20–39-yr age-group contribute tithe more than 21 times per year, while 40% those aged more than 60 years contribute tithe at this frequency. Thus it is not the proportion of those who tithe across the various age-groups that varies (about the same proportion from each age-group tithes), but the frequency of giving found in each age-group. As large a proportion as 53% of those who tithe in the 20–39-yr age-group tithe between 1 and 5 times per year. While some of these own their own businesses, and in consequence would be likely to tithe at this low frequency, the majority receive pay on a fortnightly cycle. The differences in giving patterns were found to be statistically significant.[1]

Figure 4.3 (below) allows a comparison between the three groups to be made readily. It is evident that each older age-group is better represented amongst those that contribute more frequently.

Fig 4.3: Frequency of Giving by Age-group (WAC Tithe Receipts)

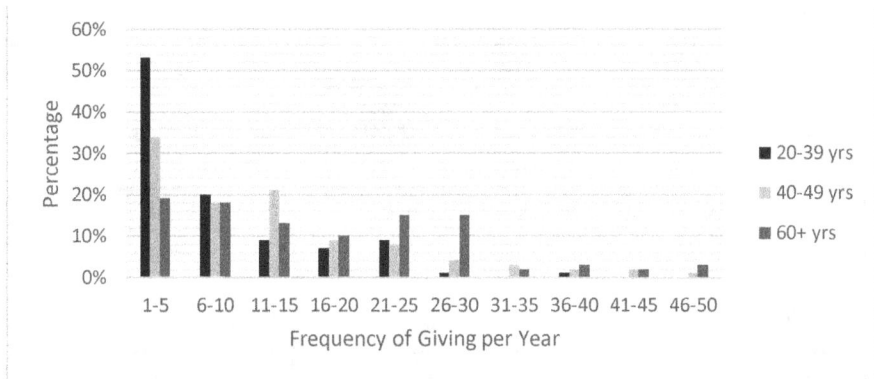

Summing up: (i) approximately the same proportion of each age-group under the age of 60 contributes tithe to the conference at least once in a year; (ii) as a percentage of their income, each age-group contributes less than the age-group immediately older than them; (iii) this pattern can be explained to a great extent by the frequency with which the various age-groups contribute tithe: frequency of tithe-paying increases with age. Note that if the frequency of giving is put in rank order for the three age-groups, 20–39, 40–59, and ≥ 60, the middle frequency of giving (i.e. the median) for each group is 4, 8 and 14 respectively.

_____

1 A T-test was performed on the frequency of giving data for the 20–39-yr age-group and the 40–59-yr age-group (the nil-frequency group was excluded). The test was done using the null-hypothesis that there was no difference between the giving patterns of each of the three age-groups. The two-tailed T-test assuming unequal variances (the most demanding type) revealed that if that was the case, then these types of outcomes have a probability of 1.56E-05 (i.e. it might occur randomly in one out of 156,000 times). Such an outcome is so unlikely that one must reject the null-hypothesis that there is no difference between the groups, and accept that there a statically significant difference between them.

4.6 Results from Survey: Tithing in Various Age-groups

Several questions in the survey related to tithing behavior. For example, Qu. B1 asked: "In the last 12 months, as a percentage of my income, I estimate that I have given":

Tithe	Offerings+gifts to charity	
□ 0% □ <2% □ 2-4% □ 5-7% □ 8-9% □ 10% □ 11+% of my total income	□ 0% □ ≤1% □ 2-3% □ 4-5% □ 6-9% □ 10+% of my total income	OR approximately $_____

Answers to question B1 shown in Table 4.5 reveal that 66% of respondents considered that they had returned at least 10% of their income as tithe.

Table 4.5: Tithe Given as Percent of Income (WAC)		
Tithe as % Income	Count	Percent
0%	151	10%
<2%	102	7%
2-4%	77	5%
5-7%	91	6%
8-9%	87	6%
10%	954	61%
11+%	89	6%
Total	1,553	

The previously reported analysis of conference tithe receipts reveals that the survey responses considerably overestimated the amount of tithe returned to the conference. Even so, the age-specific responses are quite illuminating. Table 4.6 provides a simplified break-down of the responses to Qu. B1 by age-group. The tithing behavior reported in Qu. B1 has been accumulated into three groups: "No tithe" (those who do not tithe at all); "1-7% of income as Tithe," "8-10%+ as Tithe." The percentage figures are for each age-group.

Table 4.6: Age vs Tithing Status (WAC)									
		Age-Group (Years)							
Tithe %		20-29	30-39	40-49	50-59	60-69	70-79	≥ 80	Total
No tithe	Count	31	25	29	21	12	5	0	150
	%	15%	11%	11%	7%	5%	3%	0%	10%
1-7% tithe	Count	71	55	38	39	24	10	1	267
	%	35%	24%	15%	14%	10%	6%	2%	17%
8-10+% tithe	Count	104	146	192	222	202	165	65	1148
	%	51%	65%	74%	79%	85%	92%	99%	73%
Total		206	226	259	282	238	180	66	1565

Fig 4.4: Age vs Tithing Status (WAC)

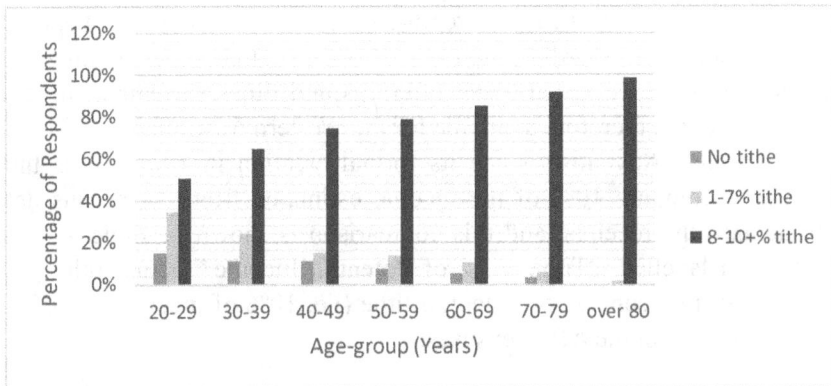

The trend in self-reported tithing is clear: each successively older age-group contained a higher proportion of those who consider they return a full 10% as tithe, and a smaller proportion of those who do not tithe.

4.7 The Proportion of Income Received in Tithe Has Declined Steadily for at Least the Last 40 Years in the Western Australia Conference

Two data sets allow an estimate to be made of long-term tithing trends in Western Australia: census data and church reports. Since 1976 members of the Seventh-day Adventist church have been able to identify their religious denomination on the census. On the census they also indicate their yearly income. As has already been explained (see section 4.2), the Australian Bureau of Statistics is able to provide reports of special searches of the Census data. It provided statistics concerning age and income of Australians living in West Australia who had declared themselves as Seventh-day Adventists on the censuses that were collected in 1976, 1981, 1986, 1991, 1996, 2001, 2006 and 2011 (the data from the 2016 census is not yet available). From these data it is possible to estimate the total income earned by those who had declared themselves Adventists on the survey done in WAC, and the proportion of this income that was earned by each age-group. Not all of those who declare themselves to be Seventh-day Adventists on the census attend church regularly or contribute tithes and offerings. Nevertheless, the census provides the best available long-term estimate of the earning power of Seventh-day Adventists in Australia.

These figures may then be compared to total tithe receipts from the conference as they are reported in official church statistics. Since its formal organization in the 1860s, the Seventh-day Adventist Church has kept and published statistics regarding numbers of organized churches, numbers of members, ordained members, and offerings and tithes. Membership and tithing figures are therefore available for the Western Australian Conference of Seventh-day Adventists since its formal creation in 1902. It is thus possible to compare 10% of the income estimated from the census data with actual tithe receipts, and this comparison is shown in Table 4.7. In the column labelled, "Tithe as % of Potential Income," actual tithe paid is shown as a percentage of potential tithe (i.e. 10% of income), based on income reported in the ABS censuses.

Table 4.7: Tithe Compared to Potential Tithe (i.e. 10% "Census" Income; WAC)							
Year	Total Tithe (AUS$)	Mem-ber-ship	Per Capita Tithe	10% "Census Income"	No SDAs (Census)	Per Capita 10% "Census Income"	Tithe as % of Potential Tithe
1941	$30,175	1396	$21.62				
1946	$42,317	1,394	$30.36				
1951	$83,092	1,827	$45.48				
1956	$117,982	2,315	$50.96				
1961	$182,551	3,001	$60.83				
1966	$278,794	3,332	$83.67				
1971	$432,747	3,637	$118.98				

Table 4.7: Tithe Compared to Potential Tithe (i.e. 10% "Census" Income; WAC)							
Year	Total Tithe (AUS$)	Member-ship	Per Capita Tithe	10% "Census Income"	No SDAs (Census)	Per Capita 10% "Census Income"	Tithe as % of Potential Tithe
1976	$1,005,910	3,955	$254.34	$1,269,375	4,538	$280	91%
1981	$1,736,152	4,320	$401.89	$2,533,456	5,061	$501	80%
1986	$2,256,746	4,681	$482.11	$3,577,550	5,145	$695	69%
1991	$2,978,916	5,109	$583.07	$5,091,645	5,072	$1,004	58%
1996	$3,361,290	5,155	$652.04	$6,745,076	5,494	$1,228	53%
2001	$3,742,876	5,322	$703.28	$8,517,080	5,481	$1,554	45%
2006	$4,849,976	5,402	$897.81	$11,555,456	5,506	$2,099	43%
2011	$6,862,899	5,871	$1,168.95	$20,612,972	6,933	$2,973	39%

Definitions for Columns in Table 4.7

Total Tithe (AUS$): is calculated by multiplying the tithe recorded for Western Australia in the Annual Statistical Reports from the Office of Archives, Statistics and Research of the General Conference of Seventh-day Adventists (which is given in US$), by the US$ to AUS$ exchange rate for December 31 reported by http://fxtop.com/en/currency-converter-past.

Membership: of the Western Australian Conference of Seventh-day Adventists as recorded in the Annual Statistical Reports.

Per Capita Tithe: is calculated by dividing the total tithe by the membership.

10% "Census Income": is 10% of the total income for those who identified themselves as Seventh-day Adventists in the Census, from data that has been provided by the Australian Bureau of Statistics.

No SDAs (Census): is the number of those who identified themselves as Seventh-day Adventists on the Census.

Per Capita 10% "Census" Income: is calculated by dividing 10% "Census Income" by No SDAs (Census).

Figures 4.5 and 4.6 show the comparison between annual tithe receipts in the WA Conference as they are reported in official Church statistics and 10% of the total income of those who identified themselves as Seventh-day Adventists in the Australian census. The first, Figure 4.5, graphs tithe returned and 10% of census income in dollar figures. The second, Figure 4.6 shows the percentage of potential tithe that has been returned to the church since 1976, and the steady deline in the relative proportion of income that has been returned to the church over this time period.

As may be observed from Figure 4.5, the absolute value of tithe has continued to increase in Western Australia, but it is not increasing at the same rate as income. I believe that the best explanation for this lies in the differences in tithing behavior between the various age-groups. While about the same proportion of each age-group tithes, frequency of tithe-paying diminishes with each progressively younger age-group and the net result is that a smaller proportion of income is donated as tithe as age decreases. The hope that as the members of each age-group grow older they will adopt more systematic giving patterns appears to be dashed by the fact that over the long term in Western Australia, the proportion of income returned as tithe has actually decreased. The most likely explanation is that once each age-group has established its tithing pattern, that pattern tends to persist over time.

Fig. 4.5: Tithe Compared to 10% of SDA Income Reported on Census (WAC)

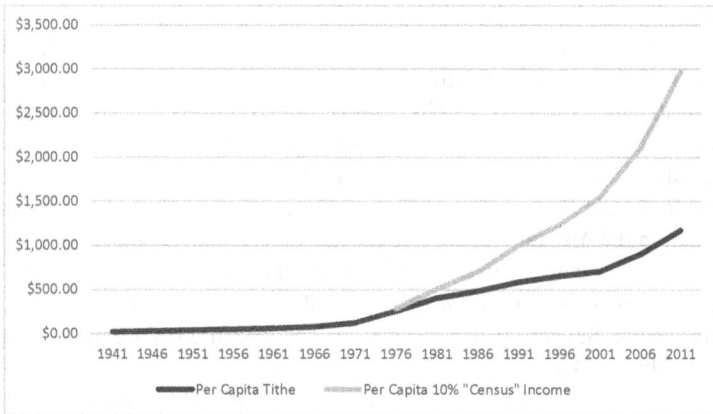

Fig. 4.6: Tithe Expressed as % of Potential Tithe since 1976 (WAC)

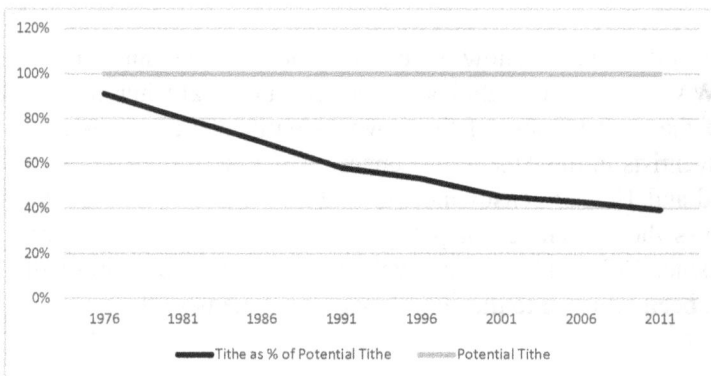

4.8 Conclusions (WAC)

Several conclusions stand out from the analysis of the tithe receipts, the survey responses and the census data from Western Australia. Figure 4.5 reveals that while tithe receipts received by the Western Australia Conference have been increasing each year, tithe returned is acutally a smaller proportion of the total income earned by Seventh-day Adventists living in the state. Table 4.7 provides figures to show that the percentage of total income earned that is returned to the church has fallen from approximately 6.7% to 4.4%. Since wages—particularly ministers' wages—constitute the bulk of the conference's expenses, the increases in the conference's expenditure reflect community wage increases rather than increases in tithe returned. Paradoxically, the end effect is that the conference has less and less funds to fund its mission despite the rise in tithe receipts expressed in Australian dollars. Unless this decline in the proportion of income returned as tithe is addressed, the potential impact on the church will be grave.

The analysis of the survey responses and tithe receipts reveals why there has been a fall in the percentage of income returned to the church as tithe. The 1,879 respondents that provided information on both their age and income on the survey enabled a good estimate to be made of the total income earned by each age-group. When data from an analysis of actual tithe receipts are compared, it is clear that each younger age cohort contributes less of their income than the immediately older age-group (see Table 4.3 and Fig. 4.2). The analysis of tithe receipts reveals also that about the same proportion of each age-group returns tithe at least once per year. In other words, there is an equivalent willingness to tithe found among every age-group. The difference in their tithing behavior lies in the frequency of giving. Each younger age cohort contributes less frequently than the cohort immediately older than it. This observation will be taken up again in Chapters 8 and 9, which will consider the best means by which tithing may be promoted.

72

5. Northern California Conference (Tithe Receipts, Survey Data, Church Rolls, CPI, Census)

5.1 Scope of Study

5.1.1 Tithe Receipts

The pastoral teams and treasurers of 21 churches in Northern California worked together to provide a report on the tithing behavior of the various age-groups as indicated in tithe receipts, using the method outlined earlier in this book. The report was generated in such a way that the identity of those who paid tithe was not known by the researchers. These 21 churches represent an official membership of 10,459, of which 4,514 were identified as being in regular attendance. Of these, 2,916 (64.5%) of regular attenders contributed tithe in a pattern which could be discerned from an analysis of the tithe receipts held at the local church.[1] As tithes and other offerings are tax deductible in northern California, members are mindful that all tithes and offerings should be documented through the church treasury, and local churches have robust systems for tracking and reporting the donations of each individual donor. Altogether, the following analysis represents 38,038 separate individual donations of tithe which amounted to a total of $10,670,310.84, as well as other donations to the amount of $7,061,210.58.[2]

---

1 The following question was asked in all versions of the survey, "In the last 12 months I have given tithe (shade all that apply); and all versions of the survey included the following options for answers: To the Conference through: the tithe envelope in my local church; Adventist e-giving; Directly to my church treasurer; Directly to the local conference." At the urging of the NCC stewardship director, the following option was included in the NCC version of the survey: "Directly to the Union Conference / NAD Division / General Conference." 2% of respondents from NCC report that they send their tithe Directly to the Union Conference / NAD Division / General Conference, and the tithe from this 2% of respondents would not appear in the receipts of their local church.

2 Uniquely amongst the tithe-receipt data reported in this study, the analysis of tithe receipts in Northern California was undertaken by already-busy volunteers who work without fanfare and with complete discretion in their local church communities. I would like to pause for a moment to thank the church treasurers who freely gave of their time to contribute to this significant data set.

5.1.2 Survey

Survey forms were received from 3,370 individuals who were at least 20 years of age, and who represent 74.7% of 4,514 members who regularly attended one of the 21 churches that participated in the research.

5.2 Data from Tithe Receipts and Church Rolls

Tithe receipts were used to derive information about the number of donors and the amount of tithe and other donations that came from each age-group. Pastors had also worked with treasurers to provided information regarding how many in each age-group were attending church regularly, and a count of those who were on a church roll but not attending regularly. These data are shown in Table 5.1.

Table 5.1 Age-group, Total Tithe, Church Roll, Attenders, CA Census (NCC)						
Age-group (Years)	Total Tithe (Receipts; US$)	Total Non-tithe (Receipts; US$)	Number of Tithers	Total Number in Age-group	Attend	Census
20-29	$164,262.89	$81,814.02	108	829	246	5,581,679
30-39	$839,071.17	$327,870.18	261	978	370	5,198,476
40-49	$1,543,249.43	$918,447.50	357	1,087	552	5,255,912
50-59	$2,410,187.80	$1,564,206.84	586	1,436	808	4,985,348
60-69	$2,104,475.48	$1,784,303.43	590	1,214	760	3,461,307
70-79	$1,498,323.23	$971,008.20	496	809	596	1,847,912
80 +	$1,459,186.46	$940,140.72	459	698	457	1,273,169
Total	$10,018,756.46	$6,587,790.89	2,857	7,051	3,789	27,603,803

Definition for columns in Table 5.1:

Age: The statistics in the row are for those in the stated age-group

Total Tithe (Receipts; US$): The total amount of tithe contributed by an age-group, expressed in US dollars

Total Non-tithe (Receipts; US$): The amount of donations other than tithe received from an age-group, expressed in US dollars

Number of Tithers: The number of discrete tithers from an age-group

Total Number in Age-group: Number of those who are on the church roll and known to the church ministerial staff well enough that they can estimate their age—attender and non-attender alike

Attend: The number of those on the church roll and who were identified as regular attenders, in that they attend the church in which they hold their membership at least once per month

Census: 2012 age profile from population estimates by the California Department of Finance and based on the 2010 Census by the United States Census Bureau – www.dof.ca.gov/research/demographic/reports/projections/P-3

5.3 Age-profiles of Church-attenders, Church-members and Population of California Compared

In Australia, Brazil and England, the criterion used for determining whether or not a church-member was an attender was set at attending three or more times per month. As may be observed in Table 3.10 (see 3.4 "Frequency of Attendance at an Adventist Church" in Chapter 3), this criterion appears to be a reasonable one for Australia and England, because in those countries (and in Kenya), 90% or more of the respondents to the Survey indicated that they attended church every week or most weeks. The number drops to 84% and 86% respectively for Brazil and the United States. Furthermore, those attending 2 or 3 times per month would be under-represented in the survey responses.

As a result of discussions with the stewardship director of the Northern California Conference, who pointed out that many members attend several different churches during any one month, it was decided that another attendance category should be added for the Californian research: those who attend the church where they hold their membership once or twice per month. Table 5.2 shows the attendance patterns noted by the church ministerial teams for those listed on their membership rolls.

Table 5.2: Attendance Patterns (NCC)						
Age-group (Years)	0 times/ month	1-2/Month	3+/month	Attend	1-2 as % of Attenders	0 as % of Total
20-29	583	95	151	246	39%	70%
30-39	608	89	281	370	24%	62%
40-49	535	126	426	552	23%	49%
50-59	628	160	648	808	20%	44%
60-69	454	127	633	760	17%	37%
70-79	213	72	524	596	12%	26%
80 +	241	59	398	457	13%	35%
Total	3262	728	3061	3789	19%	46%
Unknown	5,408					

Definition for columns in Table 5.2:

0 times/month: Number of those who are known to the church ministerial staff well enough that they can estimate their age, who attend the church at which they hold their membership *less than once per month*.

1-2/Month: Number of those who are known to the church ministerial staff well enough that they can estimate their age, who attend the church at which they hold their membership *once or twice per month*.

3+/Month: Number of those who are known to the church ministerial staff well enough that they can estimate their age, who attend the church at which they hold their membership *three or more times per month*.

Attend: The number of those who were identified as regular attenders, in that they attend the church in which they hold their membership *at least once per month*.

1-2 as % of Attenders: Number of those who attend church once or twice per month as a percentage of all those that attend church regularly (i.e. more than once per month).

0 as % of Total: Number of non-attenders whose age may be estimated as a percentage of all those who on the church roll who have a known age (attenders and non-attenders).

Row Definition: Unknown: Number of those who are on the church roll, but who are not known to the church ministerial staff well enough that they can estimate their age.

One may observe from Table 5.2 that 81% of members of the 22 Northern California Churches in the sample who are attenders (i.e. attend at least once per month the church where they hold their membership) actually attend that church three or more times per month, while 19% of them do so one or two times per month. The ministerial teams of the churches knew a further 3262 individuals well enough to be able to estimate the ages of those who do not attend church at least once per month. From these data it was possible to generate an age-profile of the church-members in the sample, and to compare it with the age-profile of the general population of California. The age-profiles of church-members are shown in Table 5.3.

Table 5.3: Age Profile of Church-Members (≥20 yrs) Compared to Population of California (NCC)						
Age-group	Attend		Tot No in Age-group		Census	
	Count	%	Count	%	Count	%
20-29	246	6%	829	12%	5,581,679	20%
30-39	370	10%	978	14%	5,198,476	19%
40-49	552	15%	1,087	15%	5,255,912	19%
50-59	808	21%	1,436	20%	4,985,348	18%

Table 5.3: Age Profile of Church-Members (≥20 yrs) Compared to Population of California (NCC)						
Age-group	Attend		Tot No in Age-group		Census	
	Count	%	Count	%	Count	%
60-69	760	20%	1214	17%	3,461,307	13%
70-79	596	16%	809	11%	1,847,912	7%
80 +	457	12%	698	10%	1,273,169	5%
Total	3,789		7,051		27,603,803	

Definition for columns in Table 5.3:

Attend: The number of those who were identified as regular attenders, in that they attend the church in which they hold their membership at least once per month.

Census: 2012 age profile from population estimates by the California Department of Finance and based on the 2010 Census by the United States Census Bureau – www.dof.ca.gov/research/demographic/reports/projections/P-3

Count: Number of individuals

%: Number of individuals divided by column total expressed as a percentage

Figure 5.1 is a bar graph of the proportion of attenders in each age-group aged at least 20 years, all members for whom an age may be estimated, and the population of the state, allowing easy comparison between the three different age-profiles.

Fig. 5.1: Age Profile of Church-Members Compared to State Age Profile (≥20 yrs, %, NCC)

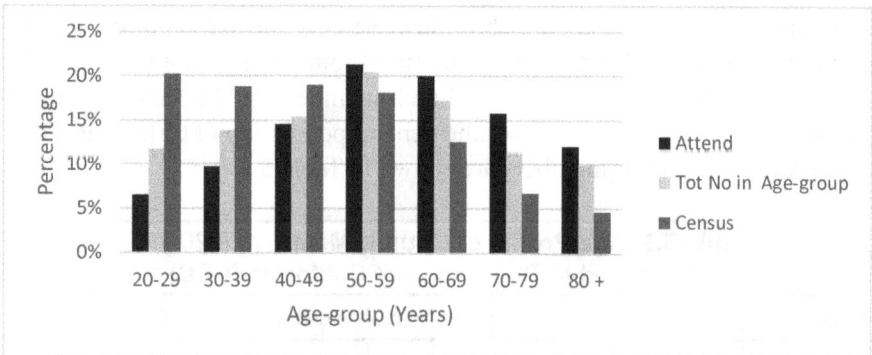

Table 5.3 and Figure 5.1 reveal that about the same proportion of the general Californian population are found in the four age-groups, 20–29, 30–39, 40–49, and 50–59 years (they differ by less than 2%—see "Census" column of Table 5.3). By way of comparison, the age-profiles of the

members and attenders of the 22 churches in the study reveal that the 20–29-yr group constitute the smallest age-group of those aged between 20 and 60, years, while the largest cohort is the 50–59-yr age-group. It appears that, when compared to the general population of California, the 20–29-yr age-group is under-represented in the church, while those aged 70 or more years are over-represented.

5.4 Approximately the Same Proportion of Church-attenders in California aged from 30 to 69 years Return Tithe

Table 5.4 shows the percentage of attenders of tither is earch age-group (column 4), the percentage of all those who are known well enough to the ministerial team for their age to be estimated and who tithe (column 6), and the percentage of those who attend out of all those known to be in a certain age-bracket (column 7).

Table 5.4: Percentage of Tithers in Each Age-group (NCC)						
Age-Group (Years)	No of Tithers	Attend	% Tithers per Attenders	Tot No in Age-group	% Tithers per Tot No	% Attenders vs Names
20-29	108	246	44%	829	13%	30%
30-39	261	370	71%	978	27%	38%
40-49	357	552	65%	1087	33%	51%
50-59	586	808	73%	1436	41%	56%
60-69	590	760	78%	1214	49%	63%
70-79	496	596	83%	809	61%	74%
80 +	459	457	100%	698	66%	65%
Total	2857	3789		7051		

Definition for columns in Table 5.4:

Age: The statistics in the row are for those in the stated age-group

No of Tithers: The number of discrete tithers from an age-group

Attend: The number of those who were identified as regular attenders, in that they attend the church in which they hold their membership at least once per month.

% Tithers per Attenders: The percentage of attenders who return tithe

Tot No in Age-group: Those who are on the church roll and known to the church ministerial staff well enough that they can estimate their age—attender and non-attender alike

% Tithers per Tot No: The number of tithers as a percentage of "Tot No in Age-group"

% Attenders vs Names: The percentage of attenders as a fraction of "Tot No in Age-group"

Figure 5.2 shows the percentage of attenders in each age-group who tithed through their local church. Three features of the graph stand out: (1) a much smaller percentage of the 20-29-yr age-group tithed compared to any other age-group; (2) all groups aged 50 years and over showed an increasing percentage of tithers; (3) it is hard to discern a difference between the tithing patterns shown by the three age-groups in the 30–59-yr age-range. Those in the 30–39-yr age-group tithed at a slightly higher rate than those in the 40–49-yr age-group. The 50–59-yr age-group tithed at a rate only 2 percent more than the 30–39-yr group, and the 60–69-yr age-group at a rate 5 percent more. Perhaps one should conclude that there is little difference between the percentage of attenders across the 30–69-yr age-range who return tithe.

Fig. 5.2: The Percentage of Attenders who Return Tithe through their Local Church in each Age-Group (NCC)

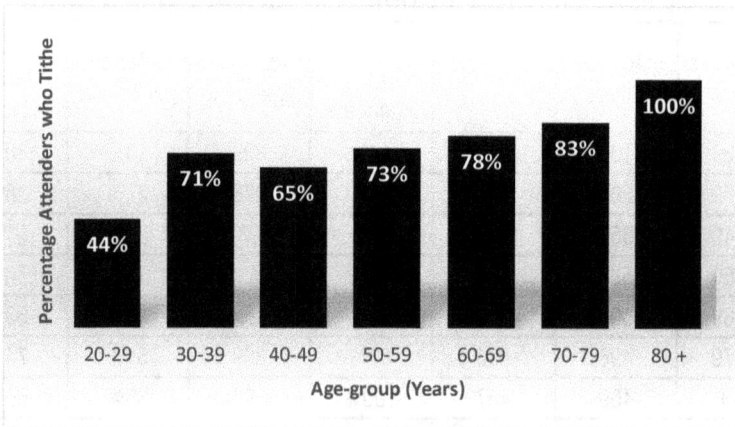

5.5 Frequency of Tithing Decreases Progressively with Each Younger Age-group

The data in Table 3.2 revealed that most Northern Californian Seventh-day Adventists intend to return tithe either monthly (i.e. 12 times per year) or semi-monthly (i.e. 26 times per year). From Table 5.5, which documents the number of tithers in the 20–29, 40–49, and 60–69-yr age-groups who tithe at each frequency, it is apparent that the actual frequency of tithing observed in the tithe receipts varies considerably from the intended frequency, particularly among the 20–29-yr age-group. The pattern of differences is apparent in the two bar charts that show tithing frequency (as found in tithe receipts) (see Figures 3.3 and 3.4), one from the 20–29-yr age-group, and one from the 60–69-yr age-group.

Table 5:5: Frequency of Returning Tithe in Each Age-group (Tithe Receipts, NCC)						
Freq	20-29		40-49		60-69	
	Count	%	Count	%	Count	%
2	37	34%	48	13%	77	13%
4	19	18%	34	9%	44	7%
6	12	11%	32	9%	48	8%
8	4	4%	18	5%	46	8%
10	6	6%	35	10%	49	8%
12	11	10%	56	16%	91	15%
14	3	3%	23	6%	49	8%
16	2	2%	12	3%	35	6%
18	3	3%	18	5%	28	5%
20	1	1%	15	4%	10	2%
22	1	1%	9	3%	10	2%
24	3	3%	16	4%	32	5%
26	2	2%	14	4%	18	3%
52	4	4%	29	8%	65	11%
Total Tithers	108		359		602	

Fig. 5.3: Tithing Frequency of 20–29-Year-Old Age-group (NCC)

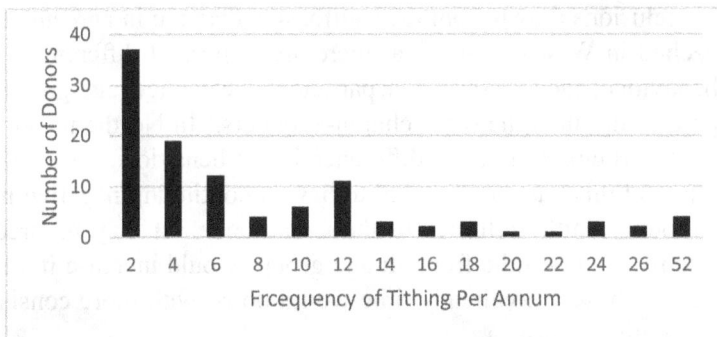

Fig. 5.4: Tithing Frequency of 60–69-Year-Old Age-group (NCC)

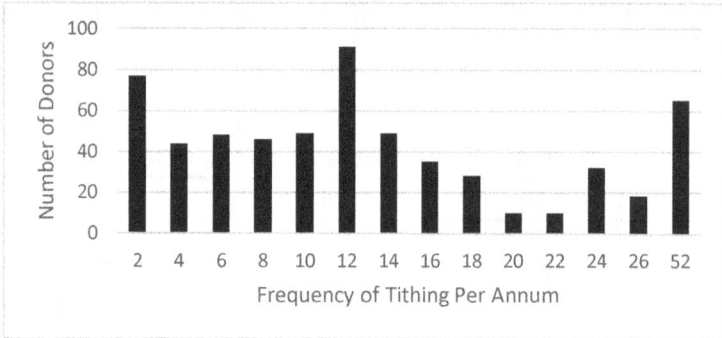

The two bar charts in Figures 5.3 and 5.4 have a different appearance that is more than superficial. The bar charts show that tithers in the younger age-group were most likely to contribute less frequently, whereas tithe-payers in the older age-group contributed across a range of frequencies. A (two-tailed) t-test comparing the giving patterns of the 20–29 year olds and the 60–69 year olds revealed that the probability of this result being random is 7.9E-08, or likely to occur less than 8 times in 10,000,000 events. In other words, there is a highly significant statistical difference between the two age-groups in the frequency of giving tithe. While the 20–29 age-group falls far short of tithing with a frequency of at least 12 times per year, not all in the 60–69 age-group meet their intention of tithing at this frequency, as they had indicated was their practice in their answer to a question on the tithing survey. Many from this older age-group do in fact tithe weekly, and some monthly, but these numbers are nearly matched by those who tithe from between 2 to 10 times per year. The survey revealed that some within this older age-group have the intention of tithing yearly or quarterly, but their numbers are much smaller than the numbers who intend to tithe weekly, semi-monthly or monthly.

The conclusions drawn from the Californian data are in agreement with those reached in Western Australia: there are important differences in the tithing behavior of each age-group, in particular, the younger age-groups tithe more sporadically than the older church-attenders. In Northern California there was a particularly notable difference in the behavior of the 20–29-yr age-group, and this has the potential to have a continuing negative impact on the amount of tithe returned to the Conference. It may be predicted from these results that tithe from all age-groups would increase if a higher percentage of those who already tithe would do so with more consistency than is currently the case.

5.6 Per-capita Income (Survey Data) Compared to Per-capita Tithe (Tithe Receipts)

Surveys were conducted in all of the churches which provided reports on tithe. One of the questions on the survey asked about income. The complete overlap between the churches that provided an analysis of tithe receipts and those churches that conducted tithe surveys enabled an estimate to be made of the total income for each age-group within the total sample. Not all those who regularly attend the churches in which the surveys were conducted completed a survey. Nevertheless, the surveys provide the best estimate of the age-related income profile of the churches involved in the analysis of the tithe receipts. It was therefore possible to compare the amount of tithe contributed with income (Table 5.6), and the per-capita tithe contributed with per-capita income of each age-group of the members attending those churches (Table 5.7).

Table 5.6: Comparison between Survey Income and Tithe Receipts (NCC)							
	Survey Data				Tithe Receipts Data		
Age-group (Years)	Number of Surveys	Estimated Tot Income (US$)	Proportion of Tot Survey Income (%)	Total Tithe (US$)	Proportion of Tot Tithe Receipts (%)	Difference between Proportion Income and Tithe	
20-29	212	$6,015,915.50	3.5	$164,262.89	1.6	-1.9	
30-39	326	$18,400,875.50	10.8	$839,071.17	8.4	-2.4	
40-49	470	$29,626,589.00	17.4	$1,543,249.43	15.4	-2	
50-59	683	$42,140,256.50	24.7	$2,410,187.80	24.1	-0.6	
60-69	735	$40,152,961.00	23.6	$2,104,475.48	21	-2.6	
70-79	484	$20,667,285.00	12.1	$1,498,323.23	15	2.9	
80 +	364	$13,470,087.50	7.9	$1,459,186.46	14.6	6.7	
Total	3274	$170,473,970.00		$10,018,756.46			

Definition for columns in Table 5.6:

Number of Surveys: The number of individuals in each age-group who completed and returned a survey

Estimated Tot Income (US$): The estimate of income was calculated by multiplying the number of individuals in a particular age-group that chose each income range by the mid-point of that income range; the result is an estimate of the total income received by a particular age-group expressed in US dollars

Proportion of Tot Survey Income (%): The percentage of total income (all age-groups) that is earned by a particular age-group

Total Tithe (US$): The total amount of tithe contributed by an age-group

Proportion of Tot Tithe Receipts (%): The figures in this column were calculated by dividing the amount of tithe for each age-group by the total amount of tithe, expressed as a percentage.

Difference between Proportion Income and Tithe: The figures in this column were calculated by subtracting the percentage column, "Proportion of Tot Survey Income (%)" from the percentage in the column, "Proportion of Tot Tithe Receipts (%)"

Table 5.6 reveals that the greatest proportion of tithe comes from the 50–69-yr age-group, which is matched by the fact that this age-group has the greatest total income and the greatest number of church-attenders (Table 5.3). The largest number of survey returns also came from this age-group (Table 5.6)..

One can compare the various age-groups by considering the per-capita income and per-capita tithe (see Table 5.7). Per-capita income was calculated by dividing the total income by the number of surveys returned by that age-group. Per-capita tithe is calculated from two perspectives in Table 5.7. "Per-capita Tithe (Tithers)" represents the total amount of tithe divided by the number of donors for each age-group. This figure provides an average measure of the income that an individual tither makes in each age-group. The column "Per-capita Tithe (Attenders)" in Table 5.7 represents the total amount of tithe divided by the number who attend church at least once per month for each age-group. This latter figure provides a measure of the proportion of the total income earned by all attenders (tithers and non-tithers alike) that is earned by each respective age-group.

Table 5.7: Comparison between Per-capita Tithe Receipts and Per-capita Survey Income USA (NCC)					
	Survey	Tithe Receipts		Comparison	
Age-group (Years)	Per-capita Income	Per-capita Tithe (Tithers; US$)	Per-capita Tithe (Attenders; US$)	Per-capita Tithe (Tithers) as % of Potential Tithe (10% Income)	Per-capita Tithe (Attenders) as % of Potential Tithe (10% Income)
20-29	$28,376.96	$1,521.00	$662.35	54%	23%
30-39	$56,444.40	$3,214.80	$2,261.60	57%	40%
40-49	$63,035.30	$4,322.80	$2,785.60	69%	44%
50-59	$61,698.77	$4,112.90	$2,975.50	67%	48%
60-69	$54,629.88	$3,566.90	$2,761.80	65%	51%
70-79	$42,701.00	$3,020.80	$2,505.60	71%	59%
80 +	$37,005.73	$3,179.10	$3,179.10	86%	86%

Definition for columns in Table 5.7

Per-capita Income: The number in this column was calculated by dividing the number in the column, "Estimated Income (Surveys)" in Table 5.6, by the "Number of Surveys" in Table 5.6

Per-capita Tithe (Tithers; US$): The number in this column was calculated by dividing the number in the column, "Amount of Tithe" by the "No of Tithers" in Table 5.1, expressed in US$

Per-capita Tithe (Attenders; US$): The number in this column was calculated by dividing the number in the column, "Amount of Tithe" by the number of "Attenders" in Table 5.1, expressed in US$

Per-capita Tithe (Tithers) as % of Potential Tithe (10% Income): The number in this column was calculated by dividing the number in the column, "Per-capita Tithe (Tithers)," by one tenth of the number in the column, "Per-capita Income" in Table 5.7, and expressing the result as a percentage

Per-capita Tithe (Tithers) as % of Potential Tithe (10% Income): The number is this column was calculated by dividing the number in the column, "Per-capita Tithe (Attenders)," by one tenth of the number in the column, "Per-capita Income" in Table 5.7, and expressing the result as a percentage

The columns in Table 5.7 allow direct comparisons of the value of 10% of the estimated income from each age-group with the tithe returned by each age-group. This comparison appears in the column headed "Per-capita Tithe (Tithers) as % of Potential Tithe (10% Income)." From the percentages in this column, it is evident that the 20–29-yr age-group returned the smallest fraction of their income as tithe (23%), which is 17% lower than the next lowest percentage. The proportion of tithe returned by those aged from 40 to 79 years shows a slow but steady increase from 40% to 59%. The highest percentage of income returned as tithe came from the 80+ age-group (86%). Figure 5.5 (below) allows these relationships to be visualized.

Fig. 5.5: Per-capita Tithe (Tithers) as % of Potential Tithe (10% Income) (NCC)

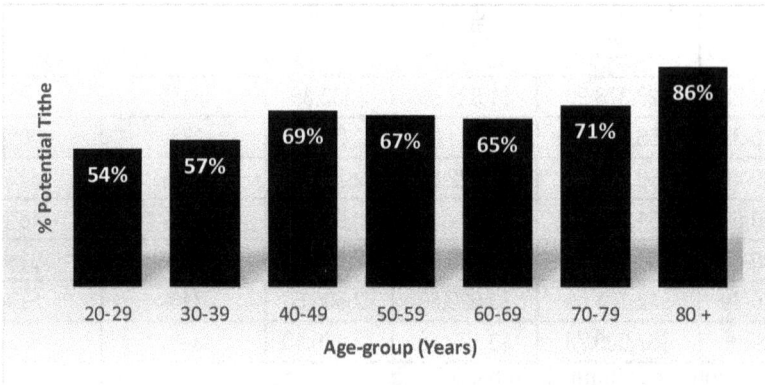

The column labelled "Per-capita Tithe (Attenders) as % of Potential Tithe (10% Income)" in Table 5.7 provides a measure of the proportion of tithe of the total income from the various age-groups. In this case there was a clear trend. Taken as a whole, the group aged 80 years or more gave the highest percentage of their income as tithe and each progressively younger age-group returned to the church progressively smaller percentages of their income as tithe. This reduction was particularly marked in the 20–29-yr age-group. Figure 5.6 (below) shows a clear trend.

Fig. 5.6: Per-capita Tithe (Attenders) as % of Potential Tithe (10% Income) (NCC)

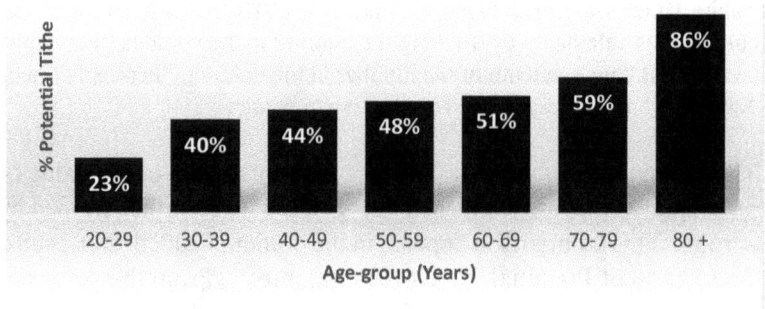

Several disparate trends worked together to produce the result visible in Figure 5.6 and Table 5.7. The percentage of their per-capita income returned as tithe by the 20–29-yr group was not that different from that returned by the 30–39-yr group (Fig. 5.7). Yet, because a greater percentage of the 30–39-yr group were returning tithe (Fig. 5.4), the net result is that, as a group, they contributed more tithe. As a percentage of their income, the per-capita tithe returned by the 40–49-yr age-group was 12% higher than the 30–39-yr age-group (Table 5.7), yet the 40–59-yr age-group had a lower rate of tithers per attenders than either the 30–39-yr group or the 60–69-yr group (65% vs 71% and 73% respectively; Table 5.4). The net result is that, as a group, the 40–49-yr group returned a greater percentage of income as tithe than the 30–39-yr group and a lesser percentage than the 60–69-yr group. In summary, there was a steady increase in the percentage of their group income contributed by each progressively older age-group.

5.7 The Proportion of Income Returned as Tithe Has Decreased Steadily for at Least the Last 40 Years in the Northern California Conference

Table 5.7 and Figure 5.6 show that the proportion of income returned as tithe decreased steadilry from the oldest age-group to the youngest. There are some implications for the church if this age-related pattern of tithing is consistent over the long term for each group. On the one hand, it could be hoped that this pattern reflects the changing giving-patterns typical of church-members as they grow older. As they age, members may be more likely to tithe, and to tithe more regularly. On the other hand, it is possible that the tithing behavior of the members in each age-group will remain relatively constant as they age. If the second possibility happens to be the case, then the long-term impact of the pattern that has been observed would be that the percentage of church member's income that is returned to the Church as tithe will decrease over time.

What is needed to determine which, if either, of the two possibilities canvassed is more likely to be correct is some measure of how tithe relates to income over longer periods of time. After all, analysis of tithe receipts written over 12 months and a survey that is conducted on one occassion in each local church provide only a snap-shot of one short period. In Australia it had been possible to use census statistics from those who self-identify as Seventh-day Adventists to determine the proportion of income returned as tithe over a period of several decades. Equivalent data are not available in the United States. What is available, though, are statistics relating to median income.

The United States Census Bureau defines median household income as "the amount which divides the income distribution into two equal groups, half having income above that amount, and half having income below that amount." Median income is, in fact, the middle income, if all incomes were arranged from smallest to highest. It is a better measure of the "middle" income than the average or statistical mean, because income has been increasing much more rapidly for those receiving the top 25% household income than it has for the other 75% of Americans.[1] This results in average income increasing at a rate much faster than is true for 75% of the population. The median income, is unaffected by the disparity of the increase in income in the top 25%.

Table 5.8 provides the median household income for the United States from the years 1950 and 1967–2014. It also provides data on the total tithe received from the North American Division and its membership.[2] This allows the calculation of per-capita tithe, which can then be compared to median household income. Particularly interesting is the percentage increase in median household income in each quinquennium compared to the percentage increase in per-capita tithe.

---

1 See graph labelled "Mean (Average) Household Income by Quintile and Top 5 Percent" at http://www.advisorperspectives.com/dshort/updates/Household-Income-Distribution.php. When accessed on 2 Feb 2015, this web page provided data from 1967 to 2014 which document the large increase in the incomes of those in the top 25%. This means that the average income of the population as a whole has increased at a faster rate than the rate of increase of income for 75% of the population. In other words, the increases in incomes of those in the highest brackets skew the average income upwards for the hole population. This distortion is avoided when the median value is chosen as the relevant statistic.

2 The North American Division (NAD) includes Canada. While separate in their history, population, currency, and economic profile, the economies of Canada and the United States track each other quite closely. Furthermore, the percentage of the tithe from the NAD that comes from the Seventh-day Adventist Church in Canada is, while substantial, a comparatively small part of the total tithe. For example, in 2014, the SDA Church in Canada contributed $64,822,539 to the NAD total tithe of $965, 591,088, or 6.7% of the total. It is therefore reasonable to compare NAD tithe with the median wages from the United States.

	US Household Income		Seventh-day Adventists (NAD)				Comparison	
Year	Median (Nominal)	Wages % Increase	Tithe (US$)	Members	Per-capita Tithe (US$)	Per-capita Tithe Increase (%)	Per-capita Tithe if Increased as Wages	Per capita tithe as a % of potential tithe
1950	$3,216		$21,137,472	250,939	$84			
1955			$31,971,346	293,448	$109	29%		
1960			$46,021,715	332,354	$138	27%		
1967	$5,968		$72,710,953	401,970	$181	31%		
1970	$7,466	25%	$93,201,151	439,726	$212	17%	$265	80%
1975	$10,257	37%	$154,365,838	620,842	$249	17%	$364	68%
1980	$16,166	58%	$243,675,524	604,430	$403	62%	$574	70%
1985	$21,580	33%	$317,233,301	689,507	$460	14%	$766	60%
1990	$27,792	29%	$408,640,139	760,148	$538	17%	$987	54%
1995	$32,422	17%	$491,795,445	838,898	$586	9%	$1,151	51%
2000	$40,199	24%	$656,938,357	933,935	$703	20%	$1,428	49%
2005	$44,406	10%	$834,926,647	1,024,035	$815	16%	$1,577	52%
2010	$47,222	6%	$887,946,937	1,126,815	$788	-3%	$1,677	47%
2014	$53,657	14%	$965,591,088	1,201,366	$804	2%	$1,906	42%

Table 5.8 Per-member Tithe Compared to Per-member Tithe if Increased at Same Rate as Average US Household Income (NAD)

Definitions for columns in Table 5.8

US Household Income: Median (Nominal): The median household income, the point at which 50% of US households have less and 50% have more than this income; for 1967 through 2010, these figures are from http://www.davemanuel. com/median-household-income.php; the figure for 1950 is from www.bls.gov/opub/uscs/1950.pdf; the 2014 figure is from http://www.deptofnumbers.com/income/us/; all accessed on 2 Feb 2016[3]

3 There are a number of different figures that are presented as median household income for the time period covered here. Many historical series start in 1967, as this set does. The United States Census Bureau publishes a number of helpful tables and graphs that provide a historical picture of what has happened to median household income (https://www.census.gov/hhes/www/income/data/historical/household), but like many other websites, they do so in terms of dollar values adjusted to take

US Household Income: % Increase: The numbers in this column were calculated by dividing the median household income for the year in question by the median household income for the previous entry, subtracting one, and expressing the result as a percentage

Seventh-day Adventists (NAD): The numbers in the columns under this heading all relate to statistics of tithing and membership of the North American Division of Seventh-day Adventists

Tithe (US$): The tithe returned to the North American Division; the numbers in this column for 1950–2010 are derived from the Annual Statistical Reports from the Seventh-day Adventist Church for 1950–2010 which may be found at http://documents.adventistarchives.org/Statistics/ASR; the NAD tithe figures for 2014 may be found at http://www.nadadventist.org/site/1/2014TitheOfferings/201412Tithe.pdf

Members: The number of members of Seventh-day Adventist Churches in the NAD; the membership numbers are derived from the Annual Statistical Reports of the Seventh-day Adventist Church

Per-Capita Tithe: The number is this column was calculated by dividing the number in the Tithe column by the number in the Members column, expressed in US dollars

Per-Capita Tithe Increase (%): The numbers in this column were calculated by dividing the per-capita tithe for the year in question by the per-capita tithe for the previous entry, subtracting one, and expressing the result as a percentage

Per-Capita Tithe if Increased as Wages: The numbers in this column were calculated from the tithe base of 1967; the increase in median household income is applied to this number successively for each period, giving an estimate of what tithe could have been if it had increased at the same rate as median household income

Per-capita tithe as a % of potential tithe: The numbers in this column were calculated by dividing the number in the column, "Per-capita Tithe," by the number in the column, "Per-capita Tithe if Increased as Wages," and expressing the result as a percentage

From the column in Table 5.8, "Per-capita tithe as a % of potential tithe", it appears that in North America, while total tithe has increased in dollar terms in each period, tithe-per-member giving has declined significantly compared to wages earned. As a proportion of the median household income, it has declined in each period. In 1970, per capita tithe was 80% of potential tithe. By 2014 this had decreased 42%.

Figure 5.6 shows the per-capita tithe for the North American Division. The same graph includes a second line that shows expected tithe returns if tithe had increased at the same rate as the median household income in North America ("Per-capita tithe as a % of potential tithe").

account of inflation. The statistics used here are for Nominal (i.e. actual) dollar figures. Most of the figures in Table 5.8 are taken from the one source, so that they are consistent.

Fig. 5.7: Per-capita and Per-capita Tithe if Increased as Wages (NAD)

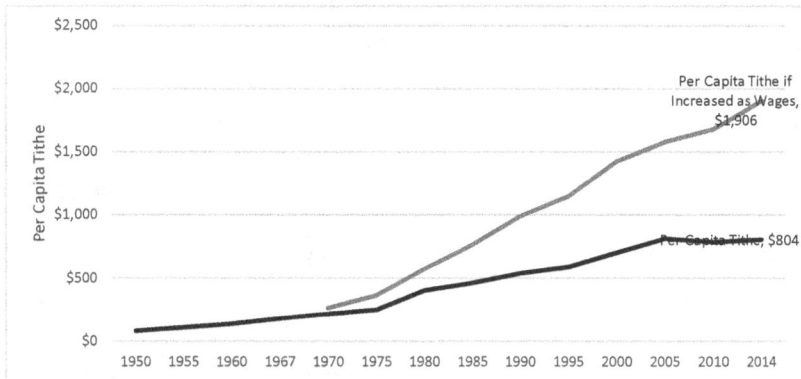

Whatever is made of the graph in Figure 5.6—and there are many assumptions that of necessity were made in its construction—it most likely should be taken as evidence that there has been a substantial reduction in the proportion of members' income that is being returned to the Church, and consequently that significant attention needs to be given to tithing education, and that efforts need to be made to make it possible to return tithe easily and consistently.

5.8 Personal Budget and Tithing

Among the new questions added to the Northern California Version of the Tithe Survey were questions about whether or not the participant had a personal budget and had followed it. As may be observed in Table 5.9, most respondents reported that they had a budget and worked to it. The responses to this question were not found to be significantly correlated to tithing behavior.

Table 5.9 Follow Personal Budget Always or Mostly (NCC)	
Age-group (Years)	"Yes" (%)
20-29	68
30-39	70
40-49	61
50-59	64
60-69	63
70-79	74
80 +	459

5.9 Conclusions (NCC)

Several conclusions have emerged from the foregoing analysis of tithe receipts and survey data from Northern California Conference:

First, compared to the general population of Northern California, the church is under-represented in the 20–49-yr age-group, and over-represented in the 60-plus age-group. This was particularly noteworthy in the 20–29-yr age-group.

Second, the 20–29-yr age-group stood out in several of the statistics that were explored. A smaller percentage of them attended church regularly, they contributed tithe with much smaller frequency, and while individual tithers in that age-group contributed about the same proportion of their income as tithe as those in the 30–49-yr bracket, a smaller percentage of them were tithing at all when compared to all other age-groups.

Third, a similar proportion of those in the age-range 30 to 69 years tithe at least once per year, although those in the older cohorts tend to tithe with greater regularity than the younger ones.

Fourth, all the various factors combined to produce the result that the percentage of income returned to the church as tithe decreased progressively from the oldest age-group to the youngest. Comparing the tithe received by the church with the median household incomes reveals that over time, the church in Northern California received less of the total income of its membership, an observation consistent with the conclusion that the pattern of tithing of each age-group appears to be consistent across many decades of their life.

Fifth, while the 20–29-yr age-group stood out as tithing more sporadically than older age-groups, irregular tithing was not limited to this age-group. How frequency of tithing might be fruitfully addressed is a topic that will be taken up again in Chapter 8.

6. São Paulo Conference (Tithe Receipts, Survey Data, Church-member Database, Census)

6.1 Scope of Study

6.1.1 Membership and Tithe Receipts

According to official church statistics, at the end of 2012 São Paulo Conference had a membership of 35,766.[1] The size of the conference meant that it was not feasible to include every church in the research project. President Sidionil Biazzi and Secretary Paulo Kokischko nominated 18 churches across the five geographic regions of the conference that would be suitable to include in the sample. These churches had a total membership of approximately 8,700. São Paulo Conference—like all of the conferences in Brazil—is blessed with well-designed and well-managed centralized computer systems that are used for the management of church membership records and tithe-receipting. At that time, membership records and tithing information were in two separate systems. By linking the data between the two systems, the conference IT team was able to provide a report (without names) on the age and tithing behavior of 3,162 tithers who attended the 18 churches in the sample and who tithed in such a manner as to appear in the tithe receipts. Based on the analysis of 22,417 tithing receipts that amounted to R$6,656,649 in total, these data are of the highest accuracy, and hence conclusions reached from these data will be highly reliable.

6.1.2 Survey

Surveys were conducted in the 18 churches which participated in this study, and 1,972 usable surveys were returned from those aged 20 years or more. The survey returns represents 23% of the approximately 8,700 members who regularly attend these churches.

6.2 Age-profile of the Church-members in the Study Compared to the Population of São Paulo

The member database of the São Paulo Conference contains exact birthdates, and the researchers were provided a report (without names)

---

1 "2014 Annual Statistical Report: 150th Report of the General Conference of Seventh-day Adventists for 2012 and 2013," 17.

of the number in each age-group in the membership of the 18 churches that participated in the study. The Churches in São Paulo Conference, like churches in other Seventh-day Adventist Conferences across Brazil, annually review membership lists for each church. Only those who are regularly attending worship services at a particular church remain on the membership list of that church. Thus the membership figures from the 18 churches reflect those who are in regular attendance at those churches. Such statistics correspond to the numbers in the column labelled "Attend" in Tables 5.1, 5.2, etc. (Chapter 5), which show the analyses of the data from the Northern California Conference. For consistency the same label is applied to the membership statistics in this chapter, viz. "Attend."

São Paulo contains such a significant component of the population of Brazil that separate demographic figures are published for the city by the Instituto Brasileiro de Geografia e Estatística. The age-profiles of the membership of the churches participating in the study and that of the general population of São Paulo may be found in Table 6.1, which shows the number of individuals in each age-group, and also provides the percentage of the total. The relationship between the age-profile of the Church membership and the wider population of São Paulo may be discerned from Figure 6.1, which shows the percentages which belong to each age-group for the church membership and for the population of São Paulo.

Table 6.1: Age Profile of Church-members and Compared to São Paulo Population				
	Attend		Census (São Paulo)	
Age-group	Count	%	Count	%
20-29	1,320	17%	2,066,241	26%
30-39	1,775	23%	1,898,761	24%
40-49	1,459	19%	1,555,699	19%
50-59	1,297	17%	1,215,771	15%
60-69	932	12%	725,393	9%
70-79	552	7%	408,270	5%
≥ 80	361	5%	204,475	3%
Totals	7,696		8,074,610	

Definition for columns in Table 6.1:

Age-group (Years): The statistics in the row are for those in the stated age-group

Attend: Number of members in age-group at the end of 2015 in membership data base in the 18 churches that participated in the research

Census (São Paulo): Number in age-group in the tables for São Paulo found on
www.cidades.ibge.gov.br in January 2016
Count: Number of individuals
%: The number of individuals in age-group divided by the total number of individuals
for all age-groups and expressed as a percentage

**Fig. 6.1: Age-profile of Members Compared
to São Paulo Population; %)**

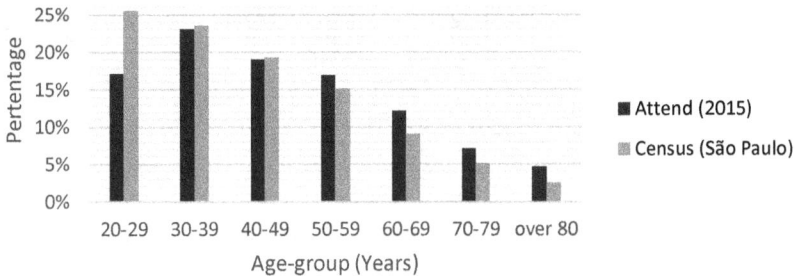

The percentages in Table 6.1 confirm what is observable in Figure 6.1.
The proportion of the members in the church who are aged from 30 to 59
years is within 2% of that for the wider population of São Paulo. Members
who are aged 60 or older are slightly over-represented. But the most striking
difference between the church membership lists and the wider population is
that the 20–29-yr age-group is under-represented in the membership of the
Seventh-day Adventist Church in São Paulo by 9%.

6.3 Percentage of Attenders Who Tithe
Decreases with Each Younger Age-group

A report was generated and provided to the researchers which gave
information on the actual tithing behavior of the members of the 18
churches which participated in the study, while maintaining the anonymity
of all respondents. The pattern of tithing and the total tithe contributed was
determined by linking the age from the membership database and the tithe
receipts from the tithe database. The tithing statistics found in Table 6.2
provide information about the number of tithers in each age-group, and the
total amount of tithe that comes from that age-group.

Age-group (Years)	No of Tithers	Total Tithe (R$)	Proportion of Total Tithe (%)	Attend	%Attenders who Tithe	Per-capita Tithe (Tithers)	Per-capita Tithe (Attenders)
20-29	412	R$ 456,446	6.9%	1,320	31%	R$ 1,108	R$ 346
30-39	598	R$ 1,466,020	22.2%	1,775	34%	R$ 2,452	R$ 826
40-49	548	R$ 1,526,703	23.1%	1,459	38%	R$ 2,786	R$ 1,046
50-59	543	R$ 1,459,714	22.1%	1,297	42%	R$ 2,688	R$ 1,125
≥ 60	834	R$ 1,695,211	25.7%	1,845	45%	R$ 2,033	R$ 919
Totals	2,935	R$ 6,604,094		7,696			

Table 6.2: Members, Tithers and Tithe (SPC)

Definition for columns in Table 6.2:

Age-group (Years): The statistics in the row are for those in the stated age-group

No of Tithers: The number of discrete tithers in an age-group

Total Tithe (R$): The total tithe that is returned by an age-group, expressed in Brazilian Reais

Proportion of Total Tithe (%): The percentage of total tithe that is returned by an age-group

Attend: Number of members in age-group at the end of 2015 in membership data base in the 18 churches that participated in the research

%Attenders who Tithe: The percentage of attenders who tithe

Per-capita Tithe (Tithers; R$): The total tithe divided by the number of discrete tithers, expressed in Brazilian Reais

Per-capita Tithe (Attenders; R$): The total tithe divided by the number who attend, expressed in Brazilian Reais

It was possible to compare the data on the number who tithed with the number of church-members of each age-group (see the column labelled "Attend"). Because church rolls are reviewed each year in São Paulo Conference and the names of those not in regular attendance are removed, the number of church- members on the membership database in each age-group is almost identical to the number in the particular age-group that regularly attend church. From this information it proved possible to calculate the percentage of each age-group who tithed (see "%Attenders who Tithe" in Table 6.2). From these numbers it is evident that the percentage of attenders who tithe steadily decreases from the oldest to the youngest age-group (see Figure 6.2).

It was possible to calculate from the statistics provided the per-capita tithe returned by tithers, and the per-capita tithe returned by attenders. This information may also be found in Table 6.2.

Fig. 6.2: Percentage of Members who Tithe in Each Age-group (SPC)

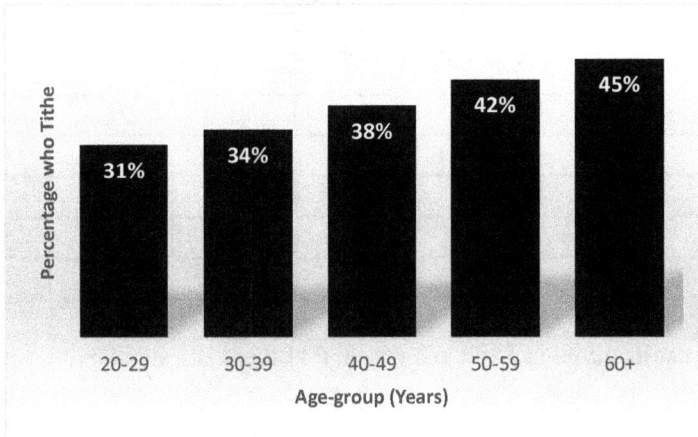

6.4 Frequency of Tithing Decreases Progressively with Each Younger Age-group

The tithe data that were provided from the analysis of the tithe receipts also included the number of times in the year that a tithe receipt had been written. Compared to the other conferences, the pattern in the frequency of tithing is much simpler in Brazil. Almost all wages and salaries are paid at monthly intervals. Furthermore, when asked on the survey their intended frequency of tithing, 83% indicated that they intended to tithe monthly, or 12 times per year (see Table 3.2 in Chapter 3). The actual frequency of tithing is recorded in Table 6.3 below.

Table 6.3: Frequency of Tithing (SPC)						
	Age					
Freq.	20-29		40-49		≥ 60	
	Count	%	Count	%	Count	%
1	60	15%	38	7%	44	5%
2	47	12%	40	7%	38	5%
3	34	8%	35	6%	41	5%
4	45	11%	33	6%	33	4%
5	29	7%	47	9%	31	4%
6	37	9%	32	6%	43	5%
7	32	8%	33	6%	46	6%
8	33	8%	50	9%	59	7%

Table 6.3: Frequency of Tithing (SPC)						
	Age					
Freq.	20-29		40-49		≥ 60	
	Count	%	Count	%	Count	%
9	31	8%	47	9%	76	9%
10	19	5%	49	9%	82	10%
11	15	4%	56	10%	120	15%
12	24	6%	88	16%	213	26%
Total	406		548		826	

The results given in Table 6.3 reveal that there is a substantial difference in the tithing behavior of the various age-groups. While most of those in the 20–29-yr age-group had indicated on the survey that they intended to tithe monthly, in actual practice very few did this. The greatest number (27%) actually tithed only once or twice per annum, and only 10% tithed eleven or twelve times per year. These trends can be seen clearly in the bar chart in Figure 6.3.

Fig. 6.3: Frequency of Tithing in 20–29-yr Age-group (SPC)

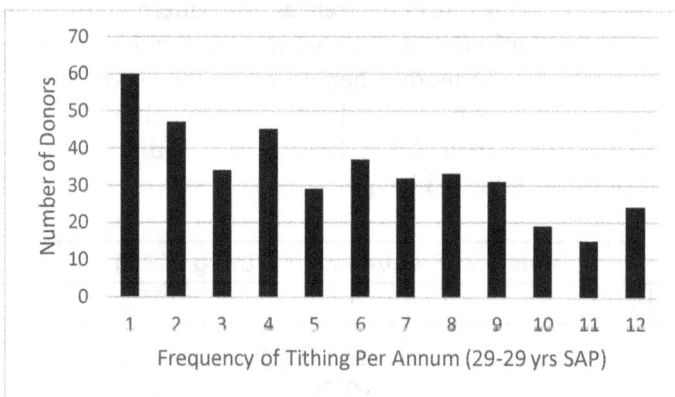

The tithing-behavior of those aged 60 years or more forms a contrast to that of the younger age-groups. They also had indicated on the survey their intention to tithe monthly, or 12 times per year. The tithe receipts provided evidence their actual practice closely matches their intent. The most common tithing frequency for this age-group was 12 times per year (true of 26% of tithers), closely followed by a tithing frequency of 11 times per year (15%). The contrast between the tithing pattern of those 60 years of age and older and that of the 20–29-yr-olds may be observed by comparing

Figure 6.4, which provides a graph of the frequency of tithing by those aged 60 and over, with Figure 6.3,which is a graph of the frequency of tithing among the 20–29-yr age-group.

Fig. 6.4: Frequency of Tithing by those Aged ≥ 60 Years (SPC)

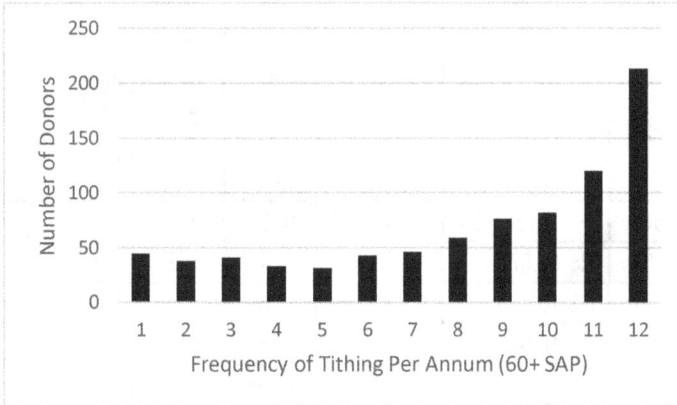

6.5 Per-capita Income for Each Age-group Estimated from Survey Data

The tithe survey included a question on the age of the participant, as well as a question on their income. The responses to these two questions enable an estimate to be made of the income from each age-group. This was done for each age-group by multiplying the number who chose a particular income range by the average of that income range, and adding the results to form an estimate of the total earnings. This total was then divided by the number in that age-group to determine the average per-capita income for each age-group. The results of these calculations are shown in Table 6.4, together with the result of a calculation of per-capita income, and some comparisons with data from the analysis of tithe receipts

Table 6.4: Survey Income Compared to Tithe Receipts (SPC)							
	Survey Data				Comparison		
Age-Group (Years)	Number of Surveys	Estimated Total Income (R$)	Per-capita Income (R$)	Proportion of Tot Income (%)	% Dif Survey Income & Tithe Receipts	Per-capita Tithe (Tithers) as % of Potential Tithe (10% Income)	Per-capita Tithe (Attenders) as % of Potential Tithe (10% Income)
20-29	319	R$ 6,188,640	R$ 19,400	10.6%	-3.7%	57.1%	17.8%
30-39	451	R$ 16,572,660	R$ 36,746	28.4%	-6.2%	66.7%	22.5%
40-49	377	R$ 16,128,840	R$ 42,782	27.6%	-4.5%	65.1%	24.5%
50-59	279	R$ 10,855,560	R$ 38,909	18.6%	3.5%	69.1%	28.9%
≥ 60	287	R$ 8,691,020	R$ 30,282	14.9%	10.8%	67.1%	30.3%
Totals	1,713	R$ 58,436,720					

Definitions for Columns in Table 6.4:

Survey Data: The statistics in the columns under this heading are derived from the tithe survey

Comparison: The statistics in the columns under this heading are derived by comparing the statistics from the tithe survey with those from the analysis of tithe receipts

Estimated Total Income (R$): The estimate of income was calculated by multiplying the number of individuals in a particular age-group that chose a particular income range by the mid-point of that income range; the result is an estimate of the total income received by a particular age-group, expressed in Brazilian Reais

Per-capita Income (R$): The numbers in this column are derived by calculating the "Estimated Total Income (R$)" by the number of surveys, expressed in Brazilian Reais

Proportion of Tot Income (%): The percentage of total income earned by a particular age-group

% Dif Survey Income & Tithe Receipts: The numbers in this column were derived by subtracting the percentages in the column "Proportion of Total Tithe (%)" in Table 6.2 from "Proportion of Tot Income (%)" in Table 6.4

Per-capita Tithe (Tithers) as % of Potential Tithe (10% Income): The number in this column was calculated by dividing the number in the column, "Per-capita Tithe (Tithers)" in Table 6.2, by one tenth of the number in the column, "Per-capita Income" in Table 6.4, and expressing the result as a percentage

Per-capita Tithe (Attenders) as % of Potential Tithe (10% Income): The numbers in this column were calculated by dividing the number in the column, "Per-capita

Tithe (Attenders)" in Table 6.2, by one tenth of the number in the column, "Per-capita Income" in Table 6.4, and expressing the result as a percentage

6.6 With the Exception of Members in the 20–29-yr Age-group, Most Tithers Return Approximately the Same Proportion of Their Income as Tithe

The column in Table 6.4 labelled, "Per-Capita Tithe (Tithers) as % of Potential Tithe (10% Income)," compares the actual tithe with 10% of the per-capita income (i.e. the potential tithe), and expresses the result as a percentage. One can make two conclusions on the basis of the figures in this column. First, there was very little variation between the percentages for each age-group 30 years and older. There is, in fact, only a difference of 4% between the highest percentage (69% for the 50–59-yr age-group) and the lowest percentage (65% for the 40–49-yr age-group). Second, the proportion of their income that is returned as tithe is noticeably lower for the 20–29-yr age-group (it is 8% lower than the next lowest figure).

6.7 The Percentage of Income Returned as Tithe Decreases Progressively from the Oldest Age-group to the Youngest

The column in Table 6.4 labelled, "Per-Capita Tithe (Attenders) as % of Potential Tithe (10% Income)," compares the per-capita tithe of all attenders with the per-capita income of the age-group. The per-capita tithe (attenders) is calculated by dividing the total amount of tithe by the total number of attenders for each age-group. Consequently, this figure provides a measure of the proportion of tithe that is returned to the church from the income earned by the whole age-group. There was a definite trend (shown clearly in Fig. 6.3): the percentage of income returned as tithe decreased progressively from the oldest age-group to the youngest.

Fig. 6.5: Per-capita Tithe (Attenders) as % of Potential Tithe (SPC)

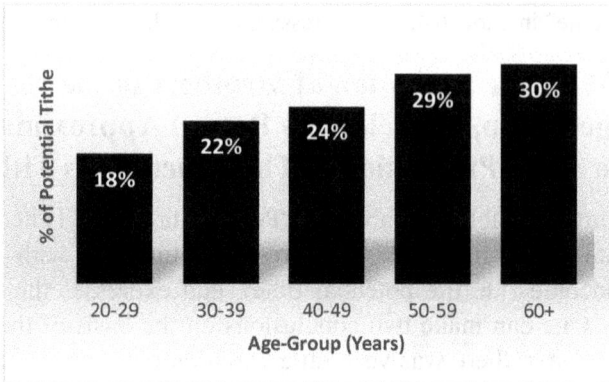

6.7 Conclusions (SPC)

There are at least three differences between the tithing pattern observed in church-members in São Paulo Conference when compared to the two other conferences examined so far. While the 20–29-yr age-group was an exception to the general rule, in both Northern California and Western Australia it was observed that approximately the same percentage of each age-group returned tithe at least once per year to the church. It was found to be different in São Paulo. Table 6.2 and Figure 6.2 reveal that, rather than being a constant, the percentage of attenders who tithe decreases progressively from the oldest to the youngest age-group.

A second difference between the data from São Paulo Conference and those of Northern California and Western Australia is seen in the relationship between the age-profile of the church membership when compared to the wider population of the city or state. In both Northern California and Western Australia the younger age-groups were under-represented and the older age-groups over-represented when compared to the general population. Figure 6.1, which shows the age-profile of the church and population side by side for São Paulo also reveals this pattern, but with the exception of the 20–29-yr age-group, there is a much closer relationship between the age-pattern of the church and the general population. The third difference may be observed in the pattern for per-capita tithe (tithers). There was much greater variation between the per-capita tithe (tithers) in Northern California (Fig. 5.5) than there was in São Paulo (Table 6.4).

Two things were constant across all the three conferences considered so far: (1) people in younger age-groups tithe much less frequently than those in older age-groups, despite their intention to tithe monthly or semi-monthly; and (2) each progressively younger age-group as a whole returns a smaller proportion of their income to the church as tithe than the older age-groups.

7. South England and Central Kenya Conferences

7.1 South England Conference of Seventh-day Adventists (Tithe & Gift Aid Receipts, Survey Data, Historical Wage Data)

7.1.1 Scope of Study

7.1.1.1 Tithe and Gift Aid Receipts

Two separate sets of receipts from the South England Conference were analyzed: tithe receipts and Gift Aid receipts. By 2014, 24 churches had adopted a common electronic means of generating tithe receipts. This data-set of 19,942 receipts represented tithe donations from 2,058 individuals. Of the 22,016 names on the official conference rolls, it had been possible to determine either the exact age (from birthdates in data base) or approximate age (by estimate of local pastor) of 6,563 individuals, 858 of whom had contributed tithe in the 24 churches in the data set. In the 2013–2014 tax year, 8,092 tithe receipts were written for these 858 individuals.[1] This equates to an average tithing frequency of 9.43 times per person per year.

In the United Kingdom it is possible for charities to participate in a program termed Gift Aid. The members of the Seventh-day Adventist Church are encouraged to register as Gift Aid donors, and to provide their Gift Aid ID on tithe envelopes when they return tithe and contribute other offerings. The Conference Treasury Department then generates a report on the Gift Aid donations and submits them to the government, which in turn then returns to the church a certain percentage of the donations. For the 2011–2012 tax year, there were 16,366 donations from 5,518 individuals which amounted to £8,271,014 in total. Of these donors, the exact or approximate age was known for 1,889 individuals, who made 5,762 separate donations that amounted to a total of £3,081,581.

---

1 The oldest tither was aged 94 years, the youngest 1 year. The youngest age for regular tithing was 13 years. In compliance with the research protocol followed by the Avondale College Human Research Ethics Committee, data relating to individuals aged less than 20 years are not reported here.

7.1.1.2 Survey

A total of 1,055 usable surveys from respondents aged 20 years and over was received from 35 of the 166 churches in the South England Conference.[2]

7.1.2 Per-capita Income Estimated from Survey Data

The Tithe Survey included a question on the age of the participant, as well as a question on their income. A total of 743 respondents answered these two questions, which enabled an estimate to be made of the per-capita income from each age-group. This was done for each age-group by multiplying the number who chose a particular income range by the average of that income range, and adding the results to form an estimate of the total earnings. This total was then divided by the number in that age-group to determine the average per-capita income for each age-group. The results of these calculations may be found in Table 7.1.

Table 7.1: Per-capita Income Estimated from Surveys (SEC)							
	Survey Data					Membership Rolls	
Age-group (Years)	Number of Surveys	Estimated Total Income (£)	Per-capita Income (£)	Proportion Total Income (%)	Proportion Respondents (%)	Number of Members	Proportion Members (%)
20-29	17	£89,649.50	£5,273.50	0.8%	2.3%	1,052	17.3%
30-39	86	£773,849.50	£8,998.25	7.3%	11.6%	1,432	23.5%
40-49	158	£2,228,049.50	£14,101.58	21.1%	21.3%	1,557	25.5%
50-59	214	£3,747,198.50	£17,510.27	35.4%	28.8%	868	14.2%
60-69	136	£2,260,850.00	£16,623.90	21.4%	18.3%	512	8.4%
70-79	70	£791,595.50	£11,308.51	7.5%	9.4%	395	6.5%
80-89	62	£686,899.00	£11,079.02	6.5%	8.3%	217	3.6%
90-99	0				0.0%	58	1.0%
100+	0				0.0%	5	0.1%
Totals	743	£10,578,091.50				6,096	

Definitions for Columns in Table 7.1
Survey: The statistics in the columns under this heading are derived from the Tithe Survey

2 It is not possible to provide a participation rate because a count was not made of those 20 years and older who were in attendance at the time the surveys were collected.

Membership Rolls: The statistics in the columns under this heading relate to the South England Conference membership list

Age-group (Years): The statistics in the row are for those in the stated age-group

Number of Surveys: Number of surveys returned from a specific age-group

Estimated Income: The estimate of income was calculated by multiplying the number of individuals in a particular age-group that chose a particular income range by the mid-point of that income range; the result is an estimate of the total income received by a particular age-group, expressed in pounds sterling

Per-capita Income: The numbers in this column are derived by calculating the "Estimated Total Income (£)" by the number of surveys, expressed in pounds sterling

Proportion Total Income (%): The percentage of total income earned by a particular age-group

Proportion Respondents (%): The percentage of surveys returned by a particular age-group

Number of Members: Number of members on church rolls whose age is known or estimated

Proportion Members (%): The percentage of members with known age in a particular age-group

The South England Conference Membership list has 22,014 names, and it was possible to identify the ages of 6,096 of these individuals. Table 7.1 shows the number of these 6,096 individuals in each of the age-groups. There are several problems with using these numbers to estimate the age-demographics of church-attenders. For example, not everyone that appears on the church rolls attends church regularly. Furthermore, while the conference has had a mechanism in place to record birth-dates of those joining the church by baptism or by confession of faith for a number of years, for those who were already members before this policy went into effect, no birth-dates have been recorded. One near-certain result of this is that the number of attenders and the number of tithers in the older age-groups have been underestimated. One may observe evidence of this by comparing the percentages in the column labelled "Proportion Respondents (%)" with the column labelled "Proportion Members." A much smaller proportion of the 20-39-yr age-group attend the churches where the tithe surveys were conducted than appear on the membership lists.

7.1.3 Tithe Receipts Reveal Giving Patterns for Each Age-group

It proved possible to identify the age-group for 858 individual tithers from 24 churches. Between them, they had returned tithe on 8,092 occasions between 1 April 2013 and 31 March 2014. These data are reported in Table 7.2 below.

Age-group (Years)	Total Tithe (£)	Per-capita Tithe (Tithers; £)	Proportion of Total Tithe (%)	Number of Tithers	Total Number of Receipts	Average Frequency of Tithing	Per-capita Tithe as % of Potential Tithe (10% income)
20-29	£54,381	£560.63	5.7%	97	600	6.2	10.6%
30-39	£219,084	£1,304.07	22.8%	168	1,160	6.9	14.5%
40-49	£317,938	£1,261.66	33.1%	252	2,398	9.5	8.9%
50-59	£218,752	£1,294.39	22.8%	169	1,619	9.6	7.4%
60-69	£65,301	£974.64	6.8%	67	775	11.6	5.9%
70-79	£60,698	£905.93	6.3%	67	1,031	15.4	8.0%
80-89	£20,719	£627.84	2.2%	33	421	12.8	5.7%
90-100	£2,910	£582.00	0.3%	5	88	17.6	
Totals	£959,783			858	8,092		

Table 7.2 Per-capita Tithe and Frequency of Tithing (Tithe Receipts; SEC)

Definitions for Columns in Table 7.1

Total Tithe (£): The total tithe that is returned by an age-group, expressed in pounds sterling

Per-capita Tithe (Tithers; £): The total tithe divided by the number of discrete tithers, expressed in pounds sterling

Proportion of Total Tithe (%): The percentage of total tithe that is returned by an age-group

Number of Tithers: Number of individual tithers whose age was known or estimated

Total Number of Receipts: Number of tithe receipts written for each age-group

Average Frequency of Tithing: The number of tithe receipts divided by the number of tithers.

Per-capita Tithe as % of Potential Tithe (10% income): The number in this column was calculated by dividing the number in the column, "Per-capita Tithe (Tithers)" in Table 6.2, by one tenth of the number in the column, "Per-capita Income" in Table 6.4, and expressing the result as a percentage

7.1.4 Gift Aid Receipts Provide an Alternative Method of Determining Giving Patterns

In some respects, analyzing the Gift Aid data might be considered to be duplicating what had already been done with the tithe receipts. Yet it is worth-while to consider these data, especially given (1) the fact that the Gift Aid data comes from the period just before the surveys were completed (1 April 2011 to 31 March 2012), and (2) the Gift Aid data provide a larger sample than that based on the tithe receipts because it was possible to determine the age-group of more of the Gift Aid donors than those represented in the tithe receipts. The tithe-receipt data are from a period two years later, at a time when 24 churches in the conference had moved to electronic means for generating receipts and reports. Given that it is a larger sample, it is tempting to think that the data from the analysis of tithe receipts could be ignored, were it not for the fact that there were two issues regarding the Gift Aid data. First, Gift Aid data include not only tithe but all donations to the church, including Sabbath School offerings, church building offerings and so on. While there are no data to back up this assertion, anecdotal evidence from those that manually entered data directly from the paper tithe-receipts suggests that the largest part of any donation that is receipted is almost always tithe, and that other donations are usually proportionate to the amount of tithe given. In other words, the Gift Aid data can stand as a proxy for tithing behavior. The second issue is that Gift Aid reporting is bi-monthly and so only six reports are given for each year. This means that frequency figures are more "grainy" than those possible to produce from the tithe-receipts, which record weekly giving (although many contribute tithe bi-weekly or monthly). In summary, the Gift Aid data are of high quality, in that they are as complete as is possible to make them, and they were associated with the correct individuals (something not always possible to guarantee with paper-based tithe receipts). The data from the Gift Aid receipts are shown in Table 7.3.

Table 7.3 Per-capita and Frequency of Gift Aid Donations (SEC)							
Age-group (Years)	Total Gift Aid (£)	Proportion of Tot Gift Aid (%)	Per-capita Giving (Donors) (£)	Number of Donors	Proportion of Donors (%)	Number of Receipts	Average Frequency of Giving
20-29	£152,730	5.1%	£1,061	144	7.6%	362	2.5
30-39	£608,963	20.4%	£1,478	412	21.9%	1,202	2.9
40-49	£1,108,294	37.0%	£1,793	618	32.8%	1,843	3.0
50-59	£576,319	19.3%	£1,623	355	18.8%	1,143	3.2
60-69	£316,511	10.6%	£1,615	196	10.4%	625	3.2
70-79	£185,431	6.2%	£1,426	130	6.9%	469	3.6
80+	£43,819	1.5%	£1,511	29	1.5%	104	3.6
Totals	£2,992,066			1,884		5,748	3.1

Definitions for Columns in Table 7.3:

Total Gift Aid: The total amount of Gift Aid that was donated by a specific age-group

Proportion of Tot Gift Aid: The percentage of cumulative total Gift Aid that was donated by a specific age-group

Per-capita Giving (Donors): The numbers in this column were calculated by dividing the "Total Gift Aid" by the number of donors

Number of Donors: Number of discrete donors

Proportion of Donors: The percentage of all donors that were from a specific age-group

Number of Receipts: Number of receipts written for a specific age-group

Average Frequency of Giving: The numbers in this column were calculated by dividing the number of receipts by the number of donors

7.1.5 Frequency of Donations Decreases
Progressively with Each Younger Age-group

An examination of the data relating to the average frequency of tithing in Table 7.2 and the average frequency of Gift Aid donations in Table 7.3 reveals that there is a very distinctive pattern, one that is similar to the patterns that have been observed in the analysis of tithe receipts from the Western Australia, Northern California and São Paulo Conferences. Frequency of tithing decreases progressively from the oldest age-group (90–99 years) to the youngest (20–29 years), with the 80–89-yr age-group somewhat anomalous. The difference between the 40–49 and the 50–59-yr age-groups is less marked than the differences between the other age-groups. This pattern may be seen clearly in Figure 7.1.

Fig. 7.1: Age-group vs Average Frequency of Tithing per Year (SEC)

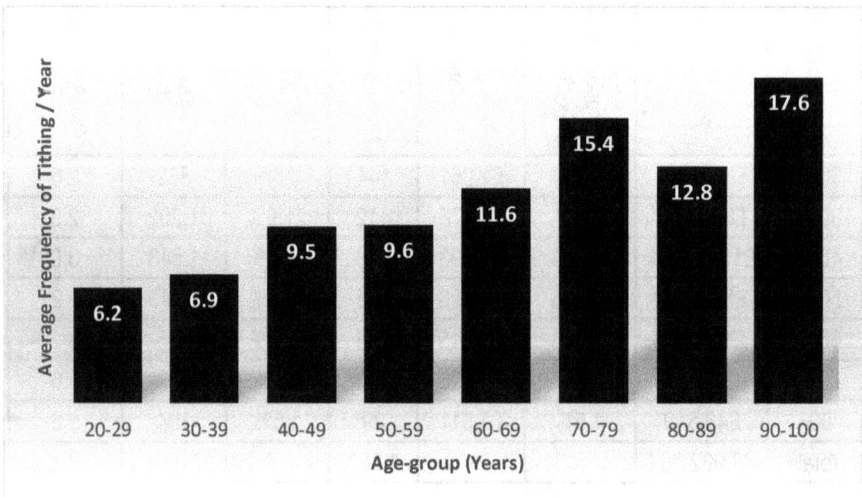

The column labelled "Average Frequency of Giving" in Table 7.3 reveals that there is a progressive decline in frequency of donating Gift Aid with each younger age-group that is very similar to the pattern already observed for tithing. This might be expected, given that the largest part of the money receipted for Gift Aid is, in fact, tithe.

Seventy-three percent of respondents to the South England Conference tithe survey indicated that they were paid wages or salaries monthly (see Table 3.1 in Chapter 3), and most indicated that they intended to tithe 12 times per year (67% chose monthly; Table 3.2) or 52 times per year (23% chose weekly). Both those who tithed monthly and those that tithed weekly would be recorded as giving with (the maximum) frequency of 6, because the Gift Aid data are consolidated and reported 6 times per year. Yet, as Table 7.4 reveals, less than 13% of any age-group succeeds in giving in all six reporting periods, and only 3% of those aged from 20 to 29 years do so.

Even though these data are more "granular" than the other data reported here, the data reported in Table 7.4 reveal a marked difference in giving behavior between the younger and older age-groups, a difference related to frequency of giving. Table 7.4 documents how many in each age-group give a donation in one or more of the six periods over which Gift Aid is reported.

Table 7.4: Age-group and Frequency of Giving for Gift Aid (SEC)						
	Age-group (Years)					
	20-29		50-59		70-79	
Freq	Count	%	Count	%	Count	%
1	40	28.0%	44	12.5%	9	7.0%
2	46	32.2%	73	20.7%	24	18.8%
3	23	16.1%	76	21.6%	26	20.3%
4	21	14.7%	83	23.6%	27	21.1%
5	9	6.3%	63	17.9%	26	20.3%
6	4	2.8%	13	3.7%	16	12.5%
Total	143		352		128	

The difference in giving patterns revealed in Table 7.4 may be observed in Figures 7.2 (for the 20–29-yr age-group) and 7.3 (for the 59–59-yr age-group).

Fig. 7.2: Frequency of Giving 20–29-yr Age-group (Gift Aid; SEC)

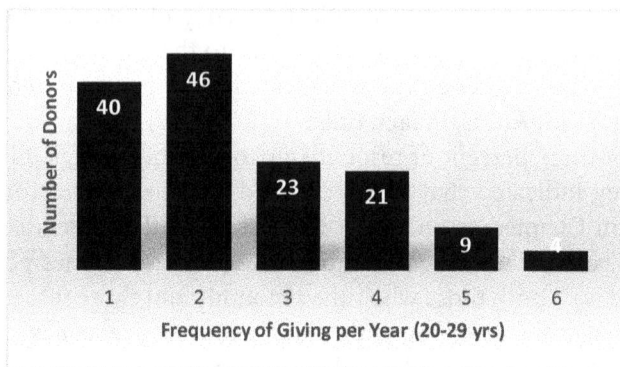

Fig. 7.3: Frequency of Giving 50–59-yr Age-group (Gift Aid; SEC)

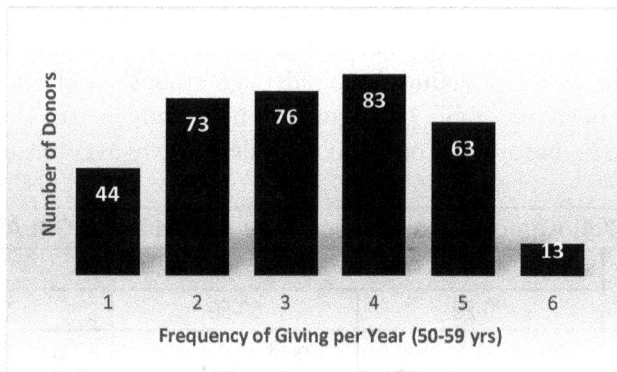

Figures 7.2 and 7.3, as well as the numbers reported in Table 7.4, confirm clearly the difference in the frequency of giving between the 20–29-yr and 50–59-yr age-groups that is evident in the Gift Aid data.   The greatest frequency of giving for the 20–29 year olds is twice per year. Survey data confirmed that most of these individuals were paid monthly and hope to tithe monthly (Table 3.2). The second-highest frequency of giving by those aged from 20 to 29 years is once per year. The situation is quite different for the 50–59-yr age-group. The highest frequency of giving for that age-group is four times per year. Yet, if everyone were to tithe monthly then the frequency of giving for everybody would be 6 times. In practice most in the age-groups represented in Table 7.4 give between two and five times per year. One easily noted conclusion is that every age-group contains many who are willing to tithe and give other donations to the church, but they do not do it with regularity. Finding ways to increase the number of times tithes

and other gifts are given to the church will inevitably have a positive impact on the total amount received by the conference and available to support the mission of the church. This is something that will be explored more thoroughly in Chapter 8.

7.1.6 The Proportion of Income Returned as Tithe Decreases Progressively from the Oldest Age-group to the Youngest

The analysis of tithe and Gift Aid provides information regarding tithing behavior over a period of one year. If each age-cohort retains a similar pattern of giving over a long period of time, it has the potential to have a significant impact on the proportion of their income that each age-cohort returns to the church over their lifetime, but, as has already been stated in considering the data from Northern California (see discussion in Chapter 5.7), this is but one possibility. A second possibility is that the differences in tithing behavior observed in the different age-groups may be part of the maturing process as one grows older. Thus, with the passage of time, as those now aged from 20 to 29 years will eventually be aged from 50 to 59 years, at which age they may become more consistent in their tithing. Which of these two options is more likely will show in the long-term trend of the proportion of total income of all age-groups that is returned to the church as tithe. A downward long-term-trend will be discovered in the proportion of member income returned to the church as tithe, which would likely indicate that the pattern of giving, once established, is consistent throughout a life-span.

Some wage data are available for the United Kingdom as far back as the year 1209.[1] Tithe data are available for the South England Conference from the year of its establishment (organized 1898; reorganized 1928[2]). Table 7.5 lists the tithe (in US$) from South England Conference and membership as they are recorded in official Seventh-day Adventist statistics, and the average income (in UK£) for the years 1950 to 2014. For comparative purposes, the average income is converted from Pounds Sterling to United States Dollars.

1 Lawrence H. Officer, "What Were the UK Earnings and Prices Then?" "Measuring Worth," 2016. https://www.measuringworth.com/datasets/ukearncpi/result2.php.

2 http://www.adventistyearbook.org/default.aspx?&page=ViewAdmField&Section=General&Search=south%20england%20conference&AdmFieldID=SEGC#Search

	South England Conference				Average Income Britain				
Year	Membership	Total Tithe (US$)	Per-capita Tithe (US$)	Per-capita Tithe Increase (%)	Average Annual Nominal Earnings (£)	Exchange rate UK£ to US$	Average Income in US$	Average Income Increase (%)	Per-capita Tithe as % of Potential Tithe
1950	3,663	$132,595	$36.20		£303				
1955	4,130	$188,173	$45.56	20.6%	£434	2.78	$1,207		37.7%
1960	5,080	$328,312	$64.63	29.5%	£545	2.80	$1,529	21.0%	42.3%
1965	5,697	$522,485	$91.71	29.5%	£751	2.80	$2,106	27.4%	43.5%
1970	6,806	$628,554	$92.35	0.7%	£1,080	2.39	$2,584	18.5%	35.7%
1975	7,363	$1,313,965	$178.46	48.2%	£2,291	2.02	$4,637	44.3%	38.5%
1980	7,998	$2,825,789	$353.31	49.5%	£4,542	2.39	$10,846	57.2%	32.6%
1985	9,637	$3,184,388	$330.43	-6.9%	£6,997	1.44	$10,072	-7.7%	32.8%
1990	10,868	$6,763,369	$622.32	46.9%	£10,601	1.93	$20,418	50.7%	30.5%
1995	12,006	$6,536,537	$544.44	-14.3%	£13,302	1.55	$20,634	1.0%	26.4%
2000	13,581	$8,969,799	$660.47	17.6%	£16,545	1.49	$24,668	16.4%	26.8%
2005	17,220	$16,043,890	$931.70	29.1%	£20,215	1.72	$34,799	29.1%	26.8%
2010	21,183	$18,122,479	$855.52	-8.9%	£23,504	1.55	$36,487	4.6%	23.4%
2014	23,309	$21,287,696	$913.28	6.3%	£25,029	1.56	$39,013	6.5%	23.4%

Table 7.5: South England Conference Tithe and Average Income in Britain 1950–2014

Definitions for Columns in Table 7.5:

South England Conference: The statistics in columns under this heading relate to the South England Conference of Seventh-day Adventists

Average Income Britain: The statistics in the columns under this heading relate to the average income in Britain

Year: The statistics in the row relate to the stated year

Membership: The membership of the South England Conference as reported in the official church statistics, starting with "Eighty-eighth Annual Statistical Report of Seventh-day Adventists, 1950" through to "2015 Annual Statistical Report: 151st Report of the General Conference of Seventh-day Adventists® for 2013 and 2014."

Total Tithe (US$): The total tithe from the South England Conference as reported in the official church statistics. Tithe figures for every conference across the world are reported in United States Dollars in the official statistics

Per-capita Tithe (US$): The total tithe divided by the number of members

Per-capita Tithe Increase (%): The percentage increase in per-capita tithe since the previously reported amount

Average Annual Nominal Earnings (£): The average annual earnings in Britain, as reported by www.measuringworth.com/datasets/ukearncpi/result2.php

Exchange rate UK£ to US$: The exchange rate at 31 December in that year as reported by http://fxtop.com/en/currency-converter-past

Average Income in US$: The figures in this column are calculated by multiplying the Average Annual Nominal Earnings (£) by the exchange rate.

Average Income Increase (%): The percentage increase in average income since the previously reported amount

Per-capita Tithe as % of Potential Tithe: The figures in this column are calculated by dividing the per-capita tithe by the average income (both in US$), and expressing the result as a percentage

The column, "Per-capita Tithe as % of Potential Tithe," in Table 7.5 provides an estimate of the proportion of member income that is being returned to the church as tithe. If all members returned a full tithe, then the potential tithe would be equivalent to 10% of average income. Hence, one might describe 10% of average income as "potential tithe." While there is some variation, the general trend is that over time the proportion of the members' income that is being returned to the Adventist Church is diminishing. This is particularly evident in Figures 7.4 and 7.5. Figure 7.4 provides a graph that tracks two statistics: (i) per-capita tithe; and (ii) 10% average income. It may be observed that there is a general trend that shows an increasing gap between the two numbers. Another way to consider the relationship between the two sets of data is to consider the per-capita tithe as a percentage of potential tithe (i.e. 10% income). The result is shown in Figure 7.5, and again, while there is some variation, the general trend downwards is clear.

Fig. 7.4: Per-capita Tithe (SEC) Compared to 10% Average Income (Britain)

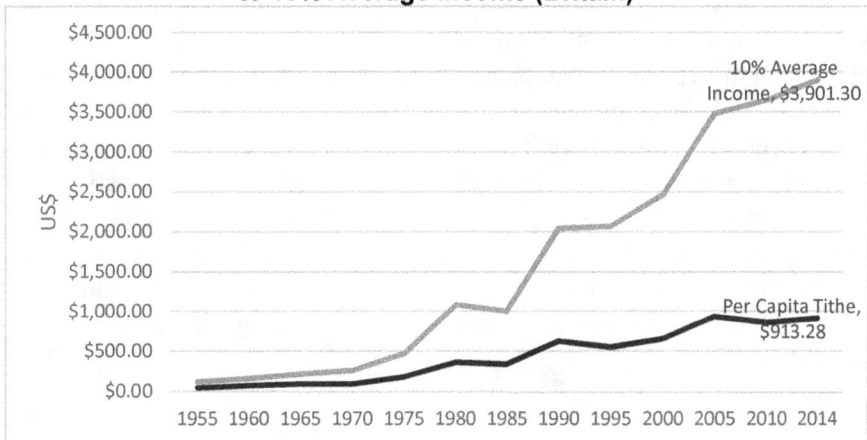

Fig. 7.5: Per-capita Tithe (SEC) as Percentage of Potential Tithe (10% Income)

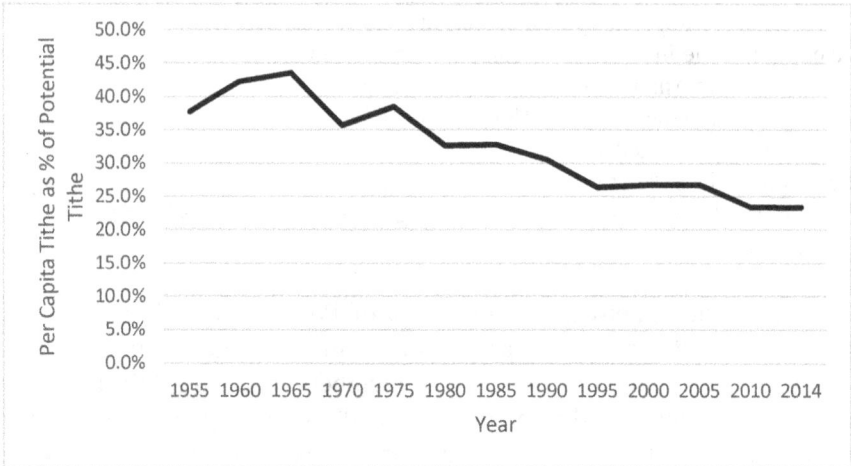

7.1.7 Conclusions (SEC)

As with the other three conferences studied (see Figures 4.5, 4.6, 5.6), there has been a long-term trend that less of the income earned by church-members in South England Conference has been returned to the church each year (see Figures 7.4 and 7.5). This trend is hidden from most observers because in terms of pounds sterling, the amount of tithe is increasing each year. Yet it is not increasing at the same rate as income. This decrease in tithe as a proportion of member income has an impact on the church's ability to maintain its ministry and outreach.

Our investigation of the giving patterns represented in both the tithe and Gift Aid receipts provides a credible explanation of the phenomena just observed. Those in the younger age-groups contribute tithe and other offerings more sporadically than the older age-groups, and it appears highly likely that this is a long-term pattern associated with a particular age cohort, not an age-related phenomenon which individuals "grow out of" as they age. This observation has within it an opportunity for the church. Even though they are more sporadic in their tithing, the attenders and members in the younger age-groups are still prepared to tithe. If done in a suitable manner, addressing the issue of regularity of giving cannot but have a positive effect on the proportion of member income that is being returned to the Church as tithe. A further consideration of this matter will occupy our attention in the next chapter.

7.2 Central Kenya Conference of Seventh-day Adventists (Tithe Receipts)

Central Kenya Conference was intended to be an important part of this project, but for various reasons I was unable to pursue research in Kenya as much as I had hoped. What can be reported is an analysis of tithe receipts from two of the larger churches. The tithing behavior of 724 adults is represented in the sample. Of these, 284 returned tithe. A summary of their statistics may be found in Table 7.6.

Table 7.6: Tithing Patterns in Kenya Central Conference						
Age-group (Years)	Number Members	Number Tithers	% Tithers	Tot Tithe (Ksh)	Per capita tithe (tithers; KSh)	Per capita Tithe (Members; Ksh)
20-29	233	65	27.9%	Ksh180,878	Ksh2,783	Ksh776
30-39	281	113	40.2%	Ksh122,824	Ksh1,087	Ksh437
40-49	143	72	50.3%	Ksh148,682	Ksh2,065	Ksh1,040
50-59	49	28	57.1%	Ksh848,753	Ksh30,313	Ksh17,321
60-69	8	3	37.5%	Ksh1,448	Ksh483	Ksh181
70+	3	0		Ksh0		
Total	724	284		Ksh1,666,948		

Definitions for Columns in Table 7.6

Age-group (Years): The statistics in the row are for those in the stated age-group

Number Members: The number of church-members for whom an age-group was known

Number of Tithers: Number of individual tithers whose age was known or estimated

% Tithers: The numbers in this column were calculated by dividing the number of tithers by the number of members and expressing the result as a percentage

Total Tithe (Ksh): The total tithe that is returned by an age-group, expressed in Kenyan shillings

Per-capita Tithe (Tithers; Ksh): The total tithe divided by the number of discrete tithers, expressed in Kenyan shillings

Per-capita Tithe (Members; Ksh): The total tithe divided by the number of members, expressed in Kenyan shillings

By combining the data into only two age-groups (20–39 years and 40–59 years), it was possible to have samples large enough to obtain a statistically valid pattern of frequency of tithing behavior. Combining the age-groups in this way produced a sample of 178 persons aged between 20 and 39 years who tithed, and a sample of 99 persons between the ages of 40 and 59 who tithed. Their reported frequency of tithing is shown in Table 7.7 and Figure 7.6.

Table 7.7: Frequency of Tithing (CKC)						
	Number of Tithers		% Tithers		Cumulative %	
Frequency Times/yr	20–39 yrs	40–59 yrs	20–39 yrs	40–59 yrs	20–39 yrs	40–59 yrs
1-2	83	36	46.6%	36.4%	46.6%	36.4%
3-4	34	24	19.1%	24.2%	65.7%	60.6%
5-6	30	22	16.9%	22.2%	82.6%	82.8%
7-8	18	9	10.1%	9.1%	92.7%	91.9%
9-10	3	5	1.7%	5.1%	94.4%	97.0%
11-12	8	2	4.5%	2.0%	98.9%	99.0%
13-14	1	1	0.6%	1.0%	99.4%	100.0%
≥15	1	0	0.6%	0.0%	100.0%	
Total	178	99				

Definitions for Columns in Figure 7.7

Number of Tithers: The number of tithers who tithed at the indicated frequency

% Tithers: The numbers in the columns under this heading are calculated by dividing the number of tithers by the total number of tithers, and expressing the result as a percentage

Cumulative %: The proportion of tithers who tithed at the indicated frequency or less; the number in the column is calculated by adding the percentage of tithers who tithe at a particular frequency to the cumulative percentage of in the row immediately above it

Fig. 7.6: Age and Frequency of Tithing (CKC)

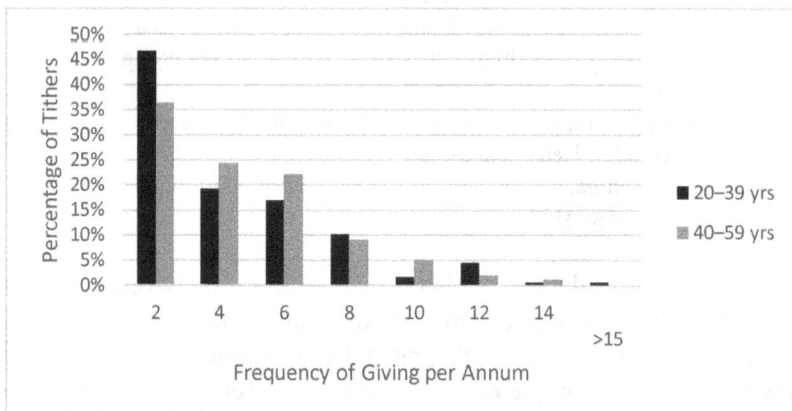

The pattern in both age-groups appears to be similar. Indeed, the average frequency of tithing for the 20–39-yr age-group was 3.8 times per year, compared to 4.1 times per year for the 49–59-yr age-group. In both age-groups, among those who tithed the most common frequency of tithing was once or twice per year. Perhaps greater percentages of the older age-group tithed more frequently, but it seems that in the two churches studied all age-groups tithe only sporadically. There can be any number of reasons for this, including sporadic employment, and future research will be needed before any real conclusions can be drawn. However the results of the small data-sample collected strongly suggest that additional research in Kenya would prove very informative.

8. "I think I should tithe, but I need to get into the habit of tithing regularly" (Survey Data)

This chapter explores one of the very significant findings of the survey, viz. the willingness of those who are not currently tithing (or not tithing a full 10% of their income), to tithe if only they could develop the habit.

Given the pressing need to keep the survey instrument as short as possible, with a few but important exceptions, almost every question on the survey related to the model being tested. Amongst those exceptions was a set of questions that assessed the willingness of those not currently returning tithe to change their behaviour. These questions were introduced by the statement, "I tithe a full 10% of my income." Respondents were given two options as follows:

○ Yes –▶ Go to question B19

○ No –▶ Go to question B18

Table 8.1 reports the numbers of those answering "Yes" and "No" to this question.

Table 8.1: Country vs "I tithe a full 10% of my income"					
	yes		no		Total
Country	Count	% within Country	Count	% within Country	
Australia (WAC)	1021	68%	472	32%	1493
England (SEC)	545	87%	80	13%	625
Brazil (SPC)	409	81%	94	19%	503
USA (NCC)	811	75%	272	25%	1083
Total	2786	75%	918	25%	3704

A total of 918 respondents (25% of those who answered this question) indicated that they did not tithe a full 10% of their income. For convenience—despite the fact that many of them return a partial tithe—these will be labelled "non-tithing respondents." The non-tithing respondents were asked the following question:

"B18. I do not currently give a full tithe, or do not give tithe. The following changes would need to happen before I would consider returning a full tithe [shade as many of the following as are true for you]":

Table 4.2 provides the list of responses that could be chosen, and shows the percentage of those who responded "No" to the statement, "I tithe a full 10% of my income", who chose a particular option.[1]

Table 8.2: "Non-tither" Responses to "The following changes would need to happen before I would consider returning a full tithe"					
	NCC	SEC	SPC	WAC	All
I think I should tithe, but I need to get into the habit of tithing regularly	117	192	62	252	623
	42%	84%	50%	50%	55%
I need to be fully financially secure before I can give any money to the church	72	74	36	113	295
	26%	57%	31%	23%	29%
The Church needs to make its worship relevant to today's youth	43	84	30	110	167
	16%	58%	26%	22%	27%
I need to be more confident that money I give as tithe actually makes it to the right place	67	23	13	Not asked	103
	24%	26%	11%		21%
Churches need to stop experimenting with worship, and restore proper reverence in worship	27	60	32	85	204
	10%	45%	27%	17%	20%
The Adventist Church needs to bring its doctrines and ideas into the 21st century	26	60	21	83	190
	9%	47%	18%	17%	19%
The Adventist Church should make it possible to ordain women to the Gospel ministry	32	38	26	90	186
	11%	34%	22%	18%	18%
The Adventist Church needs to return to the plain truth of historic Adventism	22	34	27	80	163
	8%	30%	23%	16%	16%

1 Since respondents were invited to "shade as many … as are true for you," the percentages summed down the columns add up to more than 100%. With one exception (the response, "I don't think anything would change what I do about tithing"), the table lists the more-frequently chosen options first.

Table 8.2: "Non-tither" Responses to "The following changes would need to happen before I would consider returning a full tithe"					
	NCC	SEC	SPC	WAC	All
We need a competent pastor in our local church	22	37	17	61	137
	8%	34%	14%	12%	14%
I need to be convinced from the Bible that Christians should return tithe	15	26	16	39	96
	5%	26%	14%	8%	10%
I need to know that if I tithe, more pastors will be employed and I will see a pastor more often	13	12	13	Not asked	38
	4%	14%	11%		8%
I think I should tithe, but my spouse is very strongly against giving tithe.	17	10	18	28	73
	6%	11%	15%	6%	7%
I don't think anything would change what I do about tithing	63	29	23	45	162
	22%	30%	19%	9%	16%

Note: The question, "I need to be more confident that money I give as tithe actually makes it to the right place" was developed in Kenya, and only appeared in surveys formatted after that time, viz. 9.4B in SEC, 9.6B (SPC) and 9.7B (NCC). It was not asked in versions 7.1 (WAC) and 9.1A (SEC).

The results in Table 4.2 are remarkable in many ways, not least in the fact that they reveal a great willingness to tithe from at least 55% of the respondents. Not only that, they identify clearly what may change their tithing behavior from non-tither or sporadic-tither to full-tither. The number one response as to what would need to change "before I would consider returning a full tithe" was "I think I should tithe, but I need to get into the habit of tithing regularly." No less than 55% of all non-tithing respondents indicated their willingness to tithe, and identified the thing that was stopping them as the need to form a habit of doing so. This response far outweighed the number who responded, "I don't think anything would change what I do about tithing" (16%).

Some of the other responses to the question, "The following changes would need to happen before I would consider returning a full tithe", reveal attitudes that are less amenable to change. For example, while the third-most-frequent response was, "The Church needs to make its worship relevant to today's youth" (27%), this is nearly matched by the fifth-most-frequent response, "Churches need to stop experimenting with worship, and restore proper reverence in worship" (20%).

These responses may be compared to those given in another part of the survey, reported earlier (see Tables 3.3 and 3.4 in Chapter 3), which invites respondents to reflect about their actual tithing practice. As may be observed in Table 3.3, when asked, 43% of participants in São Paulo, 20% in South England, 29% in Northern California and 33% of participants in Western Australia admitted, "Sometimes I forget to return tithe."

The most marked age-related difference in the way the question "Sometimes I forget to tithe" was answered by the various age-groups is highlighted in Table 3.4 in Chapter 3. Over all of the surveys from the different countries, 46% of respondents aged from 20 to 39 years admitted "Sometimes I forget to return tithe" (a total of 782 out of 1,686). This response drops to 32% for the 40–59-yr age-group; and to 23% for those aged 60 years or more.

The analysis of tithe receipts reported in Chapters 4–7 reveals that a very significant group of tithers tithe sporadically,[2] and this is particularly true of the 20–39-yr age-group (see Tables 4.4, 5.5, 6.3, 7.3, 7.4). While individuals who tithe sporadically could be criticized for their lack of discipline in their giving, it is nonetheless evident that these individuals are willing to tithe, and already have done so from time to time. This is confirmed by the survey data, particularly the responses to the question, "What would have to change before I return a full 10% of my income as tithe?", which revealed that the most common reason for their tithing at irregular intervals was that many individuals think they should tithe, but need to get into the habit.

The fact that a very significant number of people are saying, "I think I should tithe, but I need to get into the habit of tithing regularly", has important implications. First, the Church needs to make it as convenient as possible for tithe to be returned. This is increasingly challenging, given

---

2 Sometimes the lower frequency of giving reflected in the tithe receipts is likely to be attributable to business-related reasons (e.g. quarterly reporting), or sporadic income. This was tested by another question on the survey which asked respondents how frequently they intended to tithe: some indicated yearly or quarterly. (see Tables 3.2 and 3.3 in Chapter 3.1, which show that 17% of respondents in Northern California intended to tithe quarterly or yearly; 2% of respondents in São Paulo, 6% in South England and 21% in West Australia). But in the majority of instances amongst the younger age-groups, the actual amount of the individual tithes donations given conveys the impression that tithe is being calculated on the latest wage-interval, not on some planned giving over longer intervals. This impression is given greater credibility by the responses to such survey questions as "Sometimes I forget to return tithe." See also data in Table 3.5.

the changing habits of personal financial management. In Western societies there is a rapid move to a cashless or near-cashless economy and many are increasingly using credit or debit cards for every financial transaction. This was reflected in the responses from Northern California Conference surveys in which respondents were asked what means they usually use for purchases between $10 and $49 (they could choose more than one response).

Table 8.3: "For purchases between $10 and $49, I would usually use …" (n=2,280; NCC)											
	Raw numbers						Percentages				
Age-group	Cash	Debit Card	Credit Card	Check	Other	n for age	Cash	Debit Card	Credit Card	Check	Other
20-29	62	71	45	7	1	133	47%	53%	34%	5%	1%
30-39	96	122	77	20	4	224	43%	54%	34%	9%	2%
40-49	149	172	116	36	5	334	45%	51%	35%	11%	1%
50-59	229	228	152	58	6	471	49%	48%	32%	12%	1%
60-69	234	210	177	76	10	509	46%	41%	35%	15%	2%
70-79	167	132	111	57	4	344	49%	38%	32%	17%	1%
≥ 80	131	95	74	55	3	265	49%	36%	28%	21%	1%
Total	1,068	1,030	752	309	33	2,280					

The data reveal that the percentage of respondents using a credit card is virtually identical for all age-groups under 80 years, and that the percentage of those aged 80 years or more that use a credit card for such purchases is only a little less than credit-card use by the younger age-groups. Debit cards are more likely to be used by the younger age-groups, and checks by the older age-groups. Yet even amongst the older age-groups, the use of checks is declining.[3] In interviews conducted in California, several have shared with me that the only check they write is for their tithe payment. But the very striking thing is that cash is used by less than 50% of every age-group even for purchases of small value, and there are only minor variations in this behavior. Although a question related to the use of cash, checks, and

---

3 The results of research conducted by the US Federal Reserve System, published December 19, 2013 under the title, "The 2013 Federal Reserve Payments Study: Recent and Long-Term Payment Trends in the United States: 2003-2012 Summary Report and Initial Data Release," reveal that the relative use of cards versus cash for small purchases reported from the survey results in Northern California reflects the practices of American society as a whole. See also www.creditcards. com/creditcardnews/paymentmethodstatistics1276.php.

debit or credit cards for small transactions was not asked in the surveys used in Western Australia and South England, several lines of evidence suggest that the use of cash, checks, and cards in those places is likely to be quite similar to that in Northern California. For example, it is estimated that only 47% of all payments in Australia were made in cash in 2013, and the use of cash in Australia has continued to decline since then in favour of credit and debit cards. Worldwide cash is used in about 75% of all financial transactions, although in some countries this percentage is much smaller. For example, only 20% of all financial transactions in Sweden are in cash, and in England debit cards are used five times more often than cash for spontenous payments.[4]

Conferences, Unions, Divisions and the General Conference are naturally very cautious in their handling of tithe and other donations via electronic transactions, although the North American Division and the South Pacific Division have very sophisticated mechanisms in place that enable such transactions.

Even so, in contrast to the majority of spontaneous financial transactions in Australia and the United States, many if not most church offerings can only be donated using cash or checks while in Church. While a substantial number of members plan ahead for their tithes and offerings and can take advantage of e-giving opportunities, the group indicating "they just need to get into the habit," includes a number who would take advantage of an opportunity to use a non-cash option in a worship service. However, it is very rare that credit and/or debit-card facilities are available at a local

---

4 Shaun Drummond, "Cash Is Not Dead — Yet," *Australian Financial Review* 12 February 2016, p. 7R. It a media release from the Westpac Bank in 21 September 2015, it was noted that 53% of payments made in Australia are cashless. Compare also such publications as the "Payments and System Board Annual Report 2016," from the Reserve Bank of Australia. For the use of cash vs card for spontaneous payments in England, see Chart 1 on p. 220 of Tom Fish and Roy Whymark, "How Has Cash Usage Evolved in Recent Decades? What Might Drive Demand in the Future?" *Bank of England Quarterly Bulletin* 2015 Q3. While the use of credit and debit cards is common in Brazil and Kenya, cards are used by a much smaller percentage of the population, and much less often than cash for spontaneous transactions than they are in Australia, England and the United States. On Kenya see Justo Simiyu, Dedion Momanyi, Kiprotich Naibei and Alphonce Odondo, "Credit and Debic Card Usage and Cash Flow Management Control by Customers: Evidences from Commercial Banks Customers in Kisumi City, Kenya," *African Research Review* 6 (2012) 157–172; and "Payment Cards Grow to 12m in Kenya, but Use Stagnates," http://mgafrica.com. On Brazil see the Motley Fool, "The Massive Growth Potential of Brazilian Credit Cards," www.fool.com/investing/general/2013/10/18/thegrowthofbraziliancreditcards.aspx

church and, until recently, it has been technically challenging to provide them for a whole congregation during the offering time. This situation has changed with the opportunity to develop a cell-phone (mobile-phone) app that enables those attending to give during offering time. Such a mobile app is now being rolled out accross Australia, and is in final development in the United States.

One response to the observation, "I need to form the habit" of returning tithe, would be to provide as many overt and subtle reminders about tithing to those attending worship services as are culturally appropriate and likely to create a positive rather than negative result. Many opportunities to remind church-members about tithing exist, although practices vary widely both between and within the countries that I visited. For example, the leadership of the South England Conference identified Croydon church as a church with an outstanding record of returning tithe. Croydon church pastor, Richard Daly, shared his observations on what was happening in the church that contributed to its excellent record of tithing. He mentioned several things: the interest the church lay-leadership takes in the uses to which money is put,[5] the fact that the church is a caring church, and that it has a vibrant outreach program. He also mentioned that each Sabbath, during the five to ten minutes that it takes to collect the offering, a mini-sermon on stewardship is provided. It consists of a quotation from either the Bible or Ellen White's writings [Ellen White is an important founder of the Seventh-day Adventist Church considered by church-members to be a prophet] and "it gives a reason why we should give." This practice had been in place when Pastor Daly arrived as the pastor in the church. This type of announcement is seen as culturally appropriate in that church.[6] At the other extreme, in some other churches I attended the offering was taken up without even a notice as to the purpose of the local offering, or that tithes were included in the offering. This variety of practice may be related to the fact that in the Seventh-day Adventist Church, the local pastor is paid exactly the same whether or not he is actively promoting tithing, and whether or not the majority of the church-members are returning tithe. An increase in tithe returned by a particular congregation will not necessarily mean that extra funds are available to that

5 "At every board meeting, 11 times a year, at least 45 minutes is spent on money. People ask questions. ... When treasurer is away and we don't have a report—at least two hours earlier to finish the board meeting." Interview, Richard Daly, 27 July 2014.

6 The majority of those attending Croydon church have a West Indian heritage and about 50% are second- or third-generation British citizens (i.e. born in England).

local congregation, unless the increase is so substantial that the conference allocates another pastor to the pastoral team of the church. This is not to advocate a change is this policy—it works well for the church and allows it to act strategically in its distribution of resources, particularly pastoral and evangelistic resources.[7] But the system does provide very little motivation for local pastors to promote stewardship amongst their members, and the lack of attention to tithes and offerings in some congregations might well be traced back to this.

Some churches promote stewardship by showing on the screen activities in which their church and the wider Adventist Church has been involved while the offering is collected. One very simple idea was offered by an Australian pastor. In Australia and New Zealand it is customary to report anonymous tithe in the church bulletin (this is not true in every country in which this research took place). This pastor had observed that if the announcement was placed in the same place in the bulletin each week, then the church-members' eyes would learn to skip over that entry. As a consequence, he ensured that the announcement was moved to different locations in the bulletin each week, thus providing a subtle reminder about tithing.

The frequency and extent of regular promotion of tithe that seem appropriate appear to vary with the culture of the local congregation. Nevertheless, given the opportunity to increase tithing by reminding those who already think they should tithe, the pastor and the finance team will be able to generate new and creative ways to remind members of the importance of regular tithing. The possibilities for sensitive and positive promotion of tithing are numerous, and are likely to assist those who wish to tithe but "just need to get into the habit."

The highly significant observation is this: the majority of respondents who are not tithing 10% of their income indicated a willingness to change their tithing behavior.

---

7 Robert K. McIver, "Strategic Use of Tithe: How Does the Seventh-day Adventist Church Fare?" *Ministry* 74/10 (Oct 2001) 25–28; and Robert K. McIver and Stephen J. Currow, "Does it Make Sense to Centralise Tithe?" *[South Pacific Division] Record,* Sept 2001, pp. 8–10.

9. Motives for Tithing (Survey Data)

This chapter provides an analysis of the scales that were correlated to tithing behavior and a discussion of selected significant scales.

9.1 Correlation of Scales to Tithing Behavior

The theoretical model tested in this survey attributes a certain amount of variation in tithing behavior to demographic characteristics of the donor such as age. Indeed, it was shown that some demographic characteristics of individuals are statistically related to their reported tithing behavior — in particular, their age and being a baptized member. But the theoretical model also suggests that motives, attitudes and adoption of the "Adventist Package" also play a (statistically) significant role in predicting tithing behavior.

The statistical package SPSS was used to determine the correlation between the various scales and tithing behavior, and the results are summarized in Tables 9.1 and 9.2. A linear regression analysis was used to estimate the relationships between the scales and tithing behavior. Table 9.2 reports the probabilities that result from the progressive removal of scales that are shown not to relate to tithing behavior (the notes indicate the order in which they were removed). In other words, Table 9.2 reports the results of a backwards regression in which scales that do not correlate with the independent variable at a level that is statistically significant are removed successively. An analysis was also done using forwards regression, in which scales that most strongly correlate to tithing behavior are added one after another. The resultant set of scales that were correlated to tithing behavior were the same for both forward and backward regression.[1] The probabilities

1 The probabilities listed in Table 9.2 are based on the assumption that there is no relationship between a particular scale and reported tithing behavior. Given that assumption (termed a null hypothesis), it is possible to work out the likelihood of obtaining the data in the survey sample. For example, the likelihood that the pattern of relatedness between the feeling that it is appropriate to divert tithe and tithing behavior would occur if there was no relationship between the two (and the results were just random) is given as 0.000. This means that the probability of gaining this outcome is strictly less than 0.0005, or less than 5 times out of 10,000, or less than once in 2,000 times. It could be considerably less. This outcome is so unlikely that we reject the null hypothesis that the results are random, and for example, the analysis leads to the conclusion that there is a statistically significant relationship

in Table 9.2 show the level of statistical significance of the correlation between a scale and tithing behavior. A probability of less than 0.05 is taken as an indication of statistical correlation. Several of the probabilities are listed as 0.000. A probability of 0.000 means that the probability is less than 0.0005, or less than 5 times in 10,000; i.e. 0.000 is a strong indication of statistical correlation

Table 9.1: Probabilities that Scale and Tithing Behavior are Random					
Motive	Four Conference Data (WAC, SPC, SEC, NCC)	Australia (WAC)	Brazil (SPC)	England (SEC)	USA (NCC)
M1 Bible requirement	0.000	0.000	0.035	0.630^4	0.000
M2 God will bless	0.033	0.053^8	0.014	0.066^9	0.008
M3 Church as family	0.935^2	0.245^4	0.025	0.011	0.868^3
M4 Gratitude	0.000	0.000	0.243^7	0.000	0.000
M5 Pay your way	0.167^6	0.637^2	0.994^2	0.831^2	0.387^5
B1 Bible rule of faith	0.004	0.006	0.892^3	0.479^5	0.001
B3 Global mission	0.002	0.125^5		0.039	0.267^6
B4 Pooling tithe	0.209^7	0.009	0.035	0.197^7	0.012
B5 Church not needy	0.000	0.000	0.019	0.002	0.000
A1 Good Admin	0.799^4	0.037	0.736^4	0.000	0.069^8
A3 Comfort as SDA	0.883^5	0.007	0.426^5	0.067^8	0.042
A4 Pastor	0.000	0.004	0.436^6	0.032	0.000
A5 God is Lord of life	0.903^3	0.284^3	0.099^8	0.732^3	0.702^4
A6 OK to divert tithe	0.000	0.000	0.002	0.000	0.000
P1a No smoke alcohol	0.004	0.161^6	0.020	0.266^6	0.917^2

between believing that it is appropriate to divert tithe to unapproved destinations and tithing behavior. A more careful consideration of the statistics reveals that this is a negative correlation—the more somebody thinks that it is appropriate to divert tithe, the less likely they are to tithe at all. An important consideration is the cut-off probability where it is thought that the outcome is so unlikely we must reject the null hypothesis that there is no relationship between the scale and tithing behavior. In social science research this cut-off is usually set at the probability of an outcome being randomly produced equal to 0.05 (i.e. 95% confidence level), and this is the probability used in this chapter to determine whether or not there is a statistically significant relationship between a scale and tithing behavior. Most of the scales that turn out to be significant would also meet a much more stringent test, such as less than 0.0005, which shows the effectiveness of the survey in measuring motives and attitudes that are related to tithing.

Table 9.1: Probabilities that Scale and Tithing Behavior are Random					
Motive	Four Conference Data (WAC, SPC, SEC, NCC)	Australia (WAC)	Brazil (SPC)	England (SEC)	USA (NCC)
P1b No tea meat	0.003	0.179[7]	0.005	0.020	0.154[7]
P2 Spiritual practices	0.000	0.000	0.000	0.000	0.000

2 = removed from 2nd iteration of regression analysis
3 = removed from 3rd iteration of regression analysis
4 = removed from 4th iteration of regression analysis
5 = removed from 5th iteration of regression analysis
6 = removed from 6th iteration of regression analysis
7 = removed from 7th iteration of regression analysis
8 = removed from 8th iteration of regression analysis

Applying the criterion that any probability less than 0.05 indicates a statistically significant correlation between the scale and tithing behavior gives the results found in Table 9.2.

Table 9.2: Scales that Were Statistically Correlated to Tithing Behavior					
	Combined Data (WAC, SPC, SEC, NCC)	Australia (WAC)	Brazil (SPC)	England (SEC)	USA (NCC)
M1 Bible requirement	Yes	Yes	Yes	No	Yes
M2 God will bless	Yes	No	Yes	No	Yes
M3 Church as family	No	No	Yes	Yes	No
M4 Gratitude	Yes	Yes	No	Yes	Yes
M5 Pay your way	No	No	No	No	No
B1 Bible rule of faith	Yes	Yes	No	No	Yes
B3 Global mission	Yes	No		Yes	No
B4 Pooling tithe	No	Yes	Yes	No	Yes
B5 Church not needy	Yes	Yes	Yes	Yes	Yes
A1 Good Admin	No	Yes	No	Yes	No?
A3 Comfort as SDA	No	Yes	No	No	Yes
A4 Pastor	Yes	Yes	No	Yes	Yes
A5 God is Lord of life	No	No	No	No	No
A6 OK to divert tithe	Yes	Yes	Yes	Yes	Yes

Table 9.2: Scales that Were Statistically Correlated to Tithing Behavior					
	Combined Data (WAC, SPC, SEC, NCC)	Australia (WAC)	Brazil (SPC)	England (SEC)	USA (NCC)
P1a No smoke alcohol	Yes	No	Yes	No	No
P1b No tea meat	Yes	No	Yes	Yes	No
P2 Spiritual practices	Yes	Yes	Yes	Yes	Yes

Several things about these results are worthy of remark. For example, some of the scales are either statistically correlated with tithing behavior in all countries surveyed or not correlated in any of them.

9.1.1 Scales correlated to tithing behavior in all countries

The scales that were correlated to tithing behavior in all countries are:

P2 Spiritual practices of personal piety (e.g. study Sabbath School lesson; attend prayer meeting) (positive correlation—in other words, the more things on the list that a respondent indicated they did regularly, the more likely they were to tithe).

B5 The belief that the church has enough money to carry on without my help (negative correlation—in other words, the more the respondent thought that the church had enough money to carry on without their help, the less likely they were to tithe)

A6 The attitude that it is appropriate to divert tithe (negative correlation)

9.1.2 Scales not correlated to tithing behavior

Scales that were *not* correlated to tithing behavior in any country are:
M5 Pay your way
A5 God is Lord of my life

9.1.3 Scales that were correlated to tithing behavior in some countries and not others:

What I did not expect, but perhaps should have, was that several of the scales were significant in some countries but not in others. It might have been expected that this kind of variation would occur with one or two scales, but instead it occurred with several. Some scales that had been shown to be unrelated to tithing behavior in Australia had been reduced to one remaining question.[2] These single questions had been left in the survey on the thought-

---

2 The scales that had been reduced to one remaining question because they had proven not to be related to tithing behavior in Australia are as follows: M5 – Pay

to-be-unlikely off-chance that they might prove to be correlated to tithing behavior. Several scales, including some of only one item, did indeed prove to be correlated to tithing behavior in other countries, even if they had not done so in Australia. If further use is made of the survey instrument it is recommended that the scales having only one item should be restored to being a scale with three items.

Table 9.3 lists the scales that were significantly correlated to tithing behavior in some countries but not in others.

Table 9.3: Scales that Were Significantly Correlated to Tithing Behavior in Some Countries but not in Others (95% Confidence Interval)					
	Combined Data (WAC, SPC, SEC, NCC)	Australia (WAC)	Brazil (SPC)	England (SEC)	USA (NCC)
M1 Bible requirement	Yes	Yes	Yes	No	Yes
M2 God will bless	Yes	No	Yes	No	Yes
M3 Church as family	No	No	Yes	Yes	No
M4 Gratitude	Yes	Yes	No	Yes	Yes
B1 Bible rule of faith	Yes	Yes	No	No	Yes
B3 Global mission	Yes	No		Yes	No
B4 Pooling tithe	No	Yes	Yes	No	Yes
A1 Good Admin	No	Yes	No	Yes	No?
A3 Comfort as SDA	No	Yes	No	No	Yes
A4 Pastor	Yes	Yes	No	Yes	Yes
P1a No smoke alcohol	Yes	No	Yes	No	No
P1b No tea meat	Yes	No	Yes	Yes	No

9.2 The Adventist "Package": Spiritual Practices of Personal Piety

The survey included several scales that measured motives, beliefs and attitudes that could potentially related to patterns of tithing behavior. When

your way [which eventually was shown not to relate to tithing behavior in any of the conferences studied]; B1 – Bible rule of faith; B3 – Belief in global mission of the SDA Church; B4 – Belief that it is strategically valuable to pool tithe between churches; A1 – Confidence in financial probity and competence of SDA Church Administration; A3 – Comfort as a SDA; A4 – Attitude to local pastor; A5 – Wish to control own money vs God's lordship over money. See Appendix B.

the statistical package SPSS was programmed to identify which of the scales were related, two of them particularly stood out: "s1p2 Adventist Package – Spiritual Practices of Personal Piety" (t=14.633); and "s1a6 Attitude OK to divert tithe." They both had extraordinarily strong statistics associated with them,[3] and a movement in either scale appears to have a very large influence on tithing behavior. In very simplistic terms, in the case of "s1p2 Adventist Package – Spiritual Practices of Personal Piety", a movement in the scale is reflected in a change equivalent to 50% of that movement in tithing behavior (the footnote has a more correct technical explanation[4]).

The practical outcome is patent: an effective way to promote tithing in all the countries studied is to promote it alongside the spiritual practices of personal piety. These practices can be identified in the following questions that relate to this scale:
Which of the following is true of you?
(1 = never; 2 = sometimes; 3 = often; 4 = always/ almost always)
Do you?:
C15 Attend Sabbath school
C16 Open and close Sabbath
C17 Study the Sabbath School Quarterly
C18 Read and reflect on the Bible each day
C19 Pray often during the day
C20 Reflect on spiritual things during the day
C21 Attend prayer meetings [the wording "or small group meetings" was added to
the US survey]
The other feature of this scale which gives it practical import is that in each of the countries surveyed there is a wide variety of actual practice amongst those who filled in the survey. Responses ranged from those who

3 These two items had very high t-score indeed in the final regression model (Model 7 in Appendix H): "s1p2 Adventist Package – Spiritual Practices of Personal Piety" (t=14.633); and "s1a6 Attitude OK to divert tithe" (t=-13.921). What these t-scores mean in terms of probability might be judged from the fact that a t-score of 14.218 has a cumulative probability $P(T\leq t)=0.99999999$. (So http://stattrek.com/online-calculator/t-distribution.aspx; using 11 degrees of freedom [the web page explains what degrees of freedom means]). Putting it another way, the probability of obtaining the result t that has a t-score of 14.218 from two unrelated questions would be 1 in 100,000,000. In statistics one cannot say with absolute certainty that two things are related, but with these results, one can have a near certainty that there is a correlation between these scales and tithing behavior.
4 Strictly speaking, because S1p2 has a Beta coefficient of 0.537, a movement of one-standard deviation in the scale is reflected in a 0.537 movement in the standard deviation of tithing behavior. Standard deviation is a standardized measure of the "spread" of data.

replied "never" to each of the items, to those that said "always" to each of the items, and every intermediate step was well represented. This means that there is opportunity to promote these practices of personal piety in conjunction with tithing. Any increase in the number of church-members attending Sabbath School, studying their Sabbath School Quarterly, etc. will almost certainly be accompanied by an increase in tithing.

The scale, "Adventist Package 2" was calculated by giving values to the responses to each item (1 = never; 2 = sometimes; 3 = often; 4 = always/almost always), adding the responses to all items in the scale, and then averaging the result as a score out of 4. The result is a number between 1 and 4, which is used to give an overall reading of whether the respondents partook in the designated spiritual activities. The resultant scale has 25 different values, and is somewhat complex to explain. The results recorded in Table 9.4 have combined various intervals in the scale, so that instead of 25 separate data points there are eight. These intervals are found in the column labelled, "Scale: Adventist Package 2." These eight intervals may be conceptualized as corresponding to how many of the spiritual practices of personal piety in which the respondent participates. The respondents counted in the row labelled 1–1.3 either chose "Never" to all the items, or a combination that consisted of mainly "never," but may have included two or three "sometimes" responses. Thus the 1.0–1.3 range on the scale may be taken as roughly representing a respondent who participated in none of the practices of personal piety used to make up the scale. Similarly, values 1.4–1.7 on the scale represent responses that are largely a combination of "never," and "sometimes." Together they add up to represent an individual who participates in one of the practices of personal piety. In the same way, the further intervals roughly represent a respondent who participates in two of the practices, three, four, five, six, or seven of them. The number of practices that roughly correspond to the scale are found in the column "Equivalent No of Activities" in Table 9.4, and numbers in this column make up the x-axis of the graph in Figure 9.1, which is labelled, "Total Number of Spiritual Practices (out of 7).

Scale: Adventist Package 2	Equivalent No of Activities	Count					Percentage			
		Australia (WAC)	England (SEC)	Brazil (SPC)	USA (NCC)	All 4 Conferences	Australia (WAC)	England (SEC)	Brazil (SPC)	USA (NCC)
1.0-1.3	0	21	13	11	5	50	1.3%	1.4%	2.3%	0.5%
1.4-1.7	1	88	31	7	37	163	5.6%	3.3%	1.5%	3.6%
1.75-2.1	2	156	72	43	98	369	9.9%	7.8%	8.9%	9.5%
2.2-2.5	3	236	136	87	176	635	15.0%	14.7%	18.1%	17.1%
2.6-2.9	4	294	187	56	195	732	18.6%	20.2%	11.6%	18.9%
3.0-3.3	5	326	203	132	217	878	20.7%	21.9%	27.4%	21.0%
3.4-3.7	6	266	160	54	169	649	16.9%	17.3%	11.2%	16.4%
3.75-4.0	7	191	124	91	134	540	12.1%	13.4%	18.9%	13.0%
		1,578	926	481	1,031	4,016				

Table 9.4: Scale Adventist Package 2: Seven Spiritual Practices of Personal Piety (NCC, SEC, SPC, WAC)

Fig. 9.1: Scale Adventist Package 2: Seven Spiritual Practices of Personal Piety (NCC, SEC, SPC, WAC)

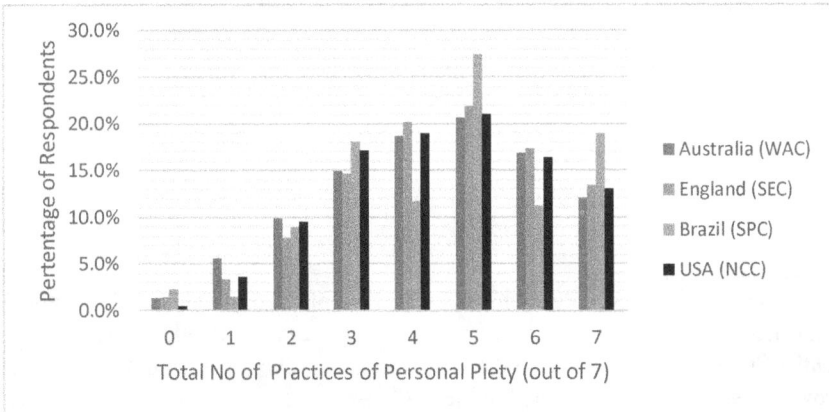

Both Table 9.4 and Figure 9.1 reveal that there is wide variation in the participation of respondents in the seven practices of personal piety that are typical of Seventh-day Adventist spirituality. These practices are strongly correlated to tithing behavior. Thus if tithing is promoted alongside of promotion of these practices of personal piety, one should expect that any increase in the number of practices of personal piety would be matched by an increase in the tithe returned to the church.

9.3 Attitude that it is OK to "Divert" Tithe

The scale "A6 Attitude that is it OK to 'Divert' Tithe" was as follows in the Northern California Conference Survey:

I feel there is nothing wrong in giving tithe ...
C9   to special projects (such as a new church building)
C10   directly to an overseas mission field
C11   to assist volunteers working in my local church
C12   to the offering that supports the local SDA school
C13   to help needy people through Adventist Community Services or ADRA[1]

This scale had a very strong negative correlation with tithing behavior. In other words, the more a respondent agreed with the items on this scale, the less likely they were to report that they returned tithe. Two considerations reveal this to be a very important scale. The first is that there is a strong linkage between changes in this scale, and changes in tithing behavior.[2] Second, and perhaps of greater importance still, is the fact that there is a very wide range of opinion as to whether it is acceptable to distribute tithe to all the destinations identified. To take but one example, Table 9.5 and Figure 9.2 (below) show how the respondents agreed or disagreed with the statement: "I feel there is nothing wrong in giving tithe to help needy people through Adventist Community Services or ADRA."

---

1 This question was worded "to help needy people through ADRA" for countries other than the United States of America. It was necessary to add the words "Adventist Community Services" in the USA, because Adventist Community Services provide assistance and relief within the USA, while ADRA provides assistance and relief outside of the USA.

2 The regression model revealed that the scale "A6 Attitude that it is OK to 'Divert' Tithe" had a beta coefficient of 0.308. In other words, a movement of 1 standard deviation on the scale is highly likely to result in a 0.308 standard deviation change in tithing behavior.

Table 9.5: "I feel there is nothing wrong in giving tithe to help needy people through ADRA"									
	Count					Percentage			
	Australia (WAC)	England (SEC)	Brazil (SPC)	USA (NCC)	All	Australia (WAC)	England (SEC)	Brazil (SPC)	USA (NCC)	All
Strongly Disagree	630	176	153	343	1,302	41%	20%	35%	34%	34%
Disagree More Than Agree	192	103	30	151	476	12%	12%	7%	15%	12%
Agree More Than Disagree	279	174	59	180	692	18%	20%	14%	18%	18%
Strongly Agree	450	424	195	337	1,406	29%	48%	45%	33%	36%
Total	1,551	877	437	1,011	3,876					

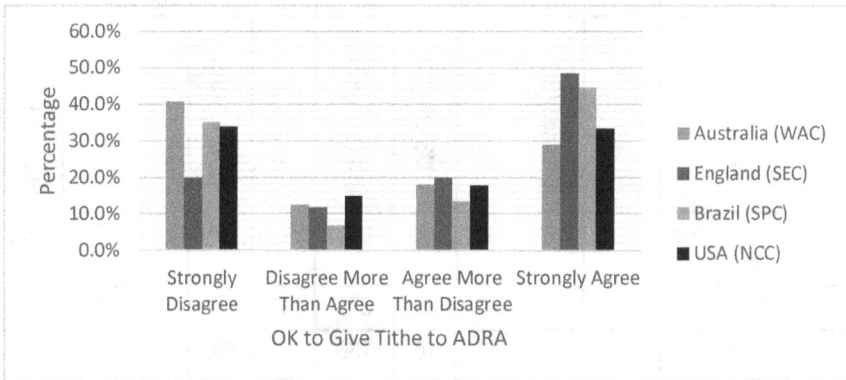

Fig. 9.2: "I feel there is nothing wrong in giving tithe to help needy people through ADRA" (%)

As may be observed in Figure 9.2 and Table 9.5, the two dominant responses to "I feel that there is nothing wrong in giving tithe to help needy people through ADRA" were either to "Strongly Disagree" or to "Strongly Agree." While the numbers were somewhat balanced between these two responses, in England and Brazil the most common response was "strongly agree," while in the US the numbers who strongly agreed and strongly disagreed were about equal. It was only in Australia that the number of those who strongly disagreed was significantly more than the number of those who strongly agreed, but there was still a very substantial minority who strongly agreed. The pattern for each of the questions varied somewhat by country, but overall, there was a very substantial number of respondents who held the opinion that it was "OK to give tithe" to the destinations identified in the five questions.

The scale A6 Attitude: "OK to Divert Tithe" was calculated by giving values to the responses to each item in the scale (1 = never; 2 = sometimes; 3 = often; 4 = always/ almost always), adding the responses to all items in the scale, and then averaging the result as a score out of 4. The result is a number between 1 and 4, which is used to give an overall reading of whether the respondents disagreed or agreed that it was acceptable to direct tithe to the places in the scale. The resultant scale has 54 different values, which is somewhat complex to explain. The results recorded in Table 9.6 have combined various intervals in the scale, so that instead of 54 separate data points, there are 7. The majority of the results fell on exactly 1, 2, 3, or 4, which appears to be the result of fairly uniform opinions from those responding to these items.

Table 9.6: Country vs Scale A6 Attitude "OK to Divert Tithe"										
	Count					Percentage				
Scale A6: "OK to divert tithe"	Australia (WAC)	England (SEC)	Brazil (SPC)	USA (NCC)	All 4 Conferences	Australia (WAC)	England (SEC)	Brazil (SPC)	USA (NCC)	All 4 Conferences
Strongly Disagree (1)	503	114	86	256	959	34%	14%	21%	26%	26%
1.1-1.9	142	66	65	106	379	10%	8%	16%	11%	10%
Disagree More Than Agree (2)	105	45	10	76	236	7%	6%	2%	8%	6%
2.1-2.9	203	114	66	123	506	14%	14%	16%	12%	14%
Agree More Than Disagree (3)	147	72	27	90	336	10%	9%	7%	9%	9%
3.1-3.9	224	245	101	166	736	15%	30%	25%	17%	20%
Strongly Agree (4)	227	225	91	174	717	16%	28%	23%	18%	20%
Total	1,551	881	446	991	3,869					

Fig. 9.3: Scale A6 Attitude "OK to Divert Tithe" (%)

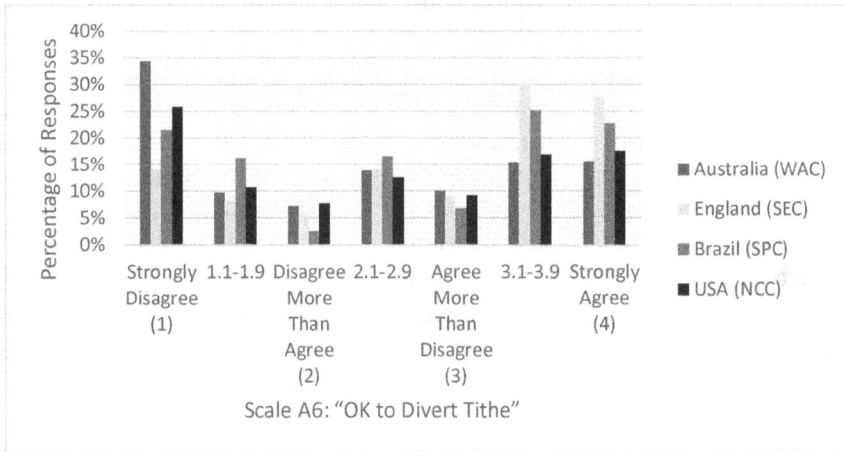

The pattern apparent in Figure 9.3 is very similar to that noticed already in Figure 9.2 (one of the items of the scale). The dominant responses fall into two clusters: one group strongly disagrees that it is acceptable to direct tithe to the destinations specified, while a larger group strongly agrees, or responded with a mixture of "Strongly Agree" and "Agree More than Disagree." What is also clear from Figure 9.3 is that there is a wide variety of opinions in the matter, which provides opportunity for change in the attitudes of a large number of people on where it is acceptable to direct tithe.

Education of the membership of the church about where tithe should be directed is likely to have a double impact. First, the evidence suggests that individuals will contribute a greater amount of tithe than had hitherto been the case and, second, the proportion of tithe that would otherwise go elsewhere would now be returned to the church.

9.4 Reported Tithe "Diversion"

The section of the survey which generated the most discussion with the leaders in the participating conferences was that dealing with tithe "diversion" (i.e. directing tithe to places other than those recommended by the church). In every country, concern was expressed by conference treasurers and/or stewardship directors that even asking this question on the survey would encourage tithe diversion. In each case, reluctant permission was granted provided that some clear indication was given as part of the question that it was not church policy that tithe should be "diverted" from official church channels. For this reason, some variation of the following language was used to introduce the question relating to tithe diversion in South England

Conference, Central Kenya Conference, São Paulo Conference and Northern California Conference (specific wording for each country may be found in Appendix C):

"C8: The Seventh-day Adventist Church considers that tithes and offerings should be treated separately. Offerings are given in addition to tithe. The Church also suggests where tithes and offerings should be directed. But this question is about what you actually do with your tithes and offerings, not what you should be doing. Next to each of the list below, fill in ...."

The argument put to the local conference directors and treasurers was that the data collected would be of such great importance that it was necessary to take the risk of the intent of the question being misunderstood. After all, what is actually happening with tithe is a very important question, and a suitable educational response can be put in place depending on what is discovered.

Table 4.13 shows what the survey respondents reported they were doing with their tithes (NCC, SEC, SPC, WAC) and offerings (for NCC, SEC and SPC).

Table 9.7: Percentage of Respondents that Report that "In the last 12 months I have given tithe ..."; "In the last 12 months I have given offerings ..."							
	Tithe				Offering		
Question	NCC	SEC	SPC	WAC	NCC	SEC	SPC
to Sabbath School (world mission) offerings		26%	40%	29%		66%	54%
to local-church-based appeals	9%	16%		9%	39%	48%	43%
to the Church Building/Plot fund/ program	18%	20%	19%	13%	56%	42%	45%
to the local SDA school offering [NCC: to the local SDA school / Education offering] [para à sistema Educacional da IASD]	10%	8%		9%	47%	31%	22%
to an independent Adventist ministry [SPC: a um ministério adventista independente]	10%	3%	16%	5%	46%	20%	22%
to support a youth volunteer/youth worker/Bible Worker in our local church	8%	4%	10%	2%	26%	19%	7%
to Sponsorships		3%	18%				
to the local church Budget/offering	51%	45%	26%	32%	78%	50%	46%

Table 9.7: Percentage of Respondents that Report that "In the last 12 months I have given tithe ..."; "In the last 12 months I have given offerings ..."							
	Tithe				Offering		
Question	NCC	SEC	SPC	WAC	NCC	SEC	SPC
to [Adventist Community Services or] ADRA	10%	15%	18%	23%	32%	41%	36%
to needs in my country or conference of origin	7%	7%	16%	5%	25%	19%	20%
to the Salvation Army or Red Cross, etc [NCC: to a non-SDA Christian ministry (e.g. the Salvation Army, World Vision); NCC: to non-SDA charity or non-profit organisation (e.g. Red Cross, American Cancer Society, United Way, etc)]	5%	5%	16%	12%	30%	15%	19%
directly to overseas mission field	8%	6%	18%	9%	30%	19%	26%
to supporting local pastors	13%	3%	18%		16%	13%	22%
NCC: to Conference Advance	9%						
SEC: to Adventist Media		2%					
SEC: to organ fund		1%					
Total Number of Respondents answering this set of questions	1,125	1,200	589	1,562	1,125	1,200	589

The results reported in Table 9.7 complement the discussion of the scale "A6 Attitude that it is OK to 'Divert' Tithe." The degree of correlation of Scale A6 with tithing behavior" reveals that there is a very widespread belief that tithe can be freely used for purposes such as donations to the mission field, to the local church school and to such worthy causes as the Red Cross. This is matched by behavior. Tithe is being directed to a wide variety of destinations. This is an area in which it would be fruitful for the Church to embark on a program to educate members about where it is appropriate to direct tithe.

9.5 Returning Tithe through Approved Church Channels

The changes to the ways that wider society handles money are reflected to a greater or lesser extent in church-member behavior in all areas, including tithes and offerings. Society as a whole has made significant progress in moving to a cashless society. Credit and debit cards are being used for purchases of quite small value, and the questions placed in the survey for

Northern California reveal that this process is widespread in all age-groups of Seventh-day Adventist church-members, so much so that less than 50% of respondents in all age-groups (including those aged $\geq$ 80 years) reported that they use cash for purchases of $10 to $49 (see Table 8.3). This process is taking place at different rates across the globe. Judging from many conversations, credit cards were virtually unknown amongst church-members in Kenya, and in Brazil their use is rare amongst church-members, especially for such purchases as fast food.

The church has been making a slow accommodation to changing practices of cash management in its membership. It is still rare for a church to make credit-card facilities available to its members. This is an important observation, given that many of those attending the church on a Sabbath morning operate entirely from credit cards, and only very rarely have cash with them, if ever. One informed minister's response was that the big donations are planned away from the church service (e.g. tithe), but that may not be an attitude shared by many who would argue that giving is an important part of the worship service. Furthermore, it makes giving something that needs to be planned. This works well for many church-members, but others are less well organized (see data on "Sometimes I forget to tithe" in Table 3.3 and Figure 3.1 in Chapter 3, as well as in Chapters 4.5, 5.5, 6.4, and 7.1.3 on the frequency of tithing revealed by tithe receipts).

While credit-card transactions are very rare in the local churches, and even in many conferences, the four conferences studied here had access to a Conference/ Union/ Division/ General Conference-sponsored system of electronic giving by means of a wage-deduction. Table 9.8 presents the percentages of survey respondents that reported they use these alternative ways of returning tithe to the church.

Table 9.8: Percentage of Respondents that Report that "In the last 12 months I have given tithe …" (%)					
	All	NCC	SEC	SPC	WAC
The tithe envelope in my local church	69%	78%	65%	72%	70%
Adventist e-giving / e-giving	7%	11%	3%	3%	8%
Directly to my church treasurer	5%	8%	8%	3%	4%
Directly to the local Conference	4%	3%	3%	1%	5%
Directly to the Union Conference / NAD Division / General Conference	N/A	2%	N/A	N/A	N/A

It is noteworthy that by far the most common way to return tithe to the church is through a tithe-envelope in the local church, either by check or by cash. More than one member reported to me that a tithe check is the only check that they still write. It could be that e-giving will become more widespread. However one concern with e-giving is that it is a transaction that is not incorporated into the worship service.

9.6 God Has Blessed Me Because I Tithe

The scale "M2 God Will Bless Me if I Tithe" was negatively correlated with tithing practice in three countries (NCC, SEC, SPC), and positively correlated with tithing practice in one country (WAC), but the linkage was only mild in all four Conferences.[1] This means, curiously enough, that in Brazil, England and the United States, the more somebody believes that God will bless them if they tithe, the less (marginally) they are likely to tithe. The responses to items in this scale may be represented by the item which stated, "I contribute tithe because God promises prosperity to those who tithe."

	Table 9.9: "I contribute tithe because God promises prosperity to those who tithe"									
	Count					Percentage				
	Australia (WAC)	England (SEC)	Brazil (SPC)	USA (NCC)	All (NCC, SEC, SPC, WAC)	Australia (WAC)	England (SEC)	Brazil (SPC)	USA (NCC)	All (NCC, SEC, SPC, WAC)
Strongly Disagree	325	143	317	243	1,028	21%	18%	46%	24%	25%
Disagree More Than Agree	272	135	114	248	769	17%	17%	17%	24%	19%
Agree More Than Disagree	456	208	106	270	1,040	29%	27%	15%	26%	26%
Strongly Agree	522	298	152	265	1,237	33%	38%	22%	26%	30%
Total	1,575	784	689	1,026	4,074					

1 For the aggregated data, the scale "M2 God will Bless" has a Beta Coefficient of -0.059. For NCC it is -0.148; for SEC it is -0.122; for SPC it is -0.164; and for WAC it is +0.083. Overall, the effect of the motive is that for every one standard deviation of change in the scale, tithing behavior is effected by less than 6% of one standard deviation; although in NCC it would be 15%.

Fig. 9.4: "I contribute tithe because God promises prosperity to those who tithe"

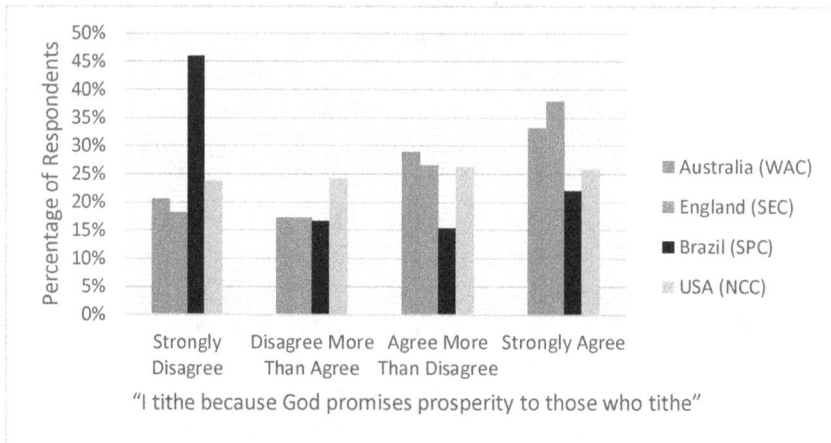

The significance of this motive varies from country to country. It is strongly believed in Australia (where is it positively correlated to increased tithing), and much less strongly believed in Brazil (where it is negatively correlated to increased tithing). But it is a factor on which there is a variety of opinions in all the countries studied. Overall it appears that to promote tithing "because God might bless you as a result" is likely to have a negative impact on the amount of tithe received by the church!

In the development of the original scale, the trial questions developed to measure the motive, "M2 God will bless" broke into two separate groups. One group of questions asked whether the participant tithed because they wished to receive a blessing, whereas the other group asked whether or not the respondent believed God had blessed them because they tithed. The items that asked whether the participant tithed because they would be blessed were kept in the scale on the grounds that this indeed was a motive for tithing, rather than a report of what they believed was a consequence of tithing. This scale was used in version 5 (that used in North New South Wales and Greater Sydney Conferences). After further reflection it was thought that it would be very interesting to discover whether or not respondents thought God had blessed them because they tithed. The question "God HAS blessed me because I tithe" was added to version 7.1 (that used in the Western Australia Conference), and was included in the surveys used in the four conferences reported here.

Tables 9.10, 9.11 and 9.12 report three different views of the data set. The first, Table 9.10, includes the responses of all who answered the question. The second, Table 9.11, shows the responses of those who said on the survey form that they did not tithe at all. The third, Table 9.12, shows the responses of those who tithe 8% or more of their income. It is perhaps noteworthy that of those who tithe 8% or more of their income, 82% either agree or strongly agree that "God HAS blessed them because they tithe." It is curious that among the group who do not tithe at all, the largest response is still "Strongly Agree." The difference between those who agree or strongly agree amongst the non-tithers (58%) and those who tithe more than 8% (82%) is quite marked. The percentages just quoted are for the whole data set. The tables also provide equivalent data for the four conferences.

	Count					Percentage				
Table 9.10: "God HAS blessed me because I tithe" **(All respondents, tither and non-tither alike)**										
	Australia (WAC)	England (SEC)	Brazil (SPC)	USA (NCC)	All (NCC, SEC, SPC, WAC)	Australia (WAC)	England (SEC)	Brazil (SPC)	USA (NCC)	All (NCC, SEC, SPC, WAC)
Strongly Disagree	325	143	317	243	1,028	21%	18%	46%	24%	25%
Disagree More Than Agree	272	135	114	248	769	17%	17%	17%	24%	19%
Agree More Than Disagree	456	208	106	270	1,040	29%	27%	15%	26%	26%
Strongly Agree	522	298	152	265	1,237	33%	38%	22%	26%	30%
Total	1,575	784	689	1,026	4,074					

Table 9.11: "God HAS blessed me because I tithe" (Those Who Do Not Tithe)									
	Count					Percentage			
	Australia (WAC)	England (SEC)	Brazil (SPC)	USA (NCC)	All (NCC, SEC, SPC, WAC)	Australia (WAC)	England (SEC)	Brazil (SPC)	USA (NCC)	All (NCC, SEC, SPC, WAC)
Strongly Disagree	56	29	18	27	130	20%	18%	18%	28%	20%
Disagree More Than Agree	69	28	20	20	137	25%	17%	20%	21%	21%
Agree More Than Disagree	65	35	17	15	132	23%	22%	17%	16%	21%
Strongly Agree	91	69	46	34	240	32%	43%	46%	35%	38%
Total	281	161	101	96	639					

Fig. 9.5: "God HAS blessed me because I tithe" (Those Who Do Not Tithe)

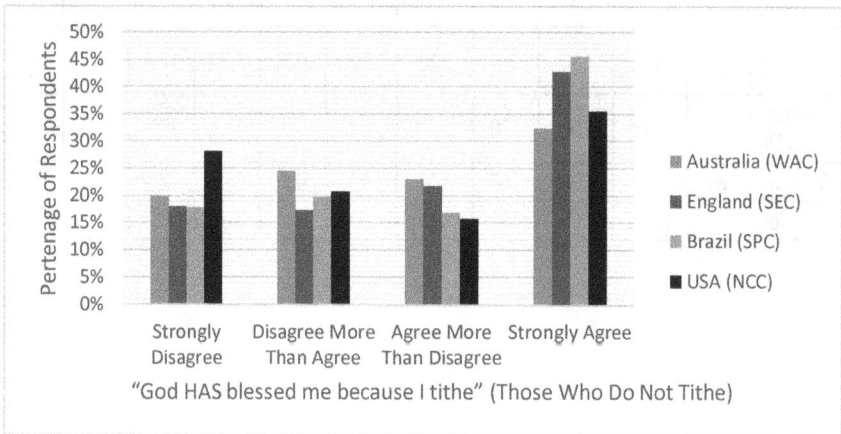

"God HAS blessed me because I tithe" (Those Who Do Not Tithe)

Table 9.12: "God HAS blessed me because I tithe" (Those Who Tithe ≥8% of Income)									
	Count					Percentage			
	Australia (WAC)	England (SEC)	Brazil (SPC)	USA (NCC)	All (NCC, SEC, SPC, WAC)	Australia (WAC)	England (SEC)	Brazil (SPC)	USA (NCC)	All (NCC, SEC, SPC, WAC)
Strongly Disagree	107	53	74	46	280	9%	9%	14%	6%	9%
Disagree More Than Agree	150	43	52	55	300	12%	7%	10%	7%	10%
Agree More Than Disagree	314	119	98	181	712	25%	20%	19%	23%	23%
Strongly Agree	671	378	299	498	1,846	54%	64%	57%	64%	59%
Total	1,242	593	523	780	3,138					

Fig. 9.6: "God HAS blessed me because I tithe"
(Those Who Tithe ≥8% of Income)

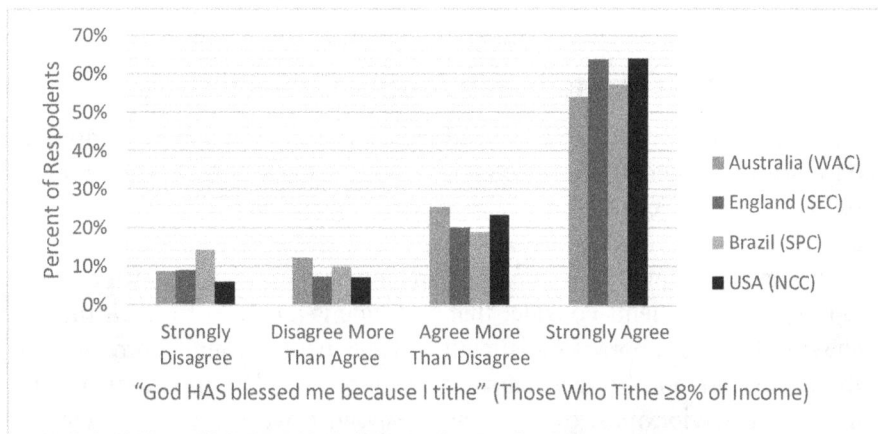

Figures 9.5 and 9.6 show how the non-tithers and tithers respond to the item, "God HAS blessed me because I tithe" for each country. The difference between the two groups is observable. Figure 9.7 allows the direct comparison between those who do not tithe and those who do tithe for the combined data from all four conferences.

Fig. 9.7: "God HAS blessed me because I tithe"
(Comparison Between Those Who Tithed 0% and those
tithed ≥8% of Income; NCC, SEC, SPC, WAC)

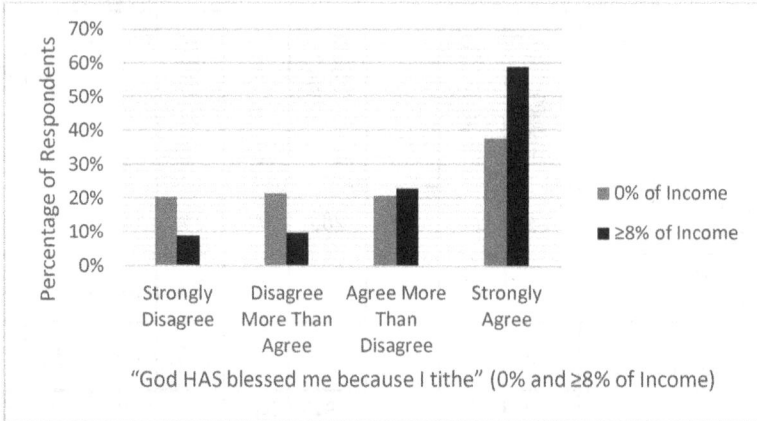

"God HAS blessed me because I tithe" (0% and ≥8% of Income)

What should not be overlooked in these statistical data is something that has become very evident to me as I have talked to people from all walks of life, and in many different countries around the world. In saying that "God HAS blessed me because I tithe," respondents are indicating that they see tangible evidence of God's activity in their lives as a result of their tithing practice. [1]

9.7 Gratitude as a Motive for Tithing

In the aggregated data from all four conferences, the motive of gratitude is strongly correlated to tithing behavior.[2] Among the individual conferences this is true in Northern California, Southern England and Western Australia, but not, for some reason, in Brazil.

The data presented in Table 9.13 and Figure 9.8 reveal that the great majority of respondents consider that gratitude is a motive for their tithing behavior (this is supported statistically). Thus, while strongly correlated to tithing behavior, and while a change in this motive had a substantial change on tithing behavior, most of those who responded were already convinced of the connection between their gratitude for God's love and forgiveness and their tithing behavior.

---

1 For examples and some further reflection, see "Should I Share These Stories?" *Adventist Review*, February 12, 2004, 25–28.

2 "Motive M3: Gratitude" has a t score of +7.518 (i.e. is a very highly reliable result) and a Beta Coefficient of +0.316 (in other words, one standard deviation change in M3 results, on average, in a 0.3 standard deviation change in tithing behavior).

Table 9.13: " I contribute tithe because I am often overwhelmed by how good God has been to me"									
	Count					Percentage			
	Australia (WAC)	England (SEC)	Brazil (SPC)	USA (NCC)	All (NCC, SEC, SPC, WAC)	Australia (WAC)	England (SEC)	Brazil (SPC)	USA (NCC)	All (NCC, SEC, SPC, WAC)
Strongly Disagree	115	70	44	88	317	7%	9%	6%	8%	8%
Disagree More Than Agree	209	84	32	145	470	13%	11%	5%	14%	11%
Agree More Than Disagree	554	203	90	343	1,190	35%	25%	13%	33%	29%
Strongly Agree	719	442	520	461	2,142	45%	55%	76%	44%	52%
Total	1,597	799	686	1,037	4,119					

Fig. 9.8: "I contribute tithe because I am often overwhelmed by how good God has been to me" (%)

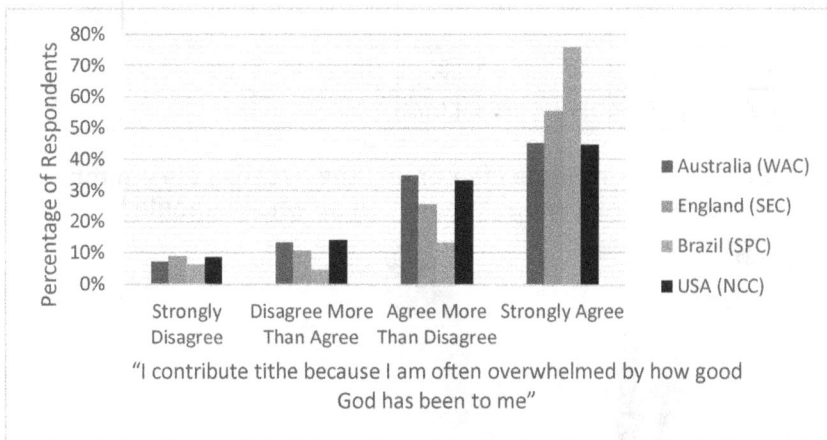

9.8 Perception that Church is Not Needy

The belief, "B4: The Church is Not Needy," was strongly negatively correlated with tithing in all four conferences studied.[1] In other words,

---

1 "B4: The Church is Not Needy" has a t-score of -8.654 (for the aggregated data), and a Beta coefficient of -0.308.

the more a respondent believed the Church was not needy, the lower the likelihood that they would tithe. On the other hand, as may be observed in Table 9.14 and Figure 9.9, most respondents disagreed with such statements as "I contribute little or no tithe because the church already has enough money to do what it should." The church appears to have been quite successful in explaining its financial needs to its members.

Table 9.14: "I contribute little or no tithe because the church already has enough money to do what it should"									
	Count					Percentage			
	Australia (WAC)	England (SEC)	Brazil (SPC)	USA (NCC)	All (NCC, SEC, SPC, WAC)	Australia (WAC)	England (SEC)	Brazil (SPC)	USA (NCC)	All (NCC, SEC, SPC, WAC)
Strongly Disagree	1,187	602	563	766	3,118	75%	78%	82%	76%	77%
Disagree More Than Agree	252	85	40	160	537	16%	11%	6%	16%	13%
Agree More Than Disagree	87	48	31	53	219	5%	6%	5%	5%	5%
Strongly Agree	60	37	52	35	184	4%	5%	8%	3%	5%
Total	1,586	772	686	1,014	4,058					

Fig. 9.9: "I contribute little or no tithe because the church already has enough money to do what it should"

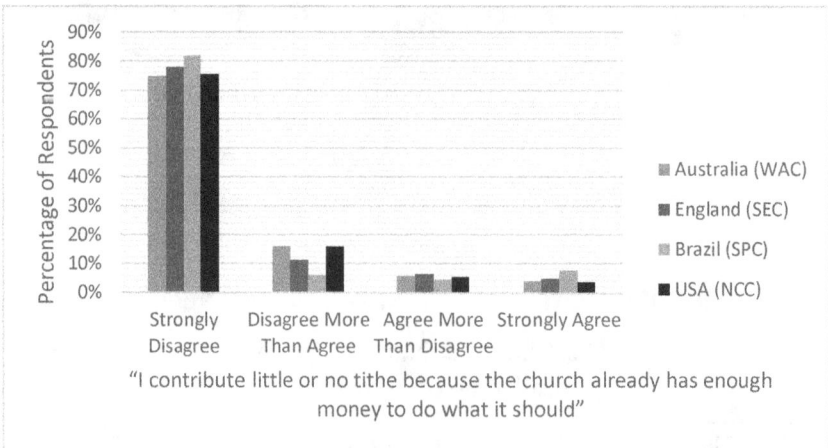

9.9 Tithe a Biblical Requirement

The motive, "M1: Tithe a Biblical Requirement," is strongly positively correlated with tithing behavior in the combined data from the four Conferences studied,[1] and also in the individual conferences of Northern California, São Paulo, and Western Australia. Indeed, any movement on this scale has a far greater likelihood of changing tithing behavior than on any other scale tested.[2] For some reason, this motive does not correlate with tithing behavior in South England. Nonetheless, in every conference it is a strongly-held belief that the Bible indicates that Christians should return 10% of their income to the Church as a tithe. This may be observed in Table 9.15, which gives the responses to the item, "The Bible is clear that I should give 10% of my income as tithe," and again in Figure 9.10 which shows the responses from the four countries.

Table 9.15: "The Bible is clear that I should give 10% of my income as tithe"										
	Count					Percentage				
	Australia (WAC)	England (SEC)	Brazil (SPC)	USA (NCC)	All (NCC, SEC, SPC, WAC)	Australia (WAC)	England (SEC)	Brazil (SPC)	USA (NCC)	All (NCC, SEC, SPC, WAC)
Strongly Disagree	52	48	46	40	186	3%	5%	6%	4%	4%
Disagree More Than Agree	41	14	12	37	104	3%	1%	2%	3%	2%
Agree More Than Disagree	196	59	28	99	382	12%	6%	4%	9%	9%
Strongly Agree	1,317	825	628	880	3,650	82%	87%	88%	83%	84%
Total	1,606	946	714	1,058	4,324					

---

1 The t-score of "M1: Tithe is a Biblical Requirement" is +7.518 for the aggregated data.

2 The Beta coefficient of "M1: Tithe is a Biblical Requirement" is +0.422, the largest Beta coefficient for all of the scales tested.

**Fig. 9.10: "The Bible is clear that I should
give 10% of my income as tithe"**

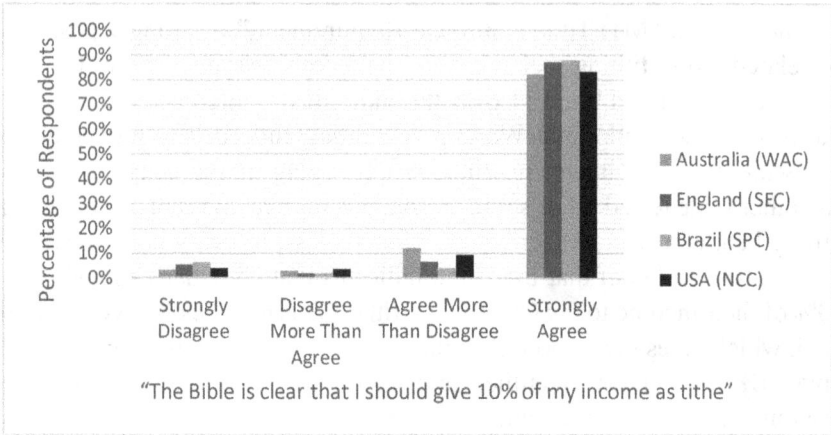

"The Bible is clear that I should give 10% of my income as tithe"

Because almost every respondent already believes that "The Bible is clear that I should give 10% of my income as tithe," even though the scale, "Tithe is a Biblical Requirement" is strongly correlated to tithing behaviour, promoting the concept heavily is unlikely to cause many to change their mind – they are already convinced. While some reminders should be made of the biblical principle of tithing, tithing promotion would be more effective if it concentrated on other factors that have been to be correlated to tithing, but on which there is a much wider spread of opinion or practice. These would include education on the places to which tithe should be directed, and encouragement of tithing practice alongside of regular prayer and Bible study.

10. Conclusions

This investigation has uncovered some disquieting data. For example, if tithe receipts from Northern California, South England and Western Australia are compared to income, it is clear that for at least the last 40 years there has been a progressive fall in the percentage of church-member income that is being returned to the church as tithe. It is indeed sobering to consider the missed opportunities for mission represented by this fall in the resources that would otherwise have been available to further the mission of the church. It is even more sobering to consider that if there is no change in the giving patterns of those returning their tithe to the church, there will be a continuous fall in the percentage of church-member income that is donated to the church well into the future. Such a result will further restrict the opportunities for the church to fulfill its mission. The analysis of tithe receipts and survey data reported in this book has revealed not only why this fall has taken place, it also reveals several clear strategies by which this trend might be reversed.

10.1 Differences in the Tithing Behavior of Various Age-groups

From its inception, this investigation was designed to investigate the relationship between donor-age and tithing behavior. The analyses of both the tithe-receipt data and the survey data provide ample confirmation that there are large differences in the tithing behavior of the various age-groups. For example, it was discovered that in the Northern California, Southern England, and Western Australia Conferences, there was a progressive decrease from the oldest to the youngest age-group in per-capita tithe expressed as a proportion of income (see Chapters 4.4, 5.6, 7.1.3). Curiously enough, about the same percentage of each age-group in Western Australia returns tithe to the church at least once per year (see Chapters 4.3), something also true of those aged between 30 and 69 years in Northern California (see Chapter 5.4). The church-members of São Paulo Conference showed a slightly different profile of giving patterns, but still one that was age-related. Those aged 30 years or older returned about the same proportion of their income to the church as tithe, but the percentage of each age-group that tithed at least once per year progressively decreased from the oldest age-group to the youngest (see Chapter 6.3 & 6.5).

10.2 Tithing Progressively More Sporadic in Each Younger Age-group

One feature of tithing practice that was common to the members of the Northern California, São Paulo, Southern England, and Western Australia Conferences: the frequency of tithing decreased progressively through the age-groups from the oldest to the youngest (see Chapters 3.1, 4.5, 5.5, 6.4, 7.1.3, 7.1.4). There is a mixture of good news and bad news for the church arising from this observation. The bad news is that if the younger age-groups continue with the pattern of tithing behavior that is currently established, then as the church population ages and the younger groups replace the older groups, in the Seventh-day Adventist Church in Australia, Brazil, Britain and the United States, the downward trend in the percentage of the income earned by its membership that is returned to the church as tithe is likely to continue. In other words, there are likely to be yet further reductions in the proportion of member-income donated to the church. This has the potential to affect greatly the church's ability to fulfill its mission. Yet there is also an element of good news in the research data. Large numbers in every age-group were tithing, and it is possible to persuade other attenders to tithe as well. It should not be overlooked that even though younger Adventists are tithing less regularly, they are still returning some proportion of income as tithe, and are convinced that they should return tithe. Consequently, one way that is very likely to increase the tithe returned to the church from these members is to find a way to assist those in the younger age-group to tithe more regularly.

10.3 Challenge of Increasing Exclusive Use of Credit/Debit Cards

Clearly, if the church is able to persuade people who are already tithing to contribute more regularly, then this would have a very positive impact on the amount of tithe contributed to the church. There are several things that might be done in this regard. In countries where regular wage-deductions can be arranged, many find that using such a facility is of great assistance to their returning tithe regularly. Much more could be done to promote such schemes where they exist.

The questions relating to use of credit and debit card asked in the Northern California version of the survey were expected to reveal that people in younger age-groups tended to use credit cards for small purchases more than those in older age-groups. In fact, the extent to which credit cards were used was similar across all age-groups in the United States. Such uses of credit cards are not restricted to Northern California. In my travels undertaken for this project, I was able to observe the impact of new technology that allows "touch and go" use of credit cards in the purchase of inexpensive meals in many different places and cultures. While not true in Kenya and Brazil, in countries such as Australia, England and the United States bank and government data reveals that the majority of financial transactions now take place using credit, debit cards or phone apps, even for such small amounts as a meal at a McDonald's fast-food outlet.

The Seventh-day Adventist Church is still thinking through its response to this new technology both at the administrative level and the local church level. Some individual churches are experimenting with having card-processing facilities available at their church. To cite one example, a large Adventist church in Auckland, New Zealand, has two card facilities in the foyer of the same type used for transactions in retail outlets. These facilities allow a debit-card transaction. Two copies of the receipt are printed: one is placed in the offering envelope, which is then annotated to direct the money as intended, while the other remains the property of the giver for their own records. This scheme has the advantage that it enables the tithe envelope to be placed in the regular church offering.

For some years, many of the Divisions, Unions and Conferences around the globe have had in place processes than enable credit cards and bank transfers to be used to donate through e-giving over the internet. To add to the giving options available, the South Pacific Division is in the early stages of itroducing a phone app accross Australia that can be used for donations at any time, including the time during which offerings are collected in a worship service. Developing this phone app has been straightforward in Australia because most local churches use a common banking framework for their tithes and offerings. The North American Division is working intensively on a native phone app as well, but in a more complex environment involving multiple banks and different state jurisdictions. Already mobile phones can be used to access the internet and donate during offering time at church services in the United States.

Which of these many options within and without the church will find wide acceptance in the Adventist Church is yet to be discovered, but it is not unlikely that many of them will need to become a more regular feature of the Adventist Church's methods of receiving offerings and tithes in the future. It is a credible hope that the application of such technology may reverse the trend in giving seen amongst the younger church-attenders, as it makes possible similar kinds of financial relationship to the Church that they use elsewhere in their lives.

10.4 Demographics of Tithing

The analysis of the survey responses revealed that amongst Seventh-day Adventists, tithing behavior is statistically correlated to a different set of demographic influences from those that have been identified in the Assemblies of God, the Baptist, the Lutheran, the Presbyterian and the Roman Catholic Churches. As in other denominations, age was found to be significantly correlated to tithing behavior, but unlike the other denominations, education-level, income-level, gender, and marital status were not. Indeed, on the basis of the survey data, it is possible to add a number of factors to the list of attributes that did not relate to tithing behavior amongst Seventh-day Adventists. Such factors as employment status, whether parents were Adventists or worked for the church, using a personal budget, use of credit card for small transactions, and how many sermons on tithing had been heard in the last 2 years were also found to be unrelated to tithing behavior.

Factors significantly and positively correlated with tithing in three countries included age, baptismal status, number of times tithe contributed each year, and frequency of attendance at worship services. Being an employee of the Adventist Church and the number of years of membership were found to be correlated with tithing behavior in Brazil.

10.5 Motives, Beliefs and Attitudes
that Correlate to Tithing

Of the scales tested by statistical analysis, several were found to be significantly correlated to tithing behavior in all countries, others in some countries, yet others in none. The scales found to be significantly correlated to tithing behavior in all countries were:

- P2 Adventist Package 2: Spiritual Practices of Personal Piety (e.g. study Sabbath School lesson; attend prayer meeting) (positive correlation – in other words, the more things on the list that a respondent indicated they did regularly, the more likely they were to tithe).
- B5 The belief that the church has enough money to carry on without my help (negative correlation – in other words, the more the respondent thought that the church had enough money to carry on without their help, the less likely they were to tithe)
- A6 the attitude that it is acceptable to divert tithe (negative correlation)

10.5.1 Practices of Personal Piety Positively Correlated to Tithing

Amongst Seventh-day Adventists, tithing behavior is very closely related to a range of other practices relating to their religion, such as whether they attend Sabbath School, open and close Sabbath, study the Sabbath School Quarterly, read and reflect on the Bible each day, and pray often during the day. It would seem that a natural strategy to increase tithing would be to encourage more Bible study, more prayer, more study of the Sabbath School Quarterly, and to include tithing as part of the practices that make up personal piety for Seventh-day Adventists.

10.5.2 Attitude that Tithe "Diversion" Is Acceptable Is Negatively Correlated to any Tithing

The more respondents felt that it was appropriate to direct tithe to destinations other than the tithe envelope or other official ways to return tithe, the less they tithed. One might expect, therefore, that much more effort needs to be given to educating church-members about where it is appropriate to direct tithe. In this study the places to which tithe was being directed in practice were traced. Within officially approved channels, the tithe envelope was still the most common method used to return tithe, although a number were using electronic methods of giving where donations were possible using the internet.

10.5.3 Belief "The Church Does Not Need My Money to Operate" Is Negatively Correlated to Tithing

Unsurprisingly, the more a respondent felt that the church had "enough money to carry on without my help," the less likely they were to tithe. Most respondents strongly disagreed with the statement, although it would no doubt be beneficial if further information was provided to church-members about the uses to which tithe is put, and how it enables the church to fulfill its mission.

10.5.4 Belief Tithe is a Biblical Requirement Is Positively Correlated to Tithing

The motive or belief that had the strongest effect on tithing behavior was the belief that tithing is a biblical requirement. The overwhelming majority of respondents already strongly agreed that tithing is indeed a biblical requirement. Thus, while tithe promotion to church-members should continue to contain an element of education of the biblical principle of tithing, it should not be stressed too much because most who hear will be already convinced that such is the case. Finding and expediting ways to make the habit of tithing natural and ensuring that the means of giving tithe to the Church are convenient, straightforward and transparent are more likely to bring about changes in tithing behavior. Furthermore, continuing to promote tithing in the wider context of bible study, regular prayer, attending Sabbath school, etc., is also likely to be highly effective. Promotion of tithing should emphasize it as being a response of gratitude to God.

10.6 God HAS Blessed Me Because I Tithe

The overwhelming majority of those who tithe 8% or more of their income, believe that "God HAS blessed them because they tithe." Of the 3,138 responses to this item, fully 1,846 (or 59%) strongly agreed, and a further 712 (23%) agreed more than disagreed. For such individuals, it is through their tithing that they can see the hand of God in their lives, and in a most practical manner. Yet there is a slight paradox in that while there was a small positive correlation between the motive for tithing "because God will bless" and tithing practice in the Western Australia Conference, in the Northern California, South England and the São Paulo Conferences there was a small negative correlation. In other words, the more the respondents thought they tithed because God will bless them, the [marginally] less likely they were to tithe. On the other hand, there was a strong correlation between the motive of tithing out of gratitude to God in all the conferences studied. Thus it appears that tithing promotion that emphasizes the motive of gratitude to God would be much more effective than promotion that emphasizes the blessings of God to those that tithe, real though those blessings are.

Tithing is indeed about money, and ten percent of an individual's income is a substantial amount of money for that person.[1] Furthermore, there is an unavoidable connection that exists between the minister that promotes tithing and the fact that tithe is mainly used to provide the wages of ministers in the Seventh-day Adventist Church. Yet for the church-member, tithing is not only about money, or even mainly about money. For them it is an

---

1 When I first starting travelling from church to church collecting surveys, I would preach on tithing after the surveys had been collected. At first I entitled by sermon, "Jesus said that this was not important," a reference to Matthew 23:23, "Woe to you, scribes and Pharisees, hypocrites! For you tithe mint, dill, and cumin, and have neglected the weightier matters of the law: justice and mercy and faith. It is these you should have practiced without neglecting the others." As I was shaking hands with members as they left the worship service at one of the churches where I had given this sermon, one kindly retired pastor said gently, "Rob, for church-members, 10 percent of their income is a significant amount of money. For them it is very important." Subsequently, I used the sermon title, "Jesus said there are more important things."

expression of their partnership with God and with the mission of the Church. It is in their tithing, and the material blessing that they see flowing from it, that most church-members see the hand of God in their lives in a tangible way.

Appendices

Appendix A: The Development of the Survey Instrument and Progress of the Research Project

Beginnings

The origins of the research reported in this book can be traced back to an almost off-hand remark made in a committee in 1999. I spent 6 years on the Executive Committee of the North New South Wales Conference of Seventh-day Adventists and found the meetings to be full of interest and educational in their own right. For much of that time the Conference was served by a President and a Secretary-Treasurer. As the Secretary-Treasurer set the agenda, the financial reports were the first item for every meeting, and much time was spent in discussing the very complex financial system that the Adventist Church used in that part of Australia to manage the money associated with the operation of its churches, its schools, its retirement villages, its camp ground, and its other activities. It was during the discussion of the conference financial reports sometime late in 1999 that the youngest member of the Executive Committee made a short speech to the effect that "My generation is not tithing as they should. Somebody should study that because if we are not careful the whole future of the conference is at risk." I clearly remember a short pause while those present digested this remark. Many significant, insightful and weighty things had been said from time to time on Executive Committee that were tangential to the matter under discussion, and usually after a short pause we would then move on to the next point that somebody wanted to raise on the agenda item under discussion. The remark, "somebody should study [tithing]," had a different outcome. I remember leaning forward to break the silence and saying, "I think that is something that should be looked at, and I think that there will be somebody at Avondale [College] who would be able to look at that for us." At the time I was a lecturer in the Faculty of Theology at Avondale, and initially thought that the topic might be of interest as a project for a research master's degree. A corridor conversation with Steve Currow, at that time a lecturer in Church Ministry at Avondale, soon established that this research would be highly sensitive, and that somebody in the SDA church with the status of an Avondale lecturer would be needed to head the project. It turned out that two lecturers did end up carrying the burden of this research – Steve Currow and myself.

And so began for me what has so far been an unexpected 15-year journey of research into tithing practice—unexpected in that up to that time my research interests had been largely in the field of New Testament studies, with a special interest in the Gospel of Matthew and in the problem of the relationships between the Synoptic Gospels. When the opportunity first arose in 1999, I was quite interested in tithe research because of its potential importance to the Church, and because it would give me a chance to dust off my skills in statistical analysis which I had thought I had left behind in 1980 when I left behind my job as a secondary teacher of Mathematics to start studying to become a minister of the Gospel.[1]

Initial Development of Theoretical Model

Early in the process of developing our methodology and survey instrument, Steve Currow and I consulted with Peter Beamish, then transitioning from Dean of Matthematics and Computing to Dean of Education at Avondale. As he had recently completed a PhD in which he had developed and used a survey instrument as his research tool, Peter was fully informed of the latest techniques of survey construction. He set us the task of designing a research model to test and worked with us on a potential set of scales by which to measure the various elements of our model.

At that time, Steve and I were able to draw upon the results of significant previous research on motivations for giving in American churches that had been funded by the Lilly Endowment, and undertaken by a team led by Dean R. Hoge. We studied the published results of this survey and also gained access to the research report.[2] As well as providing information on demographic and other trends, Hoge et al. identified the following factors that motivated the members of congregations to contribute to their churches:
1. Reciprocity with God;
2. Reciprocity with the religious group;

---

1 I had also unexpectedly found that a background that included statistics was useful in discussing aspects relating to the problem of the relationships between the synoptic Gospels. See Robert K. McIver and Marie Carroll "Experiments to Determine Distinguishing Characteristics of Orally Transmitted Material when Compared to Material Transmitted by Literary Means, and their Potential Implications for the Synoptic Problem." *Journal of Biblical Literature* 121 (2002) 667–87; and *idem.,* "Distinguishing Characteristics of Orally Transmitted Material Compared to Material Transmitted by Literary Means." *Applied Cognitive Psychology* 18 (2004) 1251–69.

2 Dean R. Hoge, Charles Zech, Patrick McNamara, and Michael J. Donahue, "Research Report of the American Congregational Giving Study," Life Cycle Institution, The Catholic University of America, Washington DC 20064, 1995. *Idem., Money Matters: Personal Giving in American Churches* (Louisville: Westminster John Knox, 1996).

3. Giving to "extensions of self" (e.g. regarding church as extended family);

4. Altruism and thankfulness.

Other published research findings that Steve and I consulted included those reported by George Barna, who identified other motivations that can underpin giving to churches:[3]

1. Shared cause;

2. Ministry efficiency;

3. Ministry influence;

4. An urgent need;

5. Gratitude for personal benefit received;

6. Relationship with ministry—involvement in ministry and operations of church; church keeps donor aware of what church is doing; significant ties with other church donors; desire to advance a particular cause or idea.

To gain information from a local Seventh-day Adventist context, Steve and I developed a short survey instrument that consisted largely of open-ended questions. We collected responses in one of the local churches that had a pastor who was sympathetic to the research, and who encouraged his congregation to engage in the survey. The responses to these surveys were then analyzed in the light of existing research. We also had access to other church survey work done in local churches, including one very detailed survey of a large suburban church that asked a wide variety of questions about worship style, attitudes and behaviors. One of the questions asked in that survey was whether or not the respondent tithed. Analysis of the responses to that survey revealed only one factor that had a statistical correlation with tithing – whether or not the individual drank tea or coffee. From this insight, it was realized that tithing is, in fact, a part of a wider set of Adventist behaviors, which we entitled commitment to the "Adventist Package."

The process of familiarizing ourselves with existing research and analyzing data specific to Seventh-day Adventists in the North New South Wales conference led Steve and I to identify a number of potential motives and beliefs that might influence the tithing behavior of those attending a Seventh-day Adventist church. They were as follows:

Motives:
Tithe a biblical requirement
God will bless

---

3 George Barna, *How to Increase Giving in Your Church* (Ventura, CA: Regal, 1997), 56–75.

Church as family
Gratitude
Pay your way

Beliefs:
Bible a rule of faith and practice
Biblical directive to use only tithe to support ministers
In global mission of SDA Church
It's strategically valuable to pool tithe between churches
Church not needy
In salvation and goodness of God

Attitudes:
Confidence in financial probity and competence of church administration
Attitude to SDA church (comfort as Adventist)
Think well of local pastor
Lordship of Jesus over money
OK to divert tithe
Sectarian view of SDA Church

Commitment to Adventist "Package":
Full adoption of Adventist lifestyle
Personal religious practices (e.g. study the Sabbath School Quarterly, attend prayer
    meeting)
Clear conception of Adventist identity
Commitment to SDA Church

Demographic items, such as age, income level, marital status and
education were also included in the theoretical model that was developed
because published research and informal reports from individuals had led to
the expectation that tithing behavior would be found to be different between
different age-groups, and between different levels of income.
    The model listed two criteria to assess tithing behavior:
1.   Respondent returned 10% of income as tithe;
2.   Respondent returned 100% of tithe through official SDA channels.

The foregoing analysis revealed that tithing is a behavior that results
from a wide range of complex motivations, beliefs and other behaviors.
Motivations and beliefs themselves are strongly shaped by the educational
background of an individual and their life experiences. This preliminary
analysis led to the development of the following theoretical model, which
is expressed diagrammatically in the two figures on the following page, and
which was used to form the basis of the questionnaire used as the research
instrument to test the model:

Theoretical Model of SDA Tithing Behavior

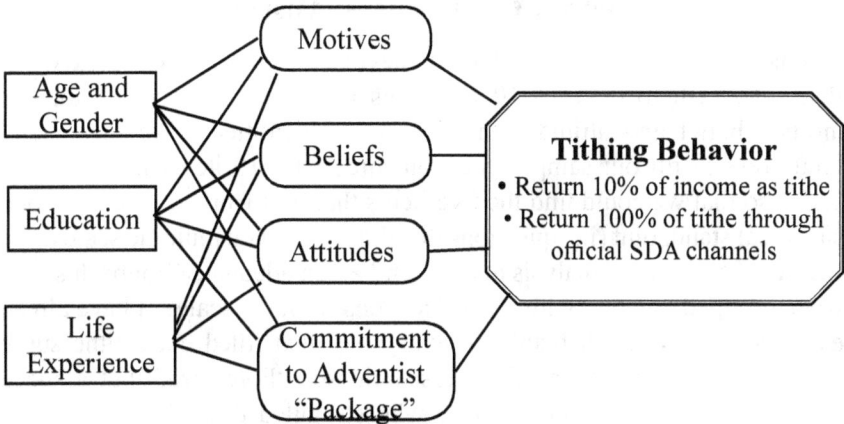

Motives

Age and Gender

Beliefs

Education

Attitudes

Life Experience

Commitment to Adventist "Package"

Tithing Behavior
• Return 10% of income as tithe
• Return 100% of tithe through official SDA channels

Theoretical Model of SDA Tithing Behavior (Detailed)

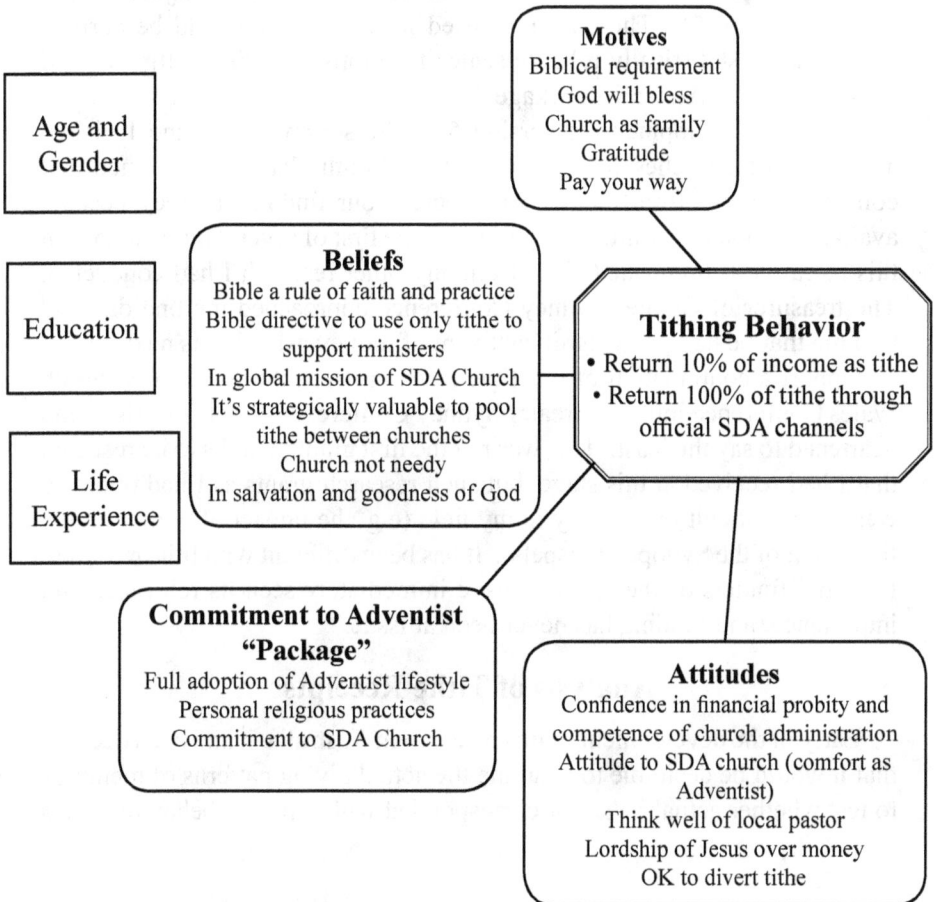

Motives
Biblical requirement
God will bless
Church as family
Gratitude
Pay your way

Age and Gender

Education

Life Experience

Beliefs
Bible a rule of faith and practice
Bible directive to use only tithe to support ministers
In global mission of SDA Church
It's strategically valuable to pool tithe between churches
Church not needy
In salvation and goodness of God

Tithing Behavior
• Return 10% of income as tithe
• Return 100% of tithe through official SDA channels

Commitment to Adventist "Package"
Full adoption of Adventist lifestyle
Personal religious practices
Commitment to SDA Church

Attitudes
Confidence in financial probity and competence of church administration
Attitude to SDA church (comfort as Adventist)
Think well of local pastor
Lordship of Jesus over money
OK to divert tithe

North New South Wales and Greater
Sydney Conferences, Australia

Once the hypothetical model was developed, Steve and I worked with Peter Beamish to develop 10 questions to make up a "scale" for each motive, belief and attitudes that had been identified. We then sought volunteers to fill out sample questionnaires with 10 items in each of the scales so that we could find the five items that best worked together from a statistical standpoint (i.e. questions that did not load on multiple scales when subjected to a factor analysis and which had an adequate Cronbach's alpha when grouped together with other questions from the scale). I have already expressed my heartfelt thanks to everybody that filled out a tithe survey for me during the course of my research (see "Foreword," but a special thanks must be exetended to those who struggled through this very long pilot survey.

The results were used to determine which five items should make up each scale to produce the version of what we thought would be the major research project (version 5). The questions used in this survey would be derived from a set of statistically reliable scales for motives, beliefs, attitudes and commitment to "Adventist package."

With the development of version 5 of the survey, Steve and I visited a number of churches in the North New South Wales Conference and collected surveys from them. We reported our findings as they became available. Soon afterwards, I experienced the first of several moments when this research distinguished itself from any other research I had conducted. The treasurer of Greater Sydney Conference approached me one day and told me that he had put a significant sum of money aside in his next budget to support a continuation of our tithe research from the North New South Wales Conference into the Greater Sydney Conference. I was surprised and heartened to say the least. This was not the first grant to underwrite research that I had received at this stage, but such research grants as I had obtained were very difficult to come by in my field (e.g. the impact of orality on the formation of the Synoptic Gospels). It has been different with tithe research. Potential funders of the research have immediately seen its relevance and importance, and funding has never been at issue.

Analysis of Tithe Receipts

Early in the development of this research in Australia, it had been decided that it would be desirable to examine the actual giving patterns of members to test whether actual behavior corresponded with reported behavior. Thus tithe receipts were analyzed to test the hypothesis that tithing behavior of older groups was different from that of younger groups. This was initially done at church-level, using reports from local church treasurers, but later at conference-level in the Greater Sydney and the Western Australian Conferences. Church pastors were asked to develop a list of those who were attending their local congregations three or more times per month together with an estimate of the age of each person. This information was linked to tithe receipts at the conference level, made anonymous, and reported back to the researchers. The results revealed that in Australia actual giving was age-related. In particular, the under-50 age-group had a different giving pattern from the those aged 50 years and over. A significantly greater percentage of those aged over 50 years returned tithe. Also, tithing was given in such patterns as to suggest that when an individual had not tithed for some weeks, when they resumed, they tithed only the current pay, and did not make an effort over the year to check whether or not 10% of the yearly income had been returned as tithe. A larger percentage of the those aged less than 50 years returned tithe sporadically when compared to those 50 or more years-of-age.

As a result of the research we did in the North New South Wales and Greater Sydney Conferences, Steve and I published a number of reports[1] and, to be frank, I was somewhat relieved to have the task finished. It had proved to be a very interesting project quite distint from the rest of my scholarly life, had taken me to all parts of the two Conferences and exposed me to aspects of Church life that I had not previously known about. But it was hard work travelling long distances on the weekend to persuade church-members to interrupt their worship services to fill out a questionnaire, and I was becoming increasingly uncomfortable about interrupting the worship hour with a survey. Experience had shown that this was the only time to

---

1 Robert K. McIver and Stephen J. Currow, "A Demographic Analysis of the Tithing Behaviour of 2,562 Seventh-day Adventists in Northern New South Wales, Australia," *Australian Religion Studies Review* 15 (2002) 115–25; *idem* "A Provocative Study of Tithing Trends in Australia," *Ministry* 74/8 (Aug 2001) 24–29; *idem,* "Does it Make Sense to Centralise Tithe?" *[South Pacific Division] Record* Sept 8, 2001, 8–10; *idem,* "Is the Church Facing a Financial Crisis?" *[South Pacific Division] Record* June 9, 2001, 8–10. Robert K. McIver, "What About those Tithing Stories?" *[South Pacific Division] Record* Sept 22, 2001, 8–9; *idem,* "Strategic Use of Tithe: How Does the Seventh-day Adventist Church Fare?" *Ministry* 74/10 (Oct 2001) 25–28; *idem,* "Should I Share These Stories?" *Adventist Review,* February 12, 2004, 25–28.

get the sample we needed,[2] but despite the fact that we usually arranged for the survey to be filled in during the time allocated to the children's story (the children were provided a story in a nearby location), it was something I was glad to finish. I felt that I had made a significant contribution to the church in that I had been able to report very widely to church administration and the stewardship directors based in Australia, and so felt that I could get back to my real job, as it were: lecturing on and researching the Synoptic Gospels. This all changed with a phone call from Lionel Smith from Western Australia.

Western Australia Conference, Australia

At that time, Lionel Smith was the stewardship director of the Western Australian Conference of Seventh-day Adventists.[3] He had heard one of my presentations on the results of the research that I had done in North New South Wales and Greater Sydney, and wanted me to come to Western Australia to do some survey work there. For the reasons given above, I was not at all keen on the idea. Towards the end of our conversation, Lionel said that even without my involvement, he would go ahead and do a survey of some kind. My thinking was that if it's going to happen, let's use a properly constructed survey instrument. So I laid down a number of things that I thought were necessary before I would become involved. I would have to be able to brief the conference leadership team, and the conference ministers, and report back. In all, that involved five visits to Western Australia, a reasonably significant expense given the five-hour flight. I wanted every church in the Conference to do the survey (something Lionel was planning in any case), and I wanted the conference copies of the tithe receipts analysed. One of the real challenges of the research in North New South Wales had been the need to find a church that had: (1) a board willing to allow an anonymous age-

---

2 On one not atypical occasion, Steve and I drove five or so hours to a church in a coastal town. We arrived in time for Sabbath school, and as I looked around I had a sinking feeling. The average age of those in attendance appeared to be about 65. This group of elderly attenders was leavened a little with a few younger worshippers by the beginning of the 11 am church service, but the average age of those in attendance was still very high. However, by the time for the children's story (about 11.20) it was completely different. The church was packed, and the majority of those present were young married couples with children. It was a living vibrant church with each age-group well represented, but the only time that it was possible to get a set of surveys filled out that represented the actual demographics of the church was after 11.20, and as part of the worship hour.

3 Since 2014 Lionel has been the Secretary of the South Pacific Division of Seventh-day Adventists.

related report to be generated from their tithe receipts; (2) a pastor willing to work with the treasurer to estimate the age of the regular church-attender; and (2) a treasurer willing to volunteer the extra work involved in analysing the receipts and producing an anonymous report. The conference leadership were all strongly behind the project,[4] and Steve and I had been given good access to the North New South Wales ministers at ministers' meetings. But arranging data to come in from the local churches had taken a great number of repeated contacts, and while we had a good participation from most of the churches we approached, some of the key churches were not represented in the data. In Greater Sydney I had tried to overcome this by getting the Conference to process their copies of tithe receipts. Because of the sensitivity of the data, they confined this work to those who were already working in the treasury. As these personnel were already very busy, little progress was made. It Western Australia, the secretary-treasurer, Warrick Long, arranged for somebody outside of treasury but with an unimpeachable background to analyse the tithe receipts. I don't know to this day who this individual was, but my thanks go to him or her for the sterling work that was done. It wasn't until I became peripherally involved in the analysis of tithe receipts myself in England and Kenya that I realized what a very large job this was. The Western Australia Conference president, Glen Townend, was willing to provide opportunity for the conference ministers to be fully briefed by myself. Given its vast territory, bringing all the ministers in for meetings was no small enterprise.

By 2010 the research in Western Australia was completed and reports written. My own research and writing had returned to the large backlog of topics that I had been neglecting and all related to Gospel studies in some way, and once again I felt that tithing research was but an interesting feature of my past research life. It had proved to be a fascinating foray into the life of churches and conferences, but something that was now behind me. That was until I received an e-mail from David Trim, who had at the time been recently appointed Director of Archives, Statistics and Research for the General Conference of Seventh-day Adventists in Washington, D.C. David and Steve Currow had been colleagues for a number of years while teaching at Newbold College in England and David had come to know about the tithe research we had done from conversations with Steve. At the time I was Dean of the Faculty of Theology at Avondale College and had more than enough on my plate with teaching, administration, and a backlog of things I wished

4 The leadership team of the North New South Wales Conference in 1999 was Peter Colquhoun (President) and Hank Penola (Secretary-Treasurer). By 2000, Hank had been succeeded by Bob Dale (Secretary) and Graeme Moffitt (Treasurer). In 2002 Peter was succeeded as president by John Lang.

to write on the Gospels. Yet two things led to me accept David's invitation to present a research grant proposal for research on tithing: (a) I felt it would be giving service to my church in an important area (money enables mission, lack of money inhibits it); and (b) Avondale College was in the process of preparing to apply to become a University. As an institution we were doing well in producing academic publications, but research grants were hard to come by, especially in the area of biblical studies and theology. So it would be good for Avondale if I was able to gain the type of substantial research grant that would be needed to underwrite tithe research that took place in several different countries. Once again, I was not particularly interested in doing this research unless it could be done correctly, which meant that I had to be released from teaching and administrative duties for 6 months, and had to visit the chosen conferences in person. As has been noted already, funding has never been an issue with regard to tithing research. Those who manage the funds instinctively can see its importance and the Future Plans Working Group of the General Conference were willing to fund research into tithing. Avondale released me from teaching, administration and other duties for the last half of 2012. During that time period I was able to visit the South England, the Central Kenyan, the São Paulo, and the Northern Californian Conferences of the Seventh-day Adventist Church.

South England Conference, United Kingdom

Between 29 June and 27 August 2012, I spent four productive weeks in the South England Conference. During this time I met with Sam Davis, the president, and with Terry Messenger, the secretary of the conference. I worked very closely with Richard de Lisser, the stewardship leader of the conference, and with Earl Ramharacksingh, the treasurer, who was kind enough to provide me with a desk in treasury, and to arrange for a suitably qualified research assistant[5] who worked on the tithe receipts for most of the four weeks I was there. I met separately for whole-day seminars with the London Ministers and the non-London ministers. I also met with Victor Pilmoor, the British Union treasurer.

I was provided with electronic membership lists with which to work. As well as this, data from the government-controlled Gift Aid program were made available. The membership list comprised over 22,156 names and the Gift Aid data tracked donations from 5,518 separate individuals. While there, I set in train the printing and distribution of the surveys in a form

---

5 She had already been engaged in working on tithe receipts at the Conference for another project, so was already in the "circle of trust" of those who had access to the tithe receipts.

that is machine-readable. I am very grateful to Mavis Bramble at the South England Conference Office for printing, distributing, recovering and finally arranging for the delivery of the South England Conference Surveys to me in Australia. Given the prohibitive cost that would have been involved in shipping or posting the completed surveys to Australia, I am also very thankful to Eddie Hypolite and his family for including these surveys along with their household goods as they moved from England to take up the role of pastor at Avondale College Church.

When I returned for a short visit to the South England Conference in 2014, I was able to meet with and brief Sam Davis, Terry Messenger and Richard de Lisser about the preliminary results of the tithe research. I was also able to ascertain that in the two years since I had last visited, a significant number of the churches had moved to generating tithe receipts by electronic means, all using the same church-sponsored software. The conference kindly allowed me to gain a report from these which enabled a larger sample of tithe receipts to be analysed.

Central Kenya Conference, Kenya

Between 21 August and 10 September 2012, I spent three extraordinary weeks in Kenya. I was able to meet with Jones Masimba the treasurer, Franklin Wariba the president, and Jean-Pierre Waiywa the executive secretary of the conference, and the stewardship director Charles Kamutu, as well as many of the pastors. I met with 145 pastors and elders on 2 September to talk over the tithe research, and brief them on the appropriate procedures for administering the tithe survey so that reliable results are obtained (given that almost all pastors have multiple parishes under their care, the elders play a very significant role in the leadership of the local churches). Compared to my experiences in the other conferences I visited, there were several different challenges for conducting my research in Kenya, such as the challenge of travelling from my overnight accommodation to the conference's office then to Nairobi to find printers that could possibly print or scan the survey forms, and back to my accommodation in the evening (a process that could take hours on some occasions). On the positive side is the fact that the conference receives detailed summaries (including names) of tithe and other receipts, which enables greater consistency in the processing of the receipts as it allows one person to process them. I was also able to hire a very well-qualified research assistant to oversee the research and undertake the analysis of the tithe receipts. On the other hand, the conference does not keep records of membership lists. Such lists are kept by the local churches. Furthermore, with the exception of six churches, these lists are handwritten, and in the order of joining the church. Then there is the sheer size of the Conference. It has more than 100,000 members spread across more than 1,000 churches and as many companies. By the end of the three weeks, I had been able to test the survey instrument, to adapt the survey for local conditions (primarily in the areas relating to income—the minimum income in the previous surveys was set far too high; and in the question relating to tithe "diversion"), arranged for the printing of surveys, and had seen the analysis of tithe receipts begin. I was also able to visit a local district camp meeting where nine churches had gathered together for a week of intensive meetings, and to see the advantage of using such an occasion for the distribution of surveys. This much progress took place while I was present, but there was very little additional progressed after I left. So while there are some figures relating to the analysis of tithe receipts from Kenya in the following chapters, insufficient numbers of surveys were completed to provide statistically significant results. Now that I have been to Kenya, seen the interesting features of the data that was collected, observed local district camp meetings and understand the local conditions so much better, I would like to return someday to complete tithe research in Kenya.

São Paulo Conference, Brazil

I visited the highly dynamic São Paulo Conference, Brazil, between 24 September and 16 October 2012. While there I met with the conference president, Sidionil Biazzi, secretary Paulo Kokischko, and treasurer Rubens Benedicto, and worked in very close cooperation with Cesar Guandalini, the stewardship director of the conference. The president and secretary identified 20 churches across the five geographic regions of the conference that would be in the sample. Between them, these churches had approximately 8,700 members in regular attendance.

All of the conferences in Brazil have access to well-designed, centralised computer systems that are used to manage church membership and tithe receipting records. In 2012 there were two separate systems – one for membership and one for tithe receipts. But it proved possible to coordinate the data from both systems to match exact birthdays of members with records of their tithing behavior. The conference IT team were able to provide a report (without names) on the age-related tithing patterns of 3,162 members who regularly attended the 20 churches in the sample. The results are very accurate and conclusions drawn from them will be very reliable.

The tithe survey was translated into Portuguese, then back into English, and then worked over until all concerned were in agreement that the Portuguese version of the survey was both an accurate representation of the English survey and that it was expressed in good Portuguese. The conference also has a system of survey processing which involves the use of specially formatted cards, and the three versions of the survey forms were stapled to specific cards. Once completed, the cards were processed by the Conference IT team, and a report was provided to me.

I wish to thank the conference leadership team of the São Paulo Conference for their expeditious support of a research project that was introduced and completed within the three weeks I was in country. At one stage, I am told, all of the various secretaries and personal assistants from the conference were collating surveys and attaching the answer cards as appropriate (the translation process had made everything very late). The IT team also need special mention—disparate data bases were linked to provide a demographic profile for the tithe receipts, the results were processed, and a report was produced very quickly and efficiently. I also thank Cesar Guandalini for hosting and guiding me so well.

Northern California Conference, United States

I visited Northern California Conference between October 21 and November 5, 2012. While there I was able to meet with Edward Fargusson, the president of the conference, Marc Woodson, the secretary, and treasurer John Rasmussen and the treasury team. Together with Gordon Botting, the stewardship director of Northern California Conference and Pacific Union Conferences, we visited two or three churches across the conference on most of the days I was in the conference, meeting with area pastors and treasurers, briefing them on the proposed research, and asking for their cooperation and their help in communicating with their respective church boards to gain permission to analyse the tithe receipts in each church and to conduct a survey.

In Northern California copies of tithe receipts are kept at the local church, not at the office of the conference. Since most treasurers were standardized on the same software package to manage the tithe receipts, most of the information needed was readily available and the remainder was available by means of some manual counting. Nevertheless, for larger churches, providing the analysis requested represented a significant investment of time on the part of the church treasurers, many of whom acted as volunteers. The church treasurers then forwarded a report to me that gave no names, but provided ages of donors and members and a summary of the frequency at which they donated and the amount donated. My thanks go to Gordon Botting for his unfailing and positive support, and to Michael Ann Sparks for printing, distributing, and recovering the completed forms and forwarding them to Australia.

Reflections

Adaptions to the Survey to fit Local Conditions:

I look back with wry amusement upon my initial over-confidence that I had a well-tested research instrument and research methodology that could seamlessly be used in any culture. Each conference has its own traditions of how tithe receipts are managed, and they each have different challenges that give them a slightly different context against which they manage their money. One example among many: in Kenya, it can take a local church up to 10 years just to purchase their own land, and thus tithe funds can be "diverted" to land purchase, something that is not an issue in any of the other conferences studied where "Church Building Fund" covered cost of both land and building. In Brazil I needed to divide the survey into three versions each small enough to be managed in a short period of time and I also used three smaller versions of the survey in the United States. All these slightly different versions of the survey meant much time was taken in reconciling the data bases generated. This was no surprise and probably unavoidable, but perhaps may have been managed better with extra time put into the setting up of the coding of the software used to read the surveys.

The implementation of the research revealed that while most of the demographic questions and all of the scales were suitable for the diverse cultures in which the surveys were administered, some aspects needed to be customized in both the demographics, and in the "tithe diversion" scale. The biggest change for demographics was in the degree of spread of income. Preliminary survey work in Kenya revealed that the question relating to income needed to include income levels much lower than initially used. The lowest level of annual income eventually was set at "Under US$1,000" (or the equivalent in local currency, rounded to a suitable multiple of 10 or 100) and was used in Kenya, England (version 9.4), Brazil and the United States. The survey initially had set The lowest annual income in the initial survey was "Less than $6,000," the lower limit that had been used in Australia and was used for about half of the surveys in England (i.e. versions 7.1 in WAC and 9.1A in SEC). The South England Conference requested that a question relating to the national "heritage" of the member be included (e.g. British, West Indian, Eastern European, etc.), while conference leadership in both Kenya and the United States specifically requested that such a question not be included. Furthermore, while the majority of the items in the scale measuring "Alternate" uses of tithe were constant across the countries, some of them needed to be varied by country (see section of Chapter 4 that deals with tithe diversion).

Length of Survey

The length of the survey continued to be an issue through England and Kenya, and proved to be nearly insurmountable in Brazil. The matter was resolved in Brazil by considering the large survey samples that were being collected. The numbers in the sample size were determined by the number of churches from which tithe receipts were analyzed, rather than the number of survey forms filled in. Large numbers in the sample size are always highly desirable, and the Australian research had revealed that a sample size over 3,000 church-members would produce a sample for the analysis of tithe receipts large enough to have sufficient numbers of each age cohort contributing to have a reliable result. It was envisaged that everybody attending the churches from which tithe receipts were analyzed would be asked to fill in a survey form. This produced many more than the minimum number of surveys needed for reliable statistical results. What resulted as a result of consultations in São Paulo was the development of three much shorter versions of the survey form (see "The Survey Instrument Version 9.6A/B/C São Paulo Conference," in "Appendix B: The Survey Instruments [by Country]"). Each survey asked questions about age, income levels and tithing behavior. Version A included additional questions relating to the scales, Version B included more-detailed demographic questions such as employment status and a lengthy question about what would be necessary to change before a non-tither would consider tithing. Version C included additional questions relating to tithe diversion and matters of religious practice. Given the numbers of surveys collected, sufficient data would be gathered for each of the demographic categories and the scales to yield statistically reliable results. The three-version form of the survey was used in Brazil and in the USA.

A Transformative Experience

I would like to acknowledge that the experience of travelling from England to Kenya to Brazil and then the United States in the few months between August and November 2012 has been nothing less than transformative at a personal level. It was extraordinary and inspiring for me to see the work of the Seventh-day Adventist Church in such diverse circumstances. As I have occasion to comment in Chapter 2, the experience of moving from Kenya, where the church prospers yet is seriously under-resourced, to Brazil, where the church has reached the critical mass of membership and resources that enables it to expand at an astonishing rate, and then to the United States, where the church has been prosperous and well established for over a century, was like seeing several centuries of the development of the Christian church compressed into a very short period of time. I have been inspired, encouraged and humbled by the men and women of faith that I have been privileged to deal with during this research project.

Appendix B: Reliability of Scales and Items in Scales

B.1 Cronbach's Alpha Statistics for the Scales Used in the Tithe Survey by Country					
Scale	Four Conference Data (WAC, SPC, SEC, NCC)	Australia (WAC)	Brazil (SPC)	England (SEC)	USA (NCC)
M1	0.793	0.835	0.732	0.695	0.82
M2	0.734	0.731	0.693	0.735	0.801
M3	0.684	0.752	0.621	0.601	0.718
M4	0.705	0.757	0.633	0.614	0.717
B5	0.696	0.747	0.655	0.62	0.702
A6	0.969	0.974	0.948	0.964	Too few cases
P1a	0.855	0.868	0.951	0.901	0.786
P1b	0.846	0.876	0.866	0.814	0.842
P2	0.704	0.721	Too few cases	0.726	0.668

B.2 Scales Used in Surveys in the South England Conference (ver 9.1A & 9.4B), the São Paulo Conference (9.6A, 9.6B, 9.6C) and the Northern California Conference (9.7A, 9.7B, 9.7C)

Note: * = item that most strongly loaded on scale for Australian Survey
First question number (e.g. B03) from Australian survey; second question number (e.g. E4 in B03/E4) is from English Version of Survey (ver 9.4)

M1. Motive: A biblical requirement
Factor analysis gives questions B03, B9; B22 as a clear factor
B03/E4 The Bible teaches that tithe is my responsibility to God

B9/E7 From the Bible I know that tithe does not belong to me, it is God's money
   already

*B22/B7 The Bible is clear that I should give 10% of my income as tithe

M2. Motive: God will bless

Factor analysis shows B4, B10, & B23 all load on one scale.

B04/E5 I contribute tithe because God promises prosperity to those who tithe

*B10/B4 God will protect me from future harm if I return tithe

B23/E9 If I give tithe God will answer my prayers

M3. Motive: Church as Family

*C1/C1 My local church feels like my extended family

C15/E11 I know just about everybody that attends my local church

[new question]/E13 My local church is like one big family

M4. Motive: Gratitude

While this was the 14th item in the 15-item factor analysis, it is clearly a distinct
   factor – nothing else loads onto this scale.

B05/E6 God has given me so much and I return tithe out of appreciation

*B11/B5 I show my gratitude to God by returning tithe

B18/E8 I contribute tithe because I am often overwhelmed by how good God has
   been to me

M5. Motive: Pay your way

1 item used: *B25/B8 I need to contribute my tithe and offerings so the church can
   continue its work

B1. Belief: Bible Rule of Faith

1 item used: *B33/B9 The Bible provides detailed guidance for my life

B2. Belief: Biblical directive to use tithe only to support ministers

(α = 0.61 on pilot study, and so this scale was discarded; retained here to answer
   question, "What was B2?")

B3. Belief: in the global mission of SDA Church

1 item (B3 had been a problem scale as it also loads on M1 & A5; why only one
   item kept): *C16/C6 I believe the SDA church has a mission to the whole world

B4. Belief: It is strategically valuable to pool tithe between churches

1 Item: *B13/B6 If tithe is not pooled by the conference the bigger churches would
   have too much money and the smaller churches not enough

B5. Belief: Church not needy

Note factor analysis shows that C3, C11 & C17 form one scale.

-C03/E10 The Adventist Church already has enough money to do what it wants to
   do without my tithe

-C11/E12   I contribute little or no tithe because the church already has enough
   money to do what it should

*C17/C7 The Adventist Church has enough money to operate without my tithe

A1. Attitude: Confidence in financial probity and competence of SDA Church administration
1 item: *C12/C5 I trust the handling and allocation of funds by the conference, union and division leaders

A2. Attitude: Expectation that church should be transparent and accountable in its use of tithe
(discarded in version 7.1)

A3. Attitude: to Church (comfort as Adventist)
Sadly – rest of version 5 scale had to go because cross-loaded badly, even though it had an $\alpha = 0.8$.
*C05/C2 I enjoy being an Adventist

A4. Attitude to local pastor
1 item: *C06/C3 Overall, my church pastor is doing a good job

A5. Attitude to wish to control over own money vs. Lordship over money
1 Item: *C20/C8 God is in control of everything in my life

A6. Attitude: OK to divert tithe
All of these are strong candidates
B34-B40/B11-17 I feel there is nothing wrong in giving tithe ...:
  ... to special projects (such as a new church building)
  ... directly to the mission field
  ... to assist volunteers working in my local church
  ... to the offering that supports the local SDA school
  ... to special appeals, such as church mission outreach overseas
  ... to help needy people through ADRA
  ... to help needy people through the red cross or the Salvation Army

A7. Attitude: Sectarian View of SDA Church
($\alpha = 0.69$ on pilot study, and so scale was discarded; retained here to answer question, "What was A7?")

P1. Adventist "Package": Full Adoption of Adventist lifestyle
3 Items package A (not smoke, drink, drugs): all equally strong
4 items (not dance, tea & coffee, meat) : all equally strong
Factor analysis reveals: Actually two scales – no alcohol, drugs & smoking forms one scale; No Pepsi, meat, coffee forms the other.
C31-C37 / C9 to C14 Do you agree (4) or disagree (1) that to be a Seventh-day Adventist, it is very important to abstain from ...
C9   Alcohol
C10 Coca Cola, Pepsi, Red Bull, etc

C11 Eating meat
C12 Tea and Coffee
C13 Smoking
C14 Illegal drugs

P2. Adventist "Package": Personal Spirituality
Study SS Quarterly strongest, others about equal
C38-C43 / C15-C21
Which of the following is true of you?
(1 = never; 2 = sometimes; 3 = often; 4 = always/ almost always)
Do you?:
 C15 Attend Sabbath school
C16 Open and close Sabbath
C17 Study the Sabbath School Quarterly
C18   Read and reflect on the Bible each day
C19 Pray often during the day
C20   Reflect on spiritual things during the day
C21 Attend prayer meetings

Miscellaneous: Things we want to ask that are not part of any scale
B08/E1 I have heard a sermon on tithe/stewardship in the last 12 months
C7 I feel a strong commitment to the Seventh-day Adventist Church

B.3 Analysis of Scales on Australian Survey Used to Choose Items for Version 9

The following data relate to scales found in the Tithe Survey versions 5.0 to 7.1, i.e. those used in the main study in New South Wales (ver 5.0, 5.1, 5.2) and Western Australia (ver 7.1). There were 3651 valid surveys in this data set. The results were used to derive questions for scales used in the South England Conference (ver 9.1A & 9.4B), the São Paulo Conference (9.6A, 9.6B, 9.6C) and the Northern California Conference (9.7A, 9.7B, 9.7C).

For each scale:
- A * has been placed next to the one item in each scale that most strongly loads onto it.
- A – has been placed next to the two items that most strongly load onto a scale (after the one marked with a *)

M1. Motive: A biblical requirement
5 questions $\alpha = 0.775$; without B27 $\alpha = 0.871$; without B9 $\alpha = 0.771$; NB: B3, B15 & B22 give $\alpha = 0.83$

Factor analysis gives questions B03, B9; B15, B22 & B27 as a clear factor; weakest is B27, but I wish to keep this neg. factor.

-B03 The Bible teaches that tithe is my responsibility to God

-B9   From the Bible I know that tithe does not belong to me, it is God's money already

 B15 The Bible teaches that I should return a regular tithe

*B22 The Bible is clear that I should give 10% of my income as tithe

B27 [neg item] I have some questions on what the Bible has to say about tithe

M2. Motive: God will bless

5 items: α =0.725; valid = 1583. Without B16 α =0.788; without B28 α =0.

Factor analysis shows B4, B10, B23 & B28 all load on one scale; but B16 only loads weakly if at all.

-B04 I contribute tithe because God promises prosperity to those who tithe

*B10 God will protect me from future harm if I return tithe

B16 [neg item] God will bless me even if I don't give tithe

-B23 If I give tithe God will answer my prayers

B28 God watches out for me if I return tithe

M3. Motive: Church as Family

5 items α = 0.804; valid = 1644; good scale; can remove C15 to give α = 0.811, and
    C21 to give items α = 0.796;

*C1 My local church feels like my extended family

C09 I feel welcome when I attend my local church

-C15 I know just about everybody that attends my local church

-C27 My local church is a family Church

NEW ITEM!:

My local church is like one big family

C21 If I had to change the local church I attend, I would feel a great sense of loss

M4. Motive: Gratitude

5 items α = 0.625; valid = 1599; without B24 (neg item) α = 0.759; without B24
    and B18, α = 0.581

While this was the 14th item in the 15-item factor analysis, it is clearly a distinct
    factor – nothing else loads onto this scale. B24 (neg item) loads relatively
    strongly.

-B05 God has given me so much and I return tithe out of appreciation

*B11 I show my gratitude to God by returning tithe

-B18 I contribute tithe because I am often overwhelmed by how good God has
    been to me

B30 I am grateful to God because he has given me so much

B24 [neg item] Tithing has little to do with gratitude

M5. Motive: Pay your way

5 Items α = 0.811; valid = 1577; good scale

Cross-loads with B4 – Don't know what can do about that.

-B06 The church cannot run its various programs without the people giving tithe
    and offerings

-B12 Tithe is important because it takes a lot of money to run this church properly

B19 If I do not return tithe the church will not be able to employ its ministers

*B25 I need to contribute my tithe and offerings so the church can continue its work

B31 Church members should all help to meet the operating needs of the whole church

B1. Belief: Bible Rule of Faith

4 items: $\alpha = 0.854$; valid = 1624; Good scale.

-B17 The Bible gives me instruction in all aspects of my life

-B29 The Bible is authoritative in all aspects of my life

*B33 The Bible provides detailed guidance for my life

B41 The Bible is the basis of my belief and practice

B2. Belief: Biblical directive to use tithe only to support ministers

($\alpha = 0.61$ BAD scale – discarded)

B3. Belief: in the global mission of SDA Church

4 items $\alpha = 0.864$; valid = 1629; good scale; B3 a problem scale: it loads on M1 & A5! Still, they are both quite different in concept, so will keep.

-C02 The Seventh-day Adventist church has a mission to the whole world

-C10 The mission of the SDA church is to take its message to the whole world

*C16 I believe the SDA church has a mission to the whole world

C22 I am very interested in the Church's work in other parts of the world

B4. Belief: It is strategically valuable to pool tithe between churches

($\alpha = 0.756$; valid = 1622)

-B07 The Conference should use some of the tithe given by bigger congregations to support ministers in smaller churches

*B13 If tithe is not pooled by the conference the bigger churches would have too much money and the smaller churches not enough

B20 If tithe is not pooled by the conference the smaller churches would not be able to afford a pastor

B26 Tithe should be sent to the conference, because that way pastors can be placed where they will do most good.

-B32 Tithe should be pooled by the conference, so that the Adventist Church can use it in the most effective way

B5. Belief: Church not needy

5 and 3 items $\alpha = 0.772$; valid = 1591.

Note factor analysis shows that C3, C11 & C17 are one scale ($\alpha = 0.78$), and that C23 & C28 are another! C3, C11 & C17

-C03 The Adventist Church already has enough money to do what it wants to do without my tithe

-C11 I contribute little or no tithe because the church already has enough money to do what it should

*C17 The Adventist Church has enough money to operate without my tithe

B6. Belief: In salvation and goodness of God
(α = 0.42; BAD scale – discarded)

A1. Attitude: Confidence financial probity and competence of SDA Church administration
(α = 0.899; valid 1596; good scale)

C04 The Conference uses the tithe it receives wisely

*C12 I trust the handling and allocation of funds by the conference, union and division leaders

-C18 I trust Church administration to manage the money I give in tithe and offerings

-C24 The SDA church uses the tithe it receives wisely

A2. Attitude: Expectation that church should be transparent and accountable in its use of tithe
(α = 0.77; BAD scale – discarded in version 7.1)

A3. Attitude: to Church (comfort as Adventist)

*C05 I enjoy being an Adventist

Sadly – rest of version 5 scale had to go because cross-loaded badly, even though it had a α = 0.8.

A4. Attitude to local pastor
(α = 0.861; valid 1572; good scale)

*C06 Overall, my church pastor is doing a good job

C13 I find the church pastor's sermons interesting and relevant

C19 I know the church pastor well

-C25 Most of the congregation thinks well of the church pastor

-C29 I am pleased to have my church pastor represent our church at community functions

A5. Attitude to wish to control over own money vs. Lordship over money
(α = 0.909; valid = 1603; good scale)

C08 Jesus is Lord of all my life, including how I spend my money

-C14 God is in control of everything in my life, including what I do with my money

*C20 God is in control of everything in my life

C30 Jesus is Lord of all my life

-C26 God is in control of everything in my life, including everything I do

A6. Attitude: OK to divert tithe
(α = 0.975; valid = 1594; good scale)

All of these are strong candidates

B34-B40 I feel there is nothing wrong in giving tithe ...:

... to special projects (such as a new church building)

... directly to the mission field

... to assist student missionaries working in my local church

... to the offering that supports the local SDA school

… to special appeals, such as church mission outreach overseas
… to help needy people through ADRA
… to help needy people through the Red Cross or the Salvation Army

A7. Attitude: Sectarian View of SDA Church
($\alpha = 0.69$ BAD scale – Discarded)

P1. Adventist "Package": Full Adoption of
Adventist lifestyle ($\alpha = 0.94$)
3 Items package A (not smoke, drink, drugs): all equally strong
4 items (not dance, tea & coffee, meat): all equally strong
C31-C37/C9 – C14 Do you agree (4) or disagree (1) that to be a Seventh-day
   Adventist, it is very important to abstain from …
Alcohol, Tea and Coffee, Coca Cola & Pepsi, Smoking, Dancing, Eating meat,
   Illegal drugs, Movies, Wearing jewelry,
Factor: Actually two scales – alcohol, drugs & smoking one scale; others another.

P2. Adventist "Package": Personal Spirituality ($\alpha = 0.755$; valid=1615)
Study SS Quarterly strongest, others about equal
C38-C43/C15-C21 Which of the following is true (1 = never; 2 = sometimes; 3 =
   often; 4 = almost always)? Do you:
Attend Sabbath school most weeks
Open and close Sabbath
**Study the Sabbath School Quarterly each day
Pray often during the day
Regularly share your faith with non-Christians
Attend prayer meetings
Education: education on use of tithe
($\alpha = 0.8+$)
B21 I understand how tithe is used by the SDA Church
Sadly—the rest of the scale was discarded in version 7

Miscellaneous: Things we want to ask that are not part of any scale
B08 I have heard a sermon on tithe/stewardship in the last 12 months
B14 It's OK to give time instead of money for tithe.
C07 I feel a strong commitment to the Seventh-day Adventist Church
Returning tithe provides the Church with funds to fulfill God's mission
By returning tithe I trust God will supply my needs

Appendix C: The Survey Instruments (by Country)

The surveys used in the four different conferences are found on the following pages. The following account traces the development of the survey instrument. The largest changes (those found between version 7 and version 9, together with the small adjustments that were made to version 9 to adapt them for each country) have been explained in the main text (see section on "Development of the Research Instrument"). Briefly, the changes are as follows:

C.1 Changes in Survey for each Version

C.1.1 Changes from Version 7.1 (Western Australia Conference) to Version 9.1A (South England Conference)
1. Reduce the scales from five to three items for scales that had shown themselves to be correlated to tithing practice in Australia, and one item for those which had not been found to be so related.
2. Discard a number of items which had been found to be of less practical use, or of no statistical significance, or which did not translate well internationally.
3. Convert dollar values (for income, etc) into pounds sterling.
4. Add questions relating to demographics requested by local conference leadership.
5. Refine the question relating to tithe diversion so that there is a separation between tithe destination approved by the church, and those that the church considers to be tithe diversion. Add a preamble to the items relating to tithe diversion. Add two items to the list of possible places to which tithe might be diverted.
6. Lay out the surveys in a manner which would enable them to be scanned and read by computer software.

C.1.2 Changes from Version 9.1A (South England Conference) to Version 9.2 (Central Kenya Conference)
1. Convert dollar and pound values to local currency for questions such as "income," plus add several "steps" at bottom of income range.
2. Add the possibility of reporting offerings as well as tithe to questions relating to where donations were directed (i.e. regarding tithe diversion).

C.1.3 Changes from Version 9.2 (Central Kenya Conference) to Version 9.4B (South England Conference)
1. Add the pound sterling equivalent of the lower income ranges developed for CKC; and also provide the option to report on offerings as well as tithe in questions relating to tithe diversion also developed for CKC.

C.1.4 Changes from Version 9.4B (South England Conference) to Versions 9.6A/B/C (São Paulo Conference)

1. Translate survey instrument into Portuguese, then back into English; further modify Portuguese to reflect what English question asked, but in language explicable to those reading the Portuguese, and then polish the resultant language to ensure high-quality grammar.
2. Produce three versions of the survey, so that each of them can be answered in a shorter amount of time (5 to 10 minutes).
3. Ensure that the options for "tithe diversion" are consistent with local opportunities and practices.
4. Convert income levels into local currency.

C.1.5 Changes from Version 9.6A/B/C (São Paulo Conference) to 9.7A/B/C (Northern California Conference)

1. Check that income levels in US$ are consistent with other surveys, and have enough options at the high end for local conditions.
2. Refine the wording of questions regarding tithe diversion to ensure they are appropriate to local conditions and opportunities, and add options unique to NCC.

C.1.6 Tracking the Changes to the Items for Self-reported Tithe "Diversion."

That individual items should stay the same for all versions of the survey is self-evident if the responses to the items are to be compared between conferences in different countries. However, local conditions led to some inevitable changes being necessary. For example, while great care was taken in translating the survey instrument into Portuguese to ensure that an equivalent meaning was maintained, different languages have, perforce, slightly different nuances. There was also one significant change in the levels of income that were tested as a result of considering income levels in Kenya. As this only affected the lowest income level, this was not a very large change. The majority of changes took place in the item that invited respondents to reflect on where they had directed tithe in the last 12 months. The items in the related scale, "A6 Attitude: OK to Divert Tithe" were kept constant, but the options provided as "alternate" tithe destinations varied by country. These items were carefully checked by the treasurers and or stewardship directors in each conference that took part in the research. Again, a serious attempt was made to keep the items either exactly the same, or equivalent, but there were a number of items that were specific to one or other country. The items that remained the same and those which varied may be tracked in Table C.1.

Table C.1: Options for "In the last 12 months I have given tithe ..."; "In the last 12 months I have given offerings ..." by Country					
Option	CKC	NCC	SEC	SPC	WAC
to Sabbath School (world mission) offerings [SPC: para ofertas da Escola Sabatina]	No	No	Yes	Yes	Yes
to local church based appeals [SPC: a outros apelos especiais da igreja]	Yes	Yes	Yes	Yes	Yes
to the Church Building/Plot fund [NCC: to the Church Building Program] [SPC: para o fundo de construção da igreja]	Yes	Yes	Yes	Yes	Yes
to the local SDA school offering [NCC: to the local SDA school / Education offering] [para â sistema Educacional da IASD]	Yes	Yes	Yes	Yes	Yes
to an independent Adventist ministry [NCC add: (e.g. Amazing Facts, It Is Written, Maranatha, Hope Chanel, etc.)] [SPC: a um ministério adventista independente]	Yes	Yes	Yes	Yes	Yes
to support a youth volunteer in our local church [NCC: to support a youth worker or Bible worker in our local church] [CYC add: (or Alive Kenya)] [SPC: para apoiar um jovem voluntário de nossa igreja local]	Yes	Yes	Yes	Yes	Yes
to Sponsorships [SEC add: (e.g. members supporting pastors)] [SPC: para patrocinar (ex: estudantes, pastores ou obreiros missionários)]	Yes	No	Yes	Yes	No
to the local church Budget/offering [CKC add: (outside of combined offering)] [SPC: ao Orçamento/Oferta igreja local]	Yes	Yes	Yes	Yes	Yes
to ADRA [NCC: to Adventist Community Services or ADRA] [CKC add: (outside of combined offerings)]	Yes	Yes	Yes	Yes	Yes
to needs in my country or conference of origin [WAC: to needs in my homeland] [SPC: para necessidades em minha terra natal]	Yes	Yes	Yes	Yes	Yes
to the Salvation Army or Red Cross, etc [NCC: to a non-SDA Christian ministry (e.g. the Salvation Army, World Vision) NCC: to non-SDA charity or non-profit organisation (e.g. Red Cross, American Cancer Society, United Way, etc)]	Yes	Yes	Yes	Yes	Yes
directly to overseas mission field	Yes	Yes	Yes	Yes	Yes
to supporting local pastors	No	Yes	Yes	Yes	No
SEC: to Adventist Media	No	No	Yes	No	No
SEC: to organ fund	No	No	Yes	No	No

Table C.1: Options for "In the last 12 months I have given tithe ..."; "In the last 12 months I have given offerings ..." by Country					
Option	CKC	NCC	SEC	SPC	WAC
NCC: to Conference Advance	No	Yes	No	No	No
CKC: to Combined Offering (Budget, Mission, ADRA, etc)	Yes	No	No	No	No
CKC: to Welfare (e.g. Barios, Funerals and Wedding)	Yes	No	No	No	No

Note: Initial feedback in England and Kenya indicated some frustration that the question asking about where tithe was directed did not allow the respondent to report on the fact that they had actually given offerings to that cause. Thus versions 9.4B (SEC) and 9.6A/B/C (SPC) were provided with three alternatives: (i) only tithe; both offerings and tithes; only offerings. In the Northern California Conference, the feedback indicated that in this conference responses to this question could be simplified to two alternatives: offerings and tithe.

C.1.7 Number of Completed Surveys by Version

Table C.2: Number of Completed Surveys (Version vs Country; ≥ 20 yrs)				
Version	Australia (WAC)	England (SEC)	Brazil (SPC)	USA (NCC)
7.1	1,660	0	0	0
9.1A	0	613	0	0
9.4B	0	442	0	0
9.6A	0	0	795	0
9.6B	0	0	589	0
9.6C	0	0	589	0
9.7A	0	0	0	1,090
9.7B	0	0	0	1,155
9.7C	0	0	0	1,125
Total	1,660	1,055	1,973	3,370

C.2 Survey Used in Western Australia (Version 7.1)

Original format: A4
Scaled: 80%

Survey of Attitudes to Tithing
and Other Church Matters

This research is very **important**.   It is completely **anonymous**.
We need to hear from both those who tithe and those who do not.
We really would like to know what you think.
We can't do this without your help.
We urge you to **answer every question**.

What is this survey about?
The Western Australian Conference of Seventh-day Adventists have asked Dr Rob
McIver and Dr Steve Currow to do some research on tithe. It is important to the
Church, and we seek your help in filling out this questionnaire. (There is more
information about this survey on the back page.)

We won't know who you are, and will make no attempt to find out
We guarantee complete confidentiality. No individual will ever be identified. We can
guarantee this because:
➢ Your survey will be one of several thousand that will be fed into a computer. We
  will only look at the overall pattern of results, not at any one return.
➢ Data entry will be by an independent person
➢ Surveys will be destroyed once results have been analyzed.
We ask you not to put your name anywhere on this questionnaire.

Returning this questionnaire indicates your willingness to participate.

Many thanks,

Rob and Steve.

PS: It is very important to answer every question (we can't use partially
finished forms for some of the things we need to do)

Version 7-1

A. About you

1. *My **Age** Group:*

☐ Under 15   ☐ 15–19   ☐ 20–29   ☐ 30–39

☐ 40–49   ☐ 50–59   ☐ 60–69   ☐ 70-79   ☐ Over 80

---

2. *I **attend** an Adventist church*:
   ☐ Most weeks   ☐ 2 to 3 times a month
   ☐ 10 to 23 times per year   ☐ 1 to 9 times per year   ☐ Never

   Today I am attending the church that I usually attend: ☐ No   ☐ **Yes**

---

3. *I am a **baptized** member* of the Seventh-day Adventist church
☐ No   ☐ Yes ➜   Number of years I have been a member of the Adventist Church:
Go to
qu. 4   ☐ 0-1   ☐ 2–4   ☐ 5-9   ☐ 10-19
⬇   ☐ 20-29   ☐ 30-39   ☐ 40-49   ☐ 50+

Qus 4-7. ***Employment***: (tick all that apply)

4. I am   **employed**
☐ No   ☐ Yes ➜   ☐ Wage/Salary earner
                    ☐ Self employed
Go to
qu. 5   ☐ Full time
⬇   ☐ Part time (hours per week: ☐ 0-9   ☐ 10-19   ☐ 20+)

5. I am   **retired**
☐ No   ☐ Yes ➜   ☐ Self-funded retiree   ☐ Receive Government benefit
Go to   ☐ Receive superannuation
qu. 6
⬇   I receive sustentation from the SDA Church: ☐ **No**   ☐ Yes

6. I am a **student**:
☐ No   ☐ Yes ➜   ☐ Full time;   ☐ Part time;   ☐ Receive Government benefit
Go to   I study at:
qu. 7   ☐ primary school   ☐ high school   ☐ TAFE college
⬇   ☐ Avondale College   ☐ University   ☐ Other _____

7. I **work for the SDA church** or one of its institutions: ☐ **No**   ☐ Yes

---

8. *My **Education*** (tick all you have completed)
☐ Primary school   ☐ Year ten, high school   ☐ Year 12, high school
☐ Trade Certificate   ☐ TAFE Certificate/Diploma   ☐ Bachelors degree
☐ Masters Degree   ☐ Doctoral degree

9. *My estimated* **income**:

Per **week** (take-home pay)		OR: *Per **year** (before tax)*	
☐ Under $120	☐ $600–$799	☐ Under $6,000	☐ $31,000–41,000
☐ $120–$199	☐ $800–$999	☐ $6,000–10,000	☐ $42,000–51,000
☐ $200-$399	☐ $1000–$1499	☐ $10,000–20,000	☐ $52,000–77,000
☐ $400-$599	☐ More than $1500	☐ $21,000–31,000	☐ $78,000-89,000
Go to qu. 10			☐ Over $90,000

10. *My* **gender**:   ☐ Female   ☐ Male

11. *Am I currently* **married?**:

☐ No   ☐ Yes ➜   11A. Does your partner attend the same congregation as you do?
Go to   ☐ No   ☐ **Yes**
qu. 12

⬇   11B When you give tithe, which of the following is usually true:
⬇   ☐ I give my own tithe;
                                     ☐ My partner gives my tithe;
                                     ☐ I give both my own tithe and that of my partner

12. *Do I have* **children?**

☐ No   ☐ Yes ➜   Are any of your children attending school or are you
Go to question 13   supporting any of them at TAFE, College or University?
                                            ☐ No   ☐ **Yes**

⬇   Do any of your children attend an **Adventist** School or
⬇   College?   ☐ No   ☐ Yes

13. One or both my **parents** was/were/are Seventh-day Adventists   ☐ **No** ☐ Yes
14. One or more of my **parents worked for the Seventh-day Adventist church** while I was
     growing up ☐ **No**   ☐ Yes

B. You and Tithes & Offerings

B1. In the last 12 months, as a percentage of my income, I estimate that I have given:

Tithe			Offerings+gifts to charity			
☐ 0%	☐ <2%	☐ 2-4%	☐ 0%	☐ ≤1%	☐ 2-3%	**OR**
☐ 5-7%	☐ 8-9%	☐ 10%	☐ 4-5%	☐ 6-9%	☐ 10+%	approximately
☐ 11+%			of my total income			$_____
of my total income						

B2. In the last 12 months I have given **tithe** (tick all that apply):
☐ through the **tithe envelope** in my local church
☐ through a **wage deduction**   ☐ through **e-giving**
☐ to **Sabbath School** offerings   ☐ to the **Local** church **Budget/offering**
☐ to **ADRA**   ☐ to the Local **SDA school Offering**
☐ directly to the **mission field**   ☐ to the **Salvation Army or Red Cross**
☐ to other **special** church based **appeals**   ☐ to needs in **my homeland**
☐ to an **independent Adventist ministry**   ☐ to the **Church Building** fund
☐ directly to my **church treasurer**   ☐ directly to the **local conference**
☐ to support a **youth volunteer** in our local church

☐ Other _____

How much do you agree with the following statements?

Circle one number for each question: 1 = strongly disagree
2 = disagree more than agree
3 = agree more than disagree
4 = strongly agree

➢ Please answer **every question**.
➢ If you do not know, just guess. In all cases, **go with your first impression**.
➢ It is important to **not leave any blanks**
➢ We ask important questions several different ways. **Don't worry about being consistent**.

B3 The Bible teaches that tithe is my responsibility to God   1 2 3 4
B4 I contribute tithe because God promises prosperity to those who tithe   1 2 3 4
B5 God has given me so much and I return tithe out of appreciation   1 2 3 4
B6 The church cannot run its various programs without people giving tithe
    and offerings   1 2 3 4

B7 The Conference should use some of the tithe given by bigger congregations
    to support ministers in smaller churches   1 2 3 4
B8 I have heard a sermon on tithe/stewardship in the last 12 months   1 2 3 4
B9 From the Bible I know that tithe does not belong to me, it is God's money
    already   1 2 3 4
B10 God will protect me from future harm if I return tithe   1 2 3 4

B11 I show my gratitude to God by returning tithe   1 2 3 4
B12 Tithe is important because it takes a lot of money to run this church
    properly   1 2 3 4
B13 If tithe is not pooled by the conference the bigger churches would have too much
    money and the smaller churches not enough   1 2 3 4
B14 It's OK to give time instead of money for tithe.   1 2 3 4

B15 The Bible teaches that I should return a regular tithe   1 2 3 4
B16 God will bless me even if I **don't** give tithe   1 2 3 4
B17   The Bible gives me instruction in all aspects of my life   1 2 3 4
B18 I contribute tithe because I am often overwhelmed by how good God has been to
    me   1 2 3 4

B19 If I do not return tithe the church will not be able to employ its ministers 1 2 3 4
B20 If tithe is not pooled by the conference the smaller churches would not be able to
    afford a pastor   1 2 3 4
B21 I understand how tithe is used by the SDA Church   1 2 3 4
B22 The Bible is clear that I should give 10% of my income as tithe   1 2 3 4

B23   If I give tithe God will answer my prayers   1 2 3 4
B24 Tithing has little to do with gratitude   1 2 3 4
B25 I need to contribute my tithe and offerings so the church can continue its
    work   1 2 3 4
B26 Tithe should be sent to the conference, because that way pastors can be placed
    where they will do most good.   1 2 3 4

B27 I have some questions on what the Bible has to say about tithe   1 2 3 4
B28 God watches out for me if I return tithe   1 2 3 4
B29 The Bible is authoritative in all aspects of my life   1 2 3 4
B30 I am grateful to God because he has given me so much   1 2 3 4

B31 Church members should all help to meet the operating needs of the whole
     church   1 2 3 4
B32 Tithe should be pooled by the conference, so that the Adventist Church can use
     it in the most effective way   1 2 3 4
B33 The Bible provides detailed guidance for my life   1 2 3 4

I feel there is nothing wrong in giving tithe . . .
    B34 ... to **special projects** (such as a new church building)   1 2 3 4
    B35 ... directly to the **mission field**   1 2 3 4
    B36 ... to assist **student missionaries** working in my local church   1 2 3 4
    B37 ... to the offering that supports the **local SDA school**   1 2 3 4
    B38 ... to **special appeals**, such as church mission outreach overseas   1 2 3 4
    B39 ... to help needy people through **ADRA**   1 2 3 4
    B40 ... to help needy people through the **Red Cross** or the **Salvation Army** 1 2 3 4

B41 The Bible is the basis of my belief and practice   1 2 3 4
B42 I know that God has blessed me because I pay tithe   1 2 3 4
B43 Returning tithe provides the Church with funds to fulfil God's mission   1 2 3 4
B44 By returning tithe I trust God will supply my needs   1 2 3 4
B45 I return tithe because I believe in my Church's purpose   1 2 3 4

B46 I try to return tithe: ☐ Weekly   ☐ Fortnightly   ☐ Quarterly   ☐ Yearly

B47 Sometimes I forget to return tithe

☐ No (I   ☐ Yes   Because I sometimes forget, I estimate that the number times
never forget,   ➜   **each year** I actually contribute tithe is about::
or only   ☐ 1-3 times   ☐ 4-6 times   ☐ 7-11 times   ☐ 12-17 times
rarely) Go to   ☐ 18-24 times ☐ 25 –29 times ☐ more than 30 times
next qu.
⬇

B48 Even though tithe should also be used to support the mission fields, youth work, and church administration, I think that at least the following percentage of tithe should be used in the local church (e.g. for local church pastor's wages):
☐ 20%   ☐ 30%   ☐ 40%   ☐ 50%   ☐ 60%   ☐ 70%   ☐ 75%   ☐ 80%   ☐ 90%

C. You and the Seventh Day Adventist Church

How much do you agree with the following statements?

1 = strongly disagree
2 = disagree more than agree
3 = agree more than disagree
4 = strongly agree

C1 My local church feels like my extended family   1 2 3 4
C2 The Seventh-day Adventist church has a mission to the whole world   1 2 3 4
C3 The Adventist Church already has enough money to do what it wants to do
    without my tithe   1 2 3 4
C4 The Conference uses the tithe it receives wisely   1 2 3 4

C5 I enjoy being an Adventist   1 2 3 4
C6 Overall, my church pastor is doing a good job   1 2 3 4
C7 I feel a strong commitment to the Seventh-day Adventist Church   1 2 3 4
C8 Jesus is Lord of all my life, including how I spend my money   1 2 3 4

C9 I feel welcome when I attend my local church   1 2 3 4
C10 The mission of the SDA church is to take its message to the whole
    world   1 2 3 4
C11 I contribute little or no tithe because the church already has enough money to do
    what it should   1 2 3 4
C12 I trust the handling and allocation of funds by the conference, union and division
    leaders   1 2 3 4

C13 I find the church pastor's sermons interesting and relevant   1 2 3 4
C14 God is in control of everything in my life, including what I do with my
    money   1 2 3 4
C15 I know just about everybody that attends my local church   1 2 3 4
C16 I believe the SDA church has a mission to the whole world   1 2 3 4

C17 The Adventist Church has enough money to operate without my tithe   1 2 3 4
C18 I trust Church administration to manage the money I give in tithe and
    offerings   1 2 3 4
C19 I know the church pastor well   1 2 3 4
C20 God is in control of everything in my life   1 2 3 4

C21 If I had to change the local church I attend, I would feel a great sense of
    loss   1 2 3 4
C22 I am very interested in the Church's work in other parts of the world   1 2 3 4
C23 The Adventist Church is wealthy   1 2 3 4
C24 The SDA church uses the tithe it receives wisely   1 2 3 4

C25 Most of the congregation thinks well of the church pastor   1 2 3 4
C26 God is in control of everything in my life, including everything I do   1 2 3 4
C27 My local church is a family Church   1 2 3 4
C28 The Adventist Church has plenty of money   1 2 3 4

C29 I am pleased to have my church pastor represent our church at community
functions   1 2 3 4
C30 Jesus is Lord of all my life   1 2 3 4

To be a Seventh-day Adventist, it is *very important* to abstain from …

C31. Alcohol	1 2 3 4	C35. Tea and Coffee	1 2 3 4
C32. Coca Cola & Pepsi	1 2 3 4	C36. Smoking	1 2 3 4
C33. Dancing	1 2 3 4	C37. Eating meat	1 2 3 4
C34. Illegal drugs	1 2 3 4		

Which of the following is true of you?
(1 = never; 2 = sometimes; 3 = often; 4 = almost always)?

Do you?:
C38. Attend **Sabbath school**   1 2 3 4
C39. **Open and close Sabbath**   1 2 3 4
C40. Study the **Sabbath School Quarterly**   1 2 3 4
C40b. **Read** and reflect on the **Bible** each day   1 2 3 4
C41. **Pray** often during the day   1 2 3 4
C41b. **Reflect on spiritual things** during the day   1 2 3 4
C42. **Share your faith** with non Seventh-day Adventists   1 2 3 4
C43. Attend **prayer meetings**   1 2 3 4

C44. I have held office in my local church in the last 12 months: ☐ Yes   ☐ No

---

C45. In the last **two** years I have done the following in the local church (tick all that
apply):

☐ Taught a Sabbath-school class	☐ Given a special item
☐ Acted as deacon / deaconess	☐ Served as Elder
☐ Served as Sabbath School Leader	☐ Served as organist / pianist
☐ Served as treasurer / church clerk	☐ Regularly accompanied song services
☐ Preached a sermon	☐ Led singing
☐ Arranged the flowers	☐ Greeted at the door
☐ Operated the PA	☐ Other _____

☐ I have joined the church in the last 2 years

C46 I feel guilty when I do not attend Church on Sabbath   1 2 3 4
C47 The Adventist Church has lots of money   1 2 3 4
C48 My local church is like one big family   1 2 3 4

D. Other important questions

D1 The number of times that I have heard a sermon on tithing or giving in the last 2
years: ☐ 0 times ☐ 1 time ☐ 2 times ☐ 3 times ☐ 4 times ☐ 5/more than 5 times

D2 I tithe a full 10% of my income

Yes ☐   No ☐ ➔   Tick as many of the following as are true for you:

Go to
qu. D3
⬇
⬇
⬇
⬇
⬇
⬇
⬇
⬇
⬇
⬇
⬇
⬇
⬇
⬇

I do not currently give a full tithe, or do not give tithe. The following changes
would need to happen before I would consider returning a full tithe
  ☐ I think I should tithe, but I need to get into the habit of tithing regularly
  ☐ I need to be fully financially secure before I can give any money to the
church
  ☐ The Adventist Church should make it possible to ordain women to the
Gospel ministry
  ☐ The Adventist Church needs to bring its doctrines and ideas into the 21st
century
  ☐ The Adventist Church needs to return to sound doctrine
  ☐ We need a competent pastor in our local church
  ☐ The Church needs to make its worship relevant to today's youth
  ☐ Churches need to stop experimenting with worship, and restore proper
reverence in worship
  ☐ I need to be convinced from the Bible that *Christians* should return tithe
  ☐ I think I should tithe, but my spouse is very strongly against giving tithe.
  ☐ Other _____
  ☐ I don't think anything would change what I do about tithing

---

D3 I have learned about tithing from the following sources:

☐ Sermons   ☐ Personal reading and study
☐ Bible studies   ☐ Video presentation
☐ Board/Business meeting   ☐ Pastoral newsletter
☐ Sabbath School classes   ☐ *Record*
☐ Parents   ☐ *Newswest* or *Conference News*
☐ Other: _____

D4. In the last **two** years I have done the following in the local community (tick all that
apply)

☐ Helped with the annual **Adra Appeal**
☐ Delivered **food parcel**
☐ Assisted in a church-sponsored **health program**
☐ Acted as **volunteer in my local community** (e.g. in Bush Fire Brigade)
☐ Collected for **Red Cross** or **Salvation Army**
☐ **Invited non-**member to Church
☐ **Invited** non-member to an **Evangelistic Program**
☐ other _____

The following questions are **optional**:

Rob & Steve, there are some things about tithe I would like to tell you that you have not really covered in your questionnaire:

_____

_____

_____

_____

_____

Other comments:

_____

_____

_____

_____

_____

Just in case you are ever asked which version of the survey you
have done ...
This is a Version 7-1 survey.
Remember the picture: 📖.

The Back Page
(more information)

What we are doing

The Western Australia, Greater Sydney and North New South Wales Conferences of Seventh-day Adventists have asked Dr Rob McIver and Dr Steve Currow of Avondale College to do some research into the patterns of tithe return for their conference. Our preliminary results indicate some trends that could have very important implications for our church in the near future. But while we can see these trends, we do not know the reasons for them. For this we need to ask questions of as many people who are willing to help us. This means we are asking you to answer the questions in this survey. You will see that we have not only asked about tithe but a number of other things as well. The research done by other people indicate that some of these may be related to patterns of giving. We don't know if they are significant for Australian Adventists until we have asked you. Many thanks for your willingness to help by answering these questions.

Special note re. ethics committee approval:

As this research involves faculty of Avondale College, a research proposal has been considered and approved by the Avondale College Human Research Ethics Committee. The HREC asked that the following notice be included in the documents given to participants:

Avondale College requires that all participants are informed that if they have any complaint concerning the manner in which a research project is conducted it may be given to the researcher [in this case – one of the members of the research group – Pr Lionel Smith at ph. (08) 9498 9127, or Dr Rob McIver, (02) 4980-2226], or if an independent person is preferred, to the College's Human Research Ethics Committee Secretary, Avondale College, PO Box 19, Cooranbong, NSW 2265, or phone (02) 4980 2121 or fax (02) 4980 2118.

C.3 Survey Used in Southern England (Version 9.4B)

Original format: A4

Scaled: 80%

Note: This version is designed to be read electronically; the ID number is changed on each individual survey.

Survey of Attitudes to Tithing and Other Church Matters

Would you help? We are seeking to understand more about why and how people tithe.

Worship and mission are much more important than money in the priorities of a Church. Yet lack of funds reduces the church's ability to fulfil its purpose.

This research is very **important**.   It is completely **confidential**.
We need to hear from both those who tithe and those who do not.
We really would like to know what you think.

We can't do this without your help.

What is this survey about?
The General Conference of Seventh-day Adventists has asked Dr Rob McIver and Dr Steve Currow to do some research on tithe in selected Conferences around the world. It is important to the Church, and we seek your help in filling out this questionnaire. (There is more information about this survey on the back page.)

We won't know who you are, and will make no attempt to find out
We guarantee confidentiality. No individual will ever be identified. We can guarantee this because:
➢ Your survey will be one of several thousand that will be fed into a computer. We will only look at the overall pattern of results, not at any one return.
➢ The results of the survey will almost certainly be entered by somebody who does not know you, or the people in the Church you attend.
➢ We ask you not to put your name anywhere on this questionnaire.

Returning this questionnaire indicates your willingness to participate.

Many thanks,

Rob and Steve.

Version 9-4 ☺

Tithe Survey: ENGLAND ver 9-4

Page: 1

Survey ID: 9100

Instructions: Please shade in the appropriate circle:
Like this: ●, not like this: ⊘ ⊗ ⊘; and cross out mistakes ✖ ② ③ ●

A. About you

A1.　*My Age Group:*
○　Under 15
○　15–19
○　20–29
○　30–39
○　40–49
○　50–59
○　60–69
○　70-79
○　Over 80

A2.　*I am a **baptized** member* of the Seventh-day Adventist church
Ⓨ　**Yes** ➔ Go to question A3
Ⓝ　No ➔ Go to question A4

A3.　Number of years I have been a member of the Adventist Church
○　0-1
○　2–4
○　5-9
○　10-19
○　20-29
○　30-39
○　40-49
○　50+

A4.　*I **attend** an Adventist church*:
○　Every week/most weeks
○　2 to 3 times a month
○　10 to 23 times per year
○　1 to 9 times per year
○　Never

A5.　Today I am attending the church that I usually attend:
Ⓨ　**Yes**
Ⓝ　No

A6.　I am **employed**
Ⓨ　Yes **Full Time**
Ⓨ　Yes **Part Time**
Ⓝ　No (go to question A9)

A7.　I am:
○　Self Employed
○　Wage/Salary earner paid **monthly**
○　Wage/Salary earner paid **fortnightly**
○　Wage/Salary earner paid **weekly**

A8.　I **work for the SDA church** or one of its institutions:
Ⓨ　Yes
Ⓝ　**No**

A9.　*My **Education*** (shade "highest" you have completed)
○　Primary School
○　High School
○　Trade Qualification
○　Further Education
○　Bachelors Degree
○　Masters Degree
○　Doctoral Degree

A10.   *My estimated **income** in Great British*
       *Pounds (answer per month **or** per year)*
       Per **MONTH** *(take-home pay)*   **OR:**   *Per **YEAR** (before tax)*

	Per MONTH		Per YEAR
O	Under £50	O	Under £600
O	£50–£99	O	£600–£1,199
O	£100-£199	O	£1,200–£2,499
O	£200-£299	O	£2,500–£3,999
O	£300–£499	O	£4,000–£5,999
O	£500–£999	O	£6,000–£11,999
O	£1,000-£1,499	O	£12,000–£17,999
O	£1,500-£1,999	O	£18,000–£23,999
O	£2,000–£2,499	O	£24,000–£29,999
O	£2,500–£2,999	O	£30,000–£39,999
O	£3,000–£3,999	O	£40,000–£49,999
O	£4,000–£6,000	O	£50,000-£70,000
O	More than £6,000	O	Over £70,000

Go to question B1

B. You and Tithes & Offerings

B1.   In the last 12 months, as a percentage of my income, I estimate that I have given
      as tithe:

O   0%
O   <2%
O   2-4%
O   5-7%
O   8-9%
O   10%
O   11+%

B2.   In the last 12 months I have given **tithe** (shade all that apply):
      To the Conference through:

O   the **tithe envelope** in my local   O   directly to my **church treasurer**
    church   O   directly to the **local conference**
O   a **wage deduction**
O   **electronic-giving** (e.g. standing
    order with bank)

Tithe Survey: ENGLAND ver 9-4

    Page: 3

Survey ID: 9100

B3. The SDA church considers that tithes and offerings should be treated separately.
Offerings are given *in addition to* tithe. The Church also suggests where tithes and offerings
should be directed. This question is a about what you *actually* do with your tithes and
offerings, *not* what you should be doing. Next to each of the list below, fill in:

the ⊙ circle for where you have given **only offerings**;
the ⓣ circle for where you have given **only tithe**, and
the ⓑ circle for where you have given **both** tithes and offerings.
Shade all that apply:

⊙ ⓣ ⓑ   to **Sabbath School (world mission)** offerings
⊙ ⓣ ⓑ   to local church based **appeals**
⊙ ⓣ ⓑ   to the **Church Building/Plot** fund
⊙ ⓣ ⓑ   to the local **SDA school Offering**
⊙ ⓣ ⓑ   to an **independent Adventist ministry**
⊙ ⓣ ⓑ   to support a **youth volunteer** in our local church
⊙ ⓣ ⓑ   to **Sponsorships** (e.g. members supporting pastors)
⊙ ⓣ ⓑ   to the **local** church **Budget/offering**
⊙ ⓣ ⓑ   to **ADRA**
⊙ ⓣ ⓑ   to needs in **my country or conference of origin**
⊙ ⓣ ⓑ   to the **Salvation Army or Red Cross, etc**
⊙ ⓣ ⓑ   directly to overseas **mission field**
⊙ ⓣ ⓑ   to Adventist **Media**
⊙ ⓣ ⓑ   to **organ fund**
⊙ ⓣ ⓑ   Other _____

How much do you agree with the following statements?
1 = strongly disagree
2 = disagree more than agree
3 = agree more than disagree
4 = strongly agree

Shade in one number for each question:

1 = strongly disagree
2 = disagree more than agree
3 = agree more than disagree
4 = strongly agree

B4 God will protect me from future harm if I return tithe — B4 ① ② ③ ④
B5 I show my gratitude to God by returning tithe — B5 ① ② ③ ④
B6 If tithe is not pooled by the conference the bigger churches
would have too much money and the smaller churches not enough — B6 ① ② ③ ④
B7 The Bible is clear that I should give 10% of my income as tithe — B7 ① ② ③ ④

How much do you agree with the following statements?
    1 = strongly disagree
    2 = disagree more than agree
    3 = agree more than disagree
    4 = strongly agree

	1 = strongly disagree	2 = disagree more than agree	3 = agree more than disagree	4 = strongly agree

Shade in one number for each question:

		1	2	3	4
B8 I need to contribute my tithe and offerings so the church can continue its work	B8	①	②	③	④
B9 The Bible provides detailed guidance for my life	B9	①	②	③	④
B10 I know that God has blessed me because I pay tithe	B10	①	②	③	④

I feel there is nothing wrong in giving tithe . . .

		1	2	3	4
B11 to **special projects** (such as a new church building)	B11	①	②	③	④
B12 directly to the overseas **mission field**	B12	①	②	③	④
B13 to assist **volunteers** working in my local church	B13	①	②	③	④
B14 to the offering that supports the **local SDA school**	B14	①	②	③	④
B15 to **special appeals**, such as church mission outreach overseas	B15	①	②	③	④
B16 to help needy people through **ADRA**	B16	①	②	③	④
B17 to help needy people through the **Red Cross** or the **Salvation Army**	B17	①	②	③	④

B18. I try to return tithe:
○   Weekly
○   Fortnightly
○   Monthly
○   Quarterly
○   Yearly

B19. Sometimes I forget to return tithe
Ⓝ   No (I never forget, or only rarely) ➔ Go to question C1
Ⓨ   Yes ➔ Go to question B20

B20. Because I sometimes forget, I estimate that the number times **each year** I actually contribute tithe is about

- ○   1-3 times
- ○   4-6 times
- ○   7-11 times
- ○   12-17 times
- ○   18-24 times
- ○   25 –29 times
- ○   more than 30 times

C. You and the Seventh-Day Adventist Church

How much do you agree with the following statements?

1 = strongly disagree
2 = disagree more than agree
3 = agree more than disagree
4 = strongly agree

Statement		1	2	3	4
C1 My local church feels like my extended family	C1	①	②	③	④
C2 I enjoy being an Adventist	C2	①	②	③	④
C3 Overall, my church pastor is doing a good job	C3	①	②	③	④
C4 I feel a strong commitment to the Seventh-day Adventist Church	C4	①	②	③	④
C5 I trust the handling and allocation of funds by the conference, union and division leaders	C5	①	②	③	④
C6 I believe the SDA church has a mission to the whole world	C6	①	②	③	④
C7 The Adventist Church has enough money to operate without my tithe	C7	①	②	③	④
C8 God is in control of everything in my life	C8	①	②	③	④

How much do you agree with the following statements?

		1 = strongly disagree	2 = disagree more than agree	3 = agree more than disagree	4 = strongly agree

To be a Seventh-day Adventist, it is *very important* to abstain from:

		1	2	3	4
C9	Alcohol	C9	①	②	③	④
C10	Coca Cola, Pepsi, Red Bull, etc	C10	①	②	③	④
C11	Eating meat	C11	①	②	③	④
C12	Tea and Coffee	C12	①	②	③	④
C13	Smoking	C13	①	②	③	④
C14	Illegal drugs	C14	①	②	③	④

Which of the following is true of you?
(1 = never; 2 = sometimes; 3 = often; 4 = always/ almost always)

		1 = never	2 = sometimes	3 = often	4 = almost always

Do you?:

		1	2	3	4
C15	Attend **Sabbath school**	C15	①	②	③	④
C16	**Open and close Sabbath**	C16	①	②	③	④
C17	Study the **Sabbath School Quarterly**	C17	①	②	③	④
C18	**Read** and reflect on the **Bible** each day	C18	①	②	③	④
C19	**Pray** often during the day	C19	①	②	③	④
C20	**Reflect on spiritual things** during the day	C20	①	②	③	④
C21	Attend **prayer meetings**	C21	①	②	③	④

D. Other questions

D1.   I tithe a full 10% of my income

Ⓨ   Yes ➔ Go to question D3

Ⓝ   No ➔ Go to question D2

D2.   I do not currently give a full tithe, or do not give tithe. The following changes would need to happen before I would consider returning a full tithe [shade as many of the following as are true for you]:

○   I think I should tithe, but I need to get into the habit of tithing regularly

○   I need to be fully financially secure before I can give any money to the church

○   I need to be more confident that money I give as tithe actually makes it to the right place

○   The Adventist Church should make it possible to ordain women to the Gospel ministry

○   The Adventist Church needs to bring its doctrines and ideas into the 21st century

○   The Adventist Church needs to return to sound doctrine

○   We need a competent pastor in our local church

○   The Church needs to make its worship relevant to today's youth

○   Churches need to stop experimenting with worship, and restore proper reverence in worship

○   I need to be convinced from the Bible that *Christians* should return tithe

○   I think I should tithe, but my spouse is very strongly against giving tithe.

○   I need to know that if I tithe, more pastors will be employed and I will see a pastor more often

○   Other _____

○   I don't think anything would change what I do about tithing

D3.   I was **born in the United Kingdom** and have lived all or most of my life here.

○   Yes➔ Go to question D4

      No➔ I have lived in the UK for

○   Most of my life

○   1-3 years

○   4-10 years

○   11-20 years

○   21-30 years

○   more than 30 years

○   I'm a visitor to the UK

D4.   *My Culture:* Culturally, I would consider myself to be

○   English/British/Welsh/Scottish

○   West Indian

○   African (e.g. Ghanaian)

○   South American (e.g. Hispanic; Portuguese)

○   Eastern European

○   Other _____

E. Optional [but very helpful] Questions

Many thanks for answering all the absolutely essential questions. If you have time, it would be *very* helpful if you could also answer the following optional questions:

E1 The number of times that I have heard a sermon on tithing or giving in the last 2 years:

- ⓪ 0 times
- ① 1 time
- ② 2 times
- ③ 3 times
- ④ 4 times
- ⑤ 5/more than 5 times

E2. I have held office in my local church in the last 12 months:

- Ⓨ Yes
- Ⓝ No

E3. *Am I currently **married?**:*

- Ⓝ No ➜ Go to question E4
- Ⓨ Yes: My partner attends the same congregation as I do
- Ⓨ Yes: My partner does **not** attend the same congregation as I do

How much do you agree with the following statements?

	1 = strongly disagree	2 = disagree more than agree	3 = agree more than disagree	4 = strongly agree
E4 The Bible teaches that tithe is my responsibility to God	①	②	③	④
E5 I contribute tithe because God promises prosperity to those who tithe	①	②	③	④
E6 God has given me so much and I return tithe out of appreciation	①	②	③	④
E7 From the Bible I know that tithe does not belong to me, it is God's money already	①	②	③	④
E8 I contribute tithe because I am often overwhelmed by how good God has been to me	①	②	③	④
E9 If I give tithe God will answer my prayers	①	②	③	④
E10 The Adventist Church already has enough money to do what it wants to do without my tithe	①	②	③	④
E11 I know just about everybody that attends my local church	①	②	③	④
E12 I contribute little or no tithe because the church already has enough money to do what it should	①	②	③	④
E13 My local church is like one big family	①	②	③	④

Tithe Survey: ENGLAND ver 9-4

Page: 9

Survey ID: 9100

E14. *My **gender***:

(F) Female

(M) Male

E15. One or both my **parents** was/were/are Seventh-day Adventists

(N) No

(Y) Yes

E16. One or more of my **parents worked for the Seventh-day Adventist church** while I was growing up

(N) **No**

(Y) Yes

E17. I am a **student**:

(N) No ➔ Go to question E20

(Y) Yes➔ I study **Full Time**

(Y) Yes➔ I study **Part Time**

E18 Do I receive a government grant?

(Y) Yes➔ I receive a **Government Grant**

(Y) No ➔ I do **not** receive a Government Grant

E19 I study at:

○ Primary School

○ Secondary School

○ College of Further Education

○ University

○ Other: _____

E20. *Do I have **children**?*

(N) No ➔ go to question E23

(Y) Yes ➔ go to question E21

E21. Are any of my children attending school or am I supporting any of them at College of Further Education or University?

(N) No ➔ go to question E23

(Y) Yes ➔ go to question E22

E22 Do any of my children attend an Adventist School, College or University?

(N) No

(Y) Yes

The following questions are **optional**:

E23. Rob & Steve, there are some things about tithe I would like to tell you that you have not really covered in your questionnaire:

_____

_____

_____

_____

_____

E24. Other comments:

_____

_____

_____

_____

_____

Just in case you are ever asked which version of the survey you
have done ...
This is a Version 9-4 survey.
Remember the picture: ☺.

The Back Page
(more information)

Who are Rob and Steve?

Associate Professor Dr. Robert K. McIver is the Head of the School of Ministry and Theology
    at Avondale College of Higher Education in Cooranbong NSW Australia.
Dr Stephen J. Currow is principal of Fulton College, Fiji.
Rob and Steve first starting researching tithe in 1999 when they were both lecturers together
    in the Faculty of Theology at Avondale College.

What we are doing

*Some of the key leaders of the General Conference of Seventh-day Adventists (the
research is funded by the Future Plans Working Group) have asked Dr Rob McIver and Dr
Steve Currow to do some research into the motives for and patterns of tithing for several
conferences from around the World. Previous research in Australia indicate some trends that
could have very important implications for the Adventist church in the near future. We need
to find out whether Adventist Church members in other countries have similar giving patterns
and motives. To discover this we need to ask questions of as many people who are willing to
help us. This means we are asking you to answer the questions in this survey. You will see
that we have not only asked about tithe but a number of other things as well. The research
done by other people indicate that some of these may be related to patterns of giving. We
don't know if they are significant for Adventists in your country until we have asked you.
Many thanks for your willingness to help by answering these questions. We plan to report
our findings in a number of places, including Church publications and academic journals.
We will never do so in a form which will enable any one individual to be identified.*

Special note re. ethics committee approval:

*As this research involves faculty of Avondale College, a research proposal has been
considered and approved by the Avondale College Human Research Ethics Committee. The
HREC asked that the following notice be included in the documents given to participants:*

Avondale College requires that all participants are informed that if they have any complaint
concerning the manner in which a research project is conducted it may be given to the
researcher [in this case – one of the members of the research group – Dr Rob McIver, (02)
4980-2226 rob.mciver@hotmail.com], or if an independent person is preferred, to the
College's Human Research Ethics Committee Secretary, Avondale College, PO Box 19,
Cooranbong, NSW 2265, or phone (02) 4980 2121 or fax (02) 4980 2118.

C.4 Survey Used in São Paulo (Version 9.6A/B/C)

Original format: A4

Scaled: 80%

Note: This version is designed to be used in conjunction with answer cards used by the São Paulo Conference as part of their standard method of collecting survey results. Each question could only have five options, which meant that some questions such as income level had to be spread accross two questions.

Pesquisa – Atitude para com o Dízimo
e Outras Questões da Igreja

O culto e a missão são mais importantes do que o dinheiro nas prioridades da Igreja. Contudo, a falta de fundos reduz a capacidade da igreja cumprir seu propósito.

Esta pesquisa é muito **importante**. Ela é totalmente **confidencial**. Necessitamos ouvir os que devolvem o dízimo e os que não o fazem. Realmente desejamos conhecer sua opinião. Não podemos fazer isso sem a sua ajuda.

Qual é o propósito desta pesquisa?
A Associação Geral dos Adventistas do Sétimo Dia pediu ao Dr. Rob McIver e ao Dr. Steve Currow para realizarem uma pesquisa a respeito do dízimo em algumas Associações ao redor do mundo. Ela é importante para a Igreja e pedimos a você para preencher este questionário. (Há mais informação a respeito da pesquisa no final deste questionário.)

Não desejamos saber quem você é, e não faremos tentativas para saber.
Garantimos o caráter confidencial. Ninguém será identificado. Podemos garantir isso porque:
➤ Suas respostas estarão entre as várias milhares que serão armazenadas no computador. Consideraremos apenas o padrão geral dos resultados e não somente a resposta de um indivíduo.
➤ Os resultados da pesquisa certamente serão lançados no programa de computador por alguém que não conhece você.
➤ Por favor não coloque o seu nome em parte alguma deste questionário.

A devolução deste questionário indica sua disposição de participar.

Muito obrigado,

Rob e Steve.

Versão 9-6A ☺

Pesquisa – Atitude para com o Dízimo e Outras Questões da Igreja

Marque suas respostas no cartão de respostas.

Questão 01 Por favor faça um círculo na letra A da questão 01 (temos três versões desta pesquisa, você está respondendo a versão A, precisamos desta informação para entender suas respostas corretamente)

Questões 02 & 03: *Minha Faixa Etária:*
Qual a sua idade? (Se você tem 50 anos ou mais responda a questão 3):
Questão 02
A. Menos de 15
B. 15–19
C. 20–29
D. 30–39
E. 40–49

Questão03
A. 50–59
B. 60–69
C. 70-79
D. Acima 80

Questão 04   *Hoje estou na igreja que frequento regularmente:*
A. Sim
B. Não

Questão 05.   *Nos últimos 12 meses, que porcentagem das minhas entradas, eu estimo ter devolvido como dizimo?*
A. 0%
B. menos de 4%
C. 5-7%
D. 8-9%
E. 10% ou +

Questões 06—08.   *Estimativa de minha renda* (responda por mês).
Por mês (valor líquido):
Se você recebe R$1.669,00 ou menos, responda a questão 06.
Se você recebe entre R$1.670,00 a R$12.499,00 responda a questão 07.
Se você recebe mais de R$12.500,00 responda a questão 08

Questão 06
A. Menos de R$170,00
B. R$170,00–R$332,00
C. R$333,00–R$749,00
D. R$750,00–R$1.159,00
E. R$1.160,00–R$1.669,00

Questão 07.
A. R$1.670,00–R$3.332,00
B. R$3.333,00–R$4.999,00
C. R$5.000,00–R$6.665,00
D. R$6.666,00–R$8.332,00
E. R$8.333,00–R$12.499,00

Questão 08.
A. R$12.500,00–R$16.665,00
B. R$16.666,00–R$20.800,00
C. Acima de R$20.800,00

Para que esta pesquisa seja mais confiável, algumas questões possuem pequenas diferenças. Você não precisa assinalar as duas alternativas, marque apenas a que parecer mais correta.

Questões 09—33: *Quanto você concorda com as seguintes declarações?*
Preencha com a letra correspondente:
A = discordo totalmente
B = discordo mais que concordo
C = concordo mais que discordo
D = concordo totalmente

Questão 09. Deus me protegerá de danos futuros se eu devolver o dízimo
Questão 10. Mostro gratidão a Deus ao devolver o dízimo
Questão 11. Se o dízimo não fosse reunido na associação, as igrejas maiores teriam mais dinheiro e as menores não teriam o suficiente
Questão 12. A Bíblia é clara ao dizer que devo dar 10% de minha renda como dízimo
Questão 13. Devo contribuir com meu dízimo e ofertas a fim de que a igreja possa seguir com sua obra

Questão 14. A Bíblia provê detalhes orientadores para minha vida
Questão 15. Sei que Deus me abençoa porque eu devolvo o dízimo
Questão 16. Para mim a igreja local me faz sentir como extensão de minha família
Questão 17. Gosto de ser adventista
Questão 18. No geral, o pastor de minha igreja está fazendo um bom trabalho

Questão 19. Sou fortemente comprometido com a Igreja Adventista
Questão 20. Confio na forma como a liderança da associação, união e divisão lidam e distribuem o dinheiro que é dado à igreja
Questão 21. Creio que a IASD tem uma missão no mundo todo
Questão 22. Creio que a Igreja Adventista tem muito dinheiro e não precisa do meu dízimo
Questão 23. Deus está no controle de tudo em minha vida

Questões 09—33: *Quanto você concorda com as seguintes declarações?*
Preencha com a letra correspondente:
A = discordo totalmente
B = discordo mais que concordo
C = concordo mais que discordo
D = concordo totalmente

Questão 24. A Bíblia ensina que o dízimo é meu dever para com Deus
Questão 25. Devolvo o dízimo porque Deus promete prosperidade aos que o
           devolvem
Questão 26. Deus me deu muito e devolvo o dízimo em gratidão
Questão 27. Pela Bíblia sei que o dízimo não me pertence, ele já é de Deus
Questão 28. Devolvo o dízimo porque sempre sinto muita gratidão pelo que Deus
           tem feito por mim

Questão 29. Se eu devolver o dízimo, Deus ouvirá minhas orações
Questão 30. A IASD já tem muito dinheiro para fazer o que deseja sem meu dízimo
Questão 31. Eu conheço quase todos os membros da minha igreja local
Questão 32. Eu devolvo parte ou não devolvo meu dízimo porque a igreja já tem
           bastante dinheiro para fazer o que ela deve
Questão 33. Minha igreja local se assemelha a uma grande família

Questão 34.   *Minha intenção é devolver o dízimo*:
A. Semanalmente
B. Quinzenalmente
C. Mensalmente
D. Trimestralmente
E. Anualmente

Questão 35. *Algumas vezes esqueço de devolver o dízimo*
A. Sim ➜ Ir para 36
B. Não (eu nunca esqueço ou raramente esqueço) ➜ Muito obrigado por sua ajuda,
você completou nossa pesquisa.

Questão 36. *Visto que esqueço algumas vezes, creio que o número de vezes que de
           fato contribuo a **cada ano** é mais ou menos*:
A. 1-3 vezes
B. 4-6 vezes
C. 7-11 vezes
D. 12 ou mais vezes
Muito obrigado por sua ajuda.

Verso da Página
(mais informação)

Quem são Rob e Steve?

Dr. Robert K. McIver, Professor Associado, é o Diretor da Escola de Ensino Superior
de Ministério e Teologia do Avondale College, em Cooranbong NSW
Austrália.

Dr Stephen J. Currow é diretor do Fulton College, Fiji.

Rob e Steve iniciaram a pesquisa sobre o dízimo, em 1999, quando ambos fizeram
palestras na Faculdade de Teologia do Avondale College.

O que Estamos Fazendo?

*Alguns dos líderes-chave da Associação Geral dos Adventistas do Sétimo Dia
solicitaram que o Dr. Rob McIver e o Dr. Steve Currow realizassem a pesquisa quanto aos
motivos para devolver o dízimo e seus padrões, em várias associações ao redor do mundo (a
pesquisa está sendo financiada pelo Grupo de Trabalho de Planos para o Futuro).*

*A pesquisa anterior, realizada na Austrália, indica algumas tendências que
poderiam ter implicações significativas para a Igreja Adventista em um futuro próximo.
Necessitamos descobrir se os membros da Igreja Adventista, em outro países, têm padrões e
motivos semelhantes.*

*Para descobrirmos isso necessitamos fazer perguntas para o maior número possível
de pessoas que estejam dispostas a nos ajudar. Isso significa que lhe estamos pedindo para
responder a esta pesquisa. Você verá que perguntamos não apenas a respeito do dízimo, mas
de outras questões também. A pesquisa feita por outra pessoa indica que algumas delas
podem estar relacionadas aos padrões de dizimar e ofertar. Não sabemos se elas são
significativas para os adventistas em seu país até obtermos suas respostas. Nossos
agradecimentos por sua disposição de ajudar ao responder às perguntas. Planejamos
informar nossas descobertas em vários lugares, incluindo as publicações acadêmicas e da
Igreja em geral. De forma alguma alguém será identificado.*

Nota Especial. Aprovação da comissão de ética:

*Visto que esta pesquisa envolve docentes do Avondale College, foi considerada a
proposta da pesquisa, e aprovada, pela* Human Research Ethics Committee
*(Comissão de Ética de Pesquisa Humana do Avondale College). Essa comissão
solicitou que a seguinte observação fosse incluída nos documentos entregues aos
participantes:*

O Avondale College requer que todos os participantes sejam informados de que se
tiverem qualquer reclamação quanto à forma pela qual o projeto de pesquisa está
sendo conduzido, poderá ser feita ao pesquisador [neste caso, um dos membros do
grupo de pesquisa – Pr. Lionel Smith, fone: (08) 9498 9127, ou Dr Rob McIver, (02)
4980-2226], se preferir uma pessoa independente, ao Secretário da Human Research
Ethics Committee do Colégio, PO Box 19, Cooranbong, NSW 2265, ou telefone (02)
4980 2121 ou fax (02) 4980 2118.

Pesquisa – Atitude para com o Dízimo e Outras Questões da Igreja

O culto e a missão são mais importantes do que o dinheiro nas prioridades da Igreja. Contudo, a falta de fundos reduz a capacidade da igreja cumprir seu propósito.

Esta pesquisa é muito **importante**. Ela é totalmente **confidencial**. Necessitamos ouvir os que devolvem o dízimo e os que não o fazem. Realmente desejamos conhecer sua opinião. Não podemos fazer isso sem a sua ajuda.

Qual é o propósito desta pesquisa?
A Associação Geral dos Adventistas do Sétimo Dia pediu ao Dr. Rob McIver e ao Dr. Steve Currow para realizarem uma pesquisa a respeito do dízimo em algumas Associações ao redor do mundo. Ela é importante para a Igreja e pedimos a você para preencher este questionário. (Há mais informação a respeito da pesquisa no final deste questionário.)

Não desejamos saber quem você é, e não faremos tentativas para saber.
Garantimos o caráter confidencial. Ninguém será identificado. Podemos garantir isso porque:
➤ Suas respostas estarão entre as várias milhares que serão armazenadas no computador. Consideraremos apenas o padrão geral dos resultados e não somente a resposta de um indivíduo.
➤ Os resultados da pesquisa certamente serão lançados no programa de computador por alguém que não conhece você.
➤ Por favor não coloque o seu nome em parte alguma deste questionário.

A devolução deste questionário indica sua disposição de participar.

Muito obrigado,

Rob e Steve.

Versão 9-6B ☺

Pesquisa – Atitude para com o Dízimo
e Outras Questões da Igreja

Marque suas respostas no cartão de respostas.

Questão 01 Por favor faça um círculo na letra B da questão 01. (temos três versões desta pesquisa, você está respondendo a versão B, precisamos desta informação para entender suas respostas corretamente)

Questões 02 & 03: *Minha Faixa Etária:*
Qual a sua idade? (Se você tem 50 anos ou mais responda a questão 3):
Questão 02
A. Menos de 15
B. 15–19
C. 20–29
D. 30–39
E. 40–49

Questão 03
A. 50–59
B. 60–69
C. 70-79
D. Acima 80

Questão 04.   *Sou membro batizado* da Igreja Adventista do Sétimo Dia
A. Sim ➜ Ir para 05
B. Não ➜ Ir para 06

Questão 05. *Há quantos anos sou membro da Igreja Adventista:*
A. 0-1
B. 2–4
C. 5-9
D. 10-29
E. 30+

Questão 06.   *Frequento a Igreja Adventista*:
A. menos de 1 vez por mês
B. 1 vez por mês
C. 2 vezes por mês
D. 3 vezes por mês
E. o mês todo

Questão 07. *Hoje estou na igreja que frequento regularmente*:
A. Sim
B. Não

Questão 08. *Estou **empregado***:
A. Sim **Tempo integral**
B. Sim **Meio período**
C. Não (ir para A9)

Questão 09. Sou:
A. Autônomo
B. Assalariado/Remunerado pago **mensalmente**
C. Assalariado/Remunerado pago **quinzenalmente**
D. Assalariado/Remunerado pago **semanalmente**

Questão 10. ***Trabalho para a Igreja Adventista** ou uma de suas instituições*:
A. Sim
B. Não

B11. *Nível Educacional*
A. Ensino Fundamental
B. Ensino Médio
C. Bacharelado
D. Mestrado
E. Doutorado

Questões 12—14. *Estimativa de minha renda* (responda por mês).
Por mês (valor liquído):
Se você recebe R$1.669,00 ou menos, responda a questão 12.
Se você recebe entre R$1.670,00 a R$12.499,00 responda a questão 13.
Se você recebe mais de R$12.500,00 responda a questão 14.

Questão 12
A. Menos de R$170,00
B. R$170,00–R$332,00
C. R$333,00–R$749,00
D. R$750,00–R$1.159,00
E. R$1.160,00–R$1.669,00

Questão 13.
A. R$1.670,00–R$3.332,00
B. R$3.333,00–R$4.999,00
C. R$5.000,00–R$6.665,00
D. R$6.666,00–R$8.332,00
E. R$8.333,00–R$12.499,00

Questão 14.
A. R$12.500,00–R$16.665,00
B. R$16.666,00–R$20.800,00
C. Acima de R$20.800,00

Questão 15. *Nos últimos 12 meses, que porcentagem das minhas entradas, eu estimo ter devolvido como dizimo?*
A. 0%
B. menos de 4%
C. 5-7%
D. 8-9%
E. 10% ou +

Questão 16. *Minha intenção é devolver o dízimo:*
A. Semanalmente
B. Quinzenalmente
C. Mensalmente
D. Trimestralmente
E. Anualmente

Questão 17. *Algumas vezes esqueço de devolver o dízimo*
A. Não (eu nunca esqueço ou raramente esqueço) → Ir para 19
B. Sim → Ir para 18

Questão 18. *Visto que esqueço algumas vezes, creio que o número de vezes que de fato contribuo a **cada ano** é mais ou menos:*
A. 1-3 vezes
B. 4-6 vezes
C. 7-11 vezes
D. 12 ou mais vezes

Questão 19. *Devolvo 10% de minha renda total*
A. Sim → Ir para 33
B. Não → Ir para 20—32

Questões 20—32. *Atualmente não devolvo meu dízimo total ou não devolvo nada. As seguintes mudanças seriam necessárias antes de eu considerar devolver meu dízimo total.*
Preencha com a letra correspondente:
A = **Não** se aplica a você
D = Aplica se a você
Questão 20. Sei que deveria devolver o dízimo, mas necessito criar o hábito de devolvê-lo regularmente
Questão 21. Necessito de segurança financeira antes de entregar qualquer dinheiro à igreja
Questão 22. Eu preciso estar mais confiante de que o dinheiro que eu devolver de dízimo vai realmente para o lugar certo
Questão 23. A Igreja Adventista deveria possibilitar a ordenação das mulheres ao ministério do evangelho
Questão 24. A IASD necessita atualizar suas doutrinas e ideias para o tempo presente.
Questão 25. A Igreja Adventista deve voltar à sólida doutrina

Questão 26. Necessitamos de um pastor competente em nossa igreja local

Questão 27. A Igreja necessita tornar o culto relevante aos jovens de hoje

Questão 28. As Igrejas necessitam parar de fazer experiências com o culto e restaurar a devida reverência neste momento de adoração

Questão 29. Necessito ser convencido pela Bíblia que os *cristãos* devem devolver o dízimo.

Questão 30. Gostaria de devolver o dízimo, mas meu cônjuge é totalmente contra.

Questão 31. Eu preciso saber que se eu devolver o dizimo mais pastores serão empregados e eu verei um pastor mais frequentemente.

Questão 32. Creio que nada mudará o que eu faço com o dízimo

Questões 33-38. *Quanto você concorda com as seguintes declarações?*
Preencha com a letra correspondente:
A = discordo totalmente
B = discordo mais que concordo
C = concordo mais que discordo
D = concordo totalmente

Para ser adventista do sétimo dia, é *muito importante* se abster de …:
Questão 33. Álcool
Questão 34. Coca Cola, Pepsi, Red Bull etc
Questão 35. Carne
Questão 36. Chá preto e café
Questão 37. Fumo
Questão 38. Drogas ilegais

Verso da Página
(mais informação)

Quem são Rob e Steve?

Dr. Robert K. McIver, Professor Associado, é o Diretor da Escola de Ensino Superior de Ministério e Teologia do Avondale College, em Cooranbong NSW Austrália.

Dr Stephen J. Currow é diretor do Fulton College, Fiji.

Rob e Steve iniciaram a pesquisa sobre o dízimo, em 1999, quando ambos fizeram palestras na Faculdade de Teologia do Avondale College.

O que Estamos Fazendo?

Alguns dos líderes-chave da Associação Geral dos Adventistas do Sétimo Dia solicitaram que o Dr. Rob McIver e o Dr. Steve Currow realizassem a pesquisa quanto aos motivos para devolver o dízimo e seus padrões, em várias associações ao redor do mundo (a pesquisa está sendo financiada pelo Grupo de Trabalho de Planos para o Futuro).

A pesquisa anterior, realizada na Austrália, indica algumas tendências que poderiam ter implicações significativas para a Igreja Adventista em um futuro próximo. Necessitamos descobrir se os membros da Igreja Adventista, em outro países, têm padrões e motivos semelhantes.

Para descobrirmos isso necessitamos fazer perguntas para o maior número possível de pessoas que estejam dispostas a nos ajudar. Isso significa que lhe estamos pedindo para responder a esta pesquisa. Você verá que perguntamos não apenas a respeito do dízimo, mas de outras questões também. A pesquisa feita por outra pessoa indica que algumas delas podem estar relacionadas aos padrões de dizimar e ofertar. Não sabemos se elas são significativas para os adventistas em seu país até obtermos suas respostas. Nossos agradecimentos por sua disposição de ajudar ao responder às perguntas. Planejamos informar nossas descobertas em vários lugares, incluindo as publicações acadêmicas e da Igreja em geral. De forma alguma alguém será identificado.

Nota Especial. Aprovação da comissão de ética:

Visto que esta pesquisa envolve docentes do Avondale College, foi considerada a proposta da pesquisa, e aprovada, pela Human Research Ethics Committee *(Comissão de Ética de Pesquisa Humana do Avondale College). Essa comissão solicitou que a seguinte observação fosse incluída nos documentos entregues aos participantes:*

O Avondale College requer que todos os participantes sejam informados de que se tiverem qualquer reclamação quanto à forma pela qual o projeto de pesquisa está sendo conduzido, poderá ser feita ao pesquisador [neste caso, um dos membros do grupo de pesquisa – Pr. Lionel Smith, fone: (08) 9498 9127, ou Dr Rob McIver, (02) 4980-2226], se preferir uma pessoa independente, ao Secretário da Human Research Ethics Committee do Colégio, PO Box 19, Cooranbong, NSW 2265, ou telefone (02) 4980 2121 ou fax (02) 4980 2118.

Pesquisa – Atitude para com o Dízimo
e Outras Questões da Igreja

O culto e a missão são mais importantes do que o dinheiro nas prioridades da Igreja. Contudo, a falta de fundos reduz a capacidade da igreja cumprir seu propósito.

Esta pesquisa é muito **importante**. Ela é totalmente **confidencial**. Necessitamos ouvir os que devolvem o dízimo e os que não o fazem. Realmente desejamos conhecer sua opinião. Não podemos fazer isso sem a sua ajuda.

Qual é o propósito desta pesquisa?
A Associação Geral dos Adventistas do Sétimo Dia pediu ao Dr. Rob McIver e ao Dr. Steve Currow para realizarem uma pesquisa a respeito do dízimo em algumas Associações ao redor do mundo. Ela é importante para a Igreja e pedimos a você para preencher este questionário. (Há mais informação a respeito da pesquisa no final deste questionário.)

Não desejamos saber quem você é, e não faremos tentativas para saber.
Garantimos o caráter confidencial. Ninguém será identificado. Podemos garantir isso porque:
➢ Suas respostas estarão entre as várias milhares que serão armazenadas no computador. Consideraremos apenas o padrão geral dos resultados e não somente a resposta de um indivíduo.
➢ Os resultados da pesquisa certamente serão lançados no programa de computador por alguém que não conhece você.
➢ Por favor não coloque o seu nome em parte alguma deste questionário.

A devolução deste questionário indica sua disposição de participar.

Muito obrigado,

Rob e Steve.

Versão 9-6C ☺

Pesquisa – Atitude para com o Dízimo
e Outras Questões da Igreja

Marque suas respostas no cartão de respostas.

Questão 01 Por favor faça um círculo na letra C da questão 01. (temos três versões desta pesquisa, você está respondendo a versão C, precisamos desta informação para entender suas respostas corretamente)

Questões 02 & 03: *Minha Faixa Etária:*
Qual a sua idade? (Se você tem 50 anos ou mais responda a questão 3):
Questão 02
A. Menos de 15
B. 15–19
C. 20–29
D. 30–39
E. 40–49

Questão03
A. 50–59
B. 60–69
C. 70-79
D. Acima 80

Questão 04. Hoje estou na igreja que frequento regularmente:
A. Sim
B. Não

Questão 05. Nos últimos 12 meses, que porcentagem das minhas entradas, eu estimo
  ter devolvido como dizimo?
A. 0%
B. menos de 4%
C. 5-7%
D. 8-9%
E. 10% ou +

Questões 06—08. Estimativa de minha renda (responda por mês).
Por mês (valor líquido):
Se você recebe R$1.669,00 ou menos, responda a questão 06.
Se você recebe entre R$1.670,00 a R$12.499,00 responda a questão 07.
Se você recebe mais de R$12.500,00 responda a questão 08

Questão 06
A. Menos de R$170,00
B. R$170,00–R$332,00
C. R$333,00–R$749,00
D. R$750,00–R$1.159,00
E. R$1.160,00–R$1.669,00

Tithe Survey: BRAZIL Ver 9.6C   Page: 2

Questão 07.
A. R$1.670,00–R$3.332,00
B. R$3.333,00–R$4.999,00
C. R$5.000,00–R$6.665,00
D. R$6.666,00–R$8.332,00
E. R$8.333,00–R$12.499,00

Questão 08.
A. R$12.500,00–R$16.665,00
B. R$16.666,00–R$20.800,00
C. Acima de R$20.800,00

Questão 09. Nos últimos 12 meses devolvi o **dízimo** (preencha tudo o que se aplica):
A. no **envelope do dízimo,** em minha igreja local
B. mediante **desconto** no meu salário
C. faço através de depósito bancário.
D. diretamente ao **tesoureiro de minha igreja**
E. diretamente à **associação local**

Questões 10—21 A igreja adventista considera que ofertas e dízimos devem ser tratados de
    forma separada. As ofertas são dadas em adição aos dízimos. A igreja também sugere
    onde os dízimos e ofertas devem ser direcionados. Mas, essa pergunta é sobre o que
    você fez com seus dízimos e ofertas nos últimos 12 meses. Não o que você deveria ter
    feito. Preencha como explicado abaixo:
    Entenda que o A. significa que você deu **somente ofertas**
    Entenda que o B. significa que você deu **somente dízimos**
    Entenda que o C. siginifica que você **deu os dois: ofertas e dízimos**
Preencha o que se aplica a você:
Questão 10. para ofertas da **Escola Sabatina** .
Questão 11. a outros **apelos especiais** da igreja
Questão 12. para o fundo de **construção da igreja**
Questão 13. para â **sistema Educacional da IASD**
Questão14. a um **ministério adventista independente**
Questão 15. para apoiar um **jovem voluntário** de nossa igreja local
Questão 16. para patrocinar (ex: estudantes, pastores ou obreiros missionários)
Questão 17. ao **Orçamento/Oferta** igreja **local**
Questão 18. para a **ADRA**
Questão19. para necessidades em minha **terra natal**
Questão 20. para o **Exército da Salvação ou Cruz Vermelha**
Questão 21. diretamente para os **campos missionários**

Questões 22—28 *Quanto você concorda com as seguintes declarações?*
Preencha com a letra correspondente:
A = discordo totalmente
B = discordo mais que concordo
C = concordo mais que discordo
D = concordo totalmente
Questões 22—28 *Sinto que não é errado dar o dízimo . . .*
Questão 22... para **projetos especiais** (como a construção de uma igreja)
Questão 23 ... diretamente ao **campo missionário**

Questão 24 … para ajudar **obreiros voluntarios** que trabalham em minha igreja local

Questão 25 … para ofertas que apoiam a **escola adventista local**

Questão 26 … para **apelos especiais**, como a missão da igreja no exterior

Questão 27 … para ajudar pessoas necessitadas através da **ADRA**

Questão 28 … para ajudar pessoas necessitadas através da **Cruz Vermelha** ou do **Exército da Salvação**

Questão 29. *Minha intenção é devolver o dízimo:*

A. Semanalmente
B. Quinzenalmente
C. Mensalmente
D. Trimestralmente
E. Anualmente

Questão 30. *Algumas vezes esqueço de devolver o dízimo*

A. Sim ➔ Ir para 31
B. Não (eu nunca esqueço ou raramente esqueço) ➔ Ir para 32

Questão 31. *Visto que esqueço algumas vezes, creio que o número de vezes que de fato contribuo a cada ano é mais ou menos:*

A. 1-3 vezes
B. 4-6 vezes
C. 7-11 vezes
D. 12 ou mais vezes

Questões 32—37. *O que é verdade para você dos itens abaixo?*

A = nunca
B = poucas vezes
C = quase sempre
D = sempre
Você
Questão 32. Frequenta a **Escola Sabatina**
Questão 33. **Abre e encerra o seu sábado com culto do lar**
Questão 34. Estuda a **Lição da Escola Sabatina**
Questão 35. **Lê** e medita na **Bíblia** a cada dia
Questão 36. **Ora**, muitas vezes, durante o dia
Questão 37. **Reflete em temas espirituais** durante o dia

Muito obrigado por sua ajuda, você completou nossa pesquisa.

Verso da Página
(mais informação)

Quem são Rob e Steve?

Dr. Robert K. McIver, Professor Associado, é o Diretor da Escola de Ensino Superior de Ministério e Teologia do Avondale College, em Cooranbong NSW Austrália.

Dr Stephen J. Currow é diretor do Fulton College, Fiji.

Rob e Steve iniciaram a pesquisa sobre o dízimo, em 1999, quando ambos fizeram palestras na Faculdade de Teologia do Avondale College.

O que Estamos Fazendo?

Alguns dos líderes-chave da Associação Geral dos Adventistas do Sétimo Dia solicitaram que o Dr. Rob McIver e o Dr. Steve Currow realizassem a pesquisa quanto aos motivos para devolver o dízimo e seus padrões, em várias associações ao redor do mundo (a pesquisa está sendo financiada pelo Grupo de Trabalho de Planos para o Futuro).

A pesquisa anterior, realizada na Austrália, indica algumas tendências que poderiam ter implicações significativas para a Igreja Adventista em um futuro próximo. Necessitamos descobrir se os membros da Igreja Adventista, em outro países, têm padrões e motivos semelhantes.

Para descobrirmos isso necessitamos fazer perguntas para o maior número possível de pessoas que estejam dispostas a nos ajudar. Isso significa que lhe estamos pedindo para responder a esta pesquisa. Você verá que perguntamos não apenas a respeito do dízimo, mas de outras questões também. A pesquisa feita por outra pessoa indica que algumas delas podem estar relacionadas aos padrões de dizimar e ofertar. Não sabemos se elas são significativas para os adventistas em seu país até obtermos suas respostas. Nossos agradecimentos por sua disposição de ajudar ao responder às perguntas. Planejamos informar nossas descobertas em vários lugares, incluindo as publicações acadêmicas e da Igreja em geral. De forma alguma alguém será identificado.

Nota Especial. Aprovação da comissão de ética:

Visto que esta pesquisa envolve docentes do Avondale College, foi considerada a proposta da pesquisa, e aprovada, pela Human Research Ethics Committee *(Comissão de Ética de Pesquisa Humana do Avondale College). Essa comissão solicitou que a seguinte observação fosse incluída nos documentos entregues aos participantes:*

O Avondale College requer que todos os participantes sejam informados de que se tiverem qualquer reclamação quanto à forma pela qual o projeto de pesquisa está sendo conduzido, poderá ser feita ao pesquisador [neste caso, um dos membros do grupo de pesquisa – Pr. Lionel Smith, fone: (08) 9498 9127, ou Dr Rob McIver, (02) 4980-2226], se preferir uma pessoa independente, ao Secretário da Human Research Ethics Committee do Colégio, PO Box 19, Cooranbong, NSW 2265, ou telefone (02) 4980 2121 ou fax (02) 4980 2118.

C.5 Survey Used in Northern California (Version 9.7A/B/C)

Original format: A4 [Slightly scaled and then printed on US letter-sized paper]
Scaled: 80%
Note: This version is designed to be read electronically; the ID number is changed
on each individual survey.

Survey of Attitudes to Tithing
and Other Church Matters

Would you help? We are seeking to understand more about why and how people tithe and give to the church.

Worship and mission are much more important than money in the priorities of a Church. Yet lack of funds reduces the church's ability to fulfil its purpose.

This research is very **important**.
It is completely **confidential**.
We need to hear from both those who tithe and those who do not.
We really would like to know what you think.

We can't do this without your help.

What is this survey about?
The General Conference of Seventh-day Adventists has asked Dr Rob McIver and Dr Steve Currow to do some research on tithe in selected Conferences around the world. It is important to the Church, and we seek your help in filling out this questionnaire. (There is more information about this survey on the back page.)

We won't know who you are, and will make no attempt to find out
We guarantee confidentiality. No individual will ever be identified. We can guarantee this because:
➤ Your survey will be one of several thousand that will be fed into a computer. We will only look at the overall pattern of results, not at any one return.
➤ The results of the survey will almost certainly be entered by somebody who does not know you, or the people in the Church you attend.
➤ We ask you not to put your name anywhere on this questionnaire.

Returning this questionnaire indicates your willingness to participate.

Many thanks,

Rob and Steve.

Version 9-7A ☺

Instructions: Please shade in the appropriate circle:
Like this: ●, not like this: ⊘ ⊗ ⊘; and cross out mistakes ✗ ② ③ ●

A1. *My Age Group:*

○ Under 15   ○ 50–59

○ 15–19   ○ 60–69

○ 20–29   ○ 70-79

○ 30–39   ○ Over 80

○ 40–49

A2   Today I am attending the church that I usually attend:

Ⓨ **Yes**

Ⓝ No

A3. **I am employed by the SDA church** or one of its institutions:

Ⓨ Yes

Ⓝ **No**

*My estimated **income** in US dollars. Answer per year (qu. A4) **or** per semi-monthly / bi-weekly (qu. A5)*

A4. *My estimated **income** per **YEAR** (before tax)*

○ Under $1,000   ○ $30,000–$39,999

○ $1,000–$1,999   ○ $40,000–$49,999

○ $2,000–$4,499   ○ $50,000–$74,999

○ $4,500–$6,999   ○ $75,000–$99,999

○ $7,000–$9,999   ○ $100,000-$125,000

○ $10,000–$19,999   ○ Over $125,000

○ $20,000–$29,999

Go to question A6

A5. *My estimated **income** per **SEMI-MONTHLY or BI-WEEKLY** (take-home pay)*

○ Under $40   ○ $1,250–$1,665

○ $40-$79   ○ $1,666-$2,079

○ $80-$189   ○ $2,080–$3,124

○ $190-$289   ○ $3,125–$4,149

○ $290-$419   ○ $4,150–$5,199

○ $420-$829   ○ More than $5,200

○ $830–$1,249

A6. In the last 12 months, as a percentage of my income, I estimate that I have given as tithe:

- ○ 0%
- ○ Less than 2%
- ○ 2-4%
- ○ 5-7%
- ○ 8-9%
- ○ 10%
- ○ 11+%

To improve the accuracy of the survey results, some of the following questions are repeated with slight variations. Don't try to be consistent in your answers. Just answer each time according to your first impression.

How much do you agree with the following statements?

1 = strongly disagree
2 = disagree more than agree
3 = agree more than disagree
4 = strongly agree

Shade in one number for each question:

		1 = strongly disagree	2 = disagree more than agree	3 = agree more than disagree	4 = strongly agree
A7. God will protect me from future harm if I return tithe	A7	①	②	③	④
A8. I show my gratitude to God by returning tithe	A8	①	②	③	④
A9. If tithe is not pooled by the conference the bigger churches would have too much money and the smaller churches not enough	A9	①	②	③	④
A10. The Bible is clear that I should give 10% of my income as tithe	A10	①	②	③	④
A11. I need to contribute my tithe and offerings so the church can continue its work	A11	①	②	③	④
A12. The Bible provides detailed guidance for my life	A12	①	②	③	④
A13. I know that God has blessed me because I pay tithe	A13	①	②	③	④
A14. My local church feels like my extended family	A14	①	②	③	④
A15. I enjoy being an Adventist	A15	①	②	③	④
A16. Overall, my church pastor is doing a good job	A16	①	②	③	④
A17. I feel a strong commitment to the Seventh-day Adventist Church	A17	①	②	③	④
A18. I trust the handling and allocation of funds by the conference, union and division leaders	A18	①	②	③	④
A19. I believe the SDA church has a mission to the whole world	A19	①	②	③	④
A20. The Adventist Church has enough money to operate without my tithe	A20	①	②	③	④

Tithe Survey: USA Ver 9-7A   Page: 3

How much do you agree with the following statements?

1 = **strongly disagree**
2 = **disagree more than agree**
3 = **agree more than disagree**
4 = **strongly agree**

Shade in one number for each question:

		1 = strongly **disagree**	2 = disagree more than agree	3 = agree more than disagree	4 = strongly **agree**
A21. God is in control of everything in my life	A21	①	②	③	④
A22. The Bible teaches that tithe is my responsibility to God	A22	①	②	③	④
A23. I contribute tithe because God promises prosperity to those who tithe	A23	①	②	③	④
A24. God has given me so much and I return tithe out of appreciation	A24	①	②	③	④
A25. From the Bible I know that tithe does not belong to me, it is God's money already	A25	①	②	③	④
A26. I contribute tithe because I am often overwhelmed by how good God has been to me	A26	①	②	③	④
A27. If I give tithe God will answer my prayers	A27	①	②	③	④
A28. The Adventist Church already has enough money to do what it wants to do without my tithe	A28	①	②	③	④
A29. I know just about everybody that attends my local church	A29	①	②	③	④
A30. I contribute little or no tithe because the church already has enough money to do what it should	A30	①	②	③	④
A31. My local church is like one big family	A31	①	②	③	④

A32. I try to return tithe:

O   Weekly

O   Bi-weekly / Semi-monthly

O   Monthly

O   Quarterly

O   Yearly

A33. Sometimes I forget to return tithe

Ⓝ   No (I never forget, or only rarely) ➜ Go to question A35

Ⓨ   Yes ➜ Go to question A34

A34. Because I sometimes forget, I estimate that the number times **each year** I actually contribute tithe is about

- ○   1-3 times
- ○   4-6 times
- ○   7-11 times
- ○   12-17 times
- ○   18-24 times
- ○   25 –29 times
- ○   more than 30 times

A35 (Optional) The following question is **optional**: Rob & Steve, there are some things about tithe I would like to tell you that you have not really covered in your questionnaire:

_____

_____

_____

_____

> Just in case you are ever asked which version of the survey you have done ...
> ## This is a Version 9-7A survey.
> ## Remember the picture: ☺.

The Back Page
(more information)

Who are Rob and Steve?

Associate Professor Dr. Robert K. McIver is the Head of the School of Ministry and
Theology at Avondale College of Higher Education in Cooranbong NSW
Australia.

Dr Stephen J. Currow is principal of Fulton College, Fiji.

Rob and Steve first starting researching tithe in 1999 when they were both lecturers
together in the Faculty of Theology at Avondale College.

What we are doing

Some of the key leaders of the General Conference of Seventh-day Adventists (the
research is funded by the Future Plans Working Group) have asked Dr Rob McIver and Dr
Steve Currow to do some research into the motives for and patterns of tithing for several
conferences from around the World. Previous research in Australia indicate some trends that
could have very important implications for the Adventist church in the near future. We need
to find out whether Adventist Church members in other countries have similar giving patterns
and motives. To discover this we need to ask questions of as many people who are willing to
help us. This means we are asking you to answer the questions in this survey. You will see
that we have not only asked about tithe but a number of other things as well. The research
done by other people indicate that some of these may be related to patterns of giving. We
don't know if they are significant for Adventists in your country until we have asked you.
Many thanks for your willingness to help by answering these questions. We plan to report
our findings in a number of places, including Church publications and academic journals. We
will never do so in a form which will enable any one individual to be identified.

Special note re. ethics committee approval:

*As this research involves faculty of Avondale College, a research proposal has been
considered and approved by the Avondale College Human Research Ethics Committee. The
HREC asked that the following notice be included in the documents given to participants:*

Avondale College requires that all participants are informed that if they have any
complaint concerning the manner in which a research project is conducted it may be
given to the researcher [in this case – one of the members of the research group – Dr
Rob McIver, (02) 4980-2226 rob.mciver@hotmail.com], or if an independent person
is preferred, to the College's Human Research Ethics Committee Secretary, Avondale
College, PO Box 19, Cooranbong, NSW 2265, or phone (02) 4980 2121 or fax (02)
4980 2118.

Survey of Attitudes to Tithing and Other Church Matters

Would you help? We are seeking to understand more about why and how people tithe and give to the church.

Worship and mission are much more important than money in the priorities of a Church. Yet lack of funds reduces the church's ability to fulfil its purpose.

This research is very **important**.
It is completely **confidential**.
We need to hear from both those who tithe and those who do not.
We really would like to know what you think.

We can't do this without your help.

What is this survey about?
The General Conference of Seventh-day Adventists has asked Dr Rob McIver and Dr Steve Currow to do some research on tithe in selected Conferences around the world. It is important to the Church, and we seek your help in filling out this questionnaire. (There is more information about this survey on the back page.)

We won't know who you are, and will make no attempt to find out
We guarantee confidentiality. No individual will ever be identified. We can guarantee this because:
➢ Your survey will be one of several thousand that will be fed into a computer. We will only look at the overall pattern of results, not at any one return.
➢ The results of the survey will almost certainly be entered by somebody who does not know you, or the people in the Church you attend.
➢ We ask you not to put your name anywhere on this questionnaire.

Returning this questionnaire indicates your willingness to participate.

Many thanks,

Rob and Steve.

Version 9-7B ☺

Instructions: Please shade in the appropriate circle:
Like this: ●, not like this: ⊘ ⊗ ⊘; and cross out mistakes ✖ ② ③ ●

B1.   *My **Age** Group:*

○   Under 15   ○   50–59
○   15–19   ○   60–69
○   20–29   ○   70-79
○   30–39   ○   Over 80
○   40–49

B2.   *I am a member* of the Seventh-day Adventist church by baptism or profession of faith.

Ⓨ   **Yes** ➔ Go to question B3
Ⓝ   No ➔ Go to question B4

B3.   Number of years I have been a member of the Adventist Church

○   0-1   ○   20-29
○   2–4   ○   30-39
○   5-9   ○   40-49
○   10-19   ○   50+

B4.   *I **attend** an Adventist church*:

○   Every week/most weeks
○   2 to 3 times a month   ○   1 to 9 times per year
○   About once a month   ○   Rarely/never

B5.   Today I am attending the church that I usually attend:

Ⓨ   **Yes**
Ⓝ   No

B6.   In the last 2 years I have attended a GYC conference (shade "No" if you do have not heard of GYC conferences)

Ⓨ   Yes
Ⓝ   No

B7.   My **employment status**

Ⓨ   Employed **Full Time**
Ⓨ   Employed **Part Time**
Ⓝ   Retired (go to question B10)
Ⓝ   I am not currently employed (go to question B10)

B8.   I am:

○   Self Employed

○   Wage/Salary earner paid **monthly**

○   Wage/Salary earner paid **bi-weekly/bi-monthly**

○   Wage/Salary earner paid **weekly**

B9.   **I am employed by the SDA church** or one of its institutions:

Ⓨ   Yes

Ⓝ   **No**

B10.   *My **Education*** (shade "highest" you have completed)

○   High School Diploma or G.E.D.

○   Trade Certificate / Trade Licence

○   Associate Degree

○   Bachelor Degree

○   Master Degree

○   Doctoral Degree

*My estimated **income** in US dollars. Answer **either** per year (qu. B11) **or** per semi-monthly / bi-weekly (qu. B12)*

B11.   *My estimated **income** per **YEAR** (before tax)*

○ Under $1,000	○ $30,000–$39,999
○ $1,000–$1,999	○ $40,000–$49,999
○ $2,000–$4,499	○ $50,000–$74,999
○ $4,500–$6,999	○ $75,000–$99,999
○ $7,000–$9,999	○ $100,000–$125,000
○ $10,000–$19,999	○ Over $125,000
○ $20,000–$29,999	

Go to question B13

B12.   *My estimated **income** per **SEMI-MONTHLY or BI-WEEKLY** (take-home pay)*

○ Under $40	○ $1,250–$1,665
○ $40–$79	○ $1,666–$2,079
○ $80–$189	○ $2,080–$3,124
○ $190–$289	○ $3,125–$4,149
○ $290–$419	○ $4,150–$5,199
○ $420–$829	○ More than $5,200
○ $830–$1,249	

Tithe Survey: USA Ver 9-7B   Page: 9

Survey ID: 82101 |||||| |||||| || |||| |||||||| || ||| || |||| ||||| |||| ||| |||||

B13. In the last 12 months, as a percentage of my income, I estimate that I have given as tithe:

- ○ 0%
- ○ <2%
- ○ 2-4%
- ○ 5-7%
- ○ 8-9%
- ○ 10%
- ○ 11+%

B14. I try to return tithe:

- ○ Weekly
- ○ Semi-monthly / bi-weekly
- ○ Monthly
- ○ Quarterly
- ○ Yearly

B15. Sometimes I forget to return tithe

- (N) No (I never forget, or only rarely) ➔ Go to question B17
- (Y) Yes ➔ Go to question B16

B16. Because I sometimes forget, I estimate that the number times **each year** I actually contribute tithe is about

- ○ 1-3 times
- ○ 4-6 times
- ○ 7-11 times
- ○ 12-17 times
- ○ 18-24 times
- ○ 25 –29 times
- ○ more than 30 times

B17. I tithe a full 10% of my income

- (Y) Yes ➔ Go to question B19
- (N) No ➔ Go to question B18

B18. I do not currently give a full tithe, or do not give tithe. The following changes would need to happen before I would consider returning a full tithe [shade as many of the following as are true for you; there are more options on the next page]:

- ○ I think I should tithe, but I need to get into the habit of tithing regularly
- ○ I need to be fully financially secure before I can give any money to the church
- ○ I need to be more confident that money I give as tithe actually makes it to the right place
- ○ The Adventist Church should make it possible to ordain women to the Gospel ministry
- ○ The Adventist Church needs to bring its doctrines and ideas into the 21st century
- ○ The Adventist Church needs to return to the plain truth of historic Adventism
- ○ We need a competent pastor in our local church
- ○ The Church needs to make its worship relevant to today's youth

○   Churches need to stop experimenting with worship, and restore proper reverence in worship

○   I need to be convinced from the Bible that *Christians* should return tithe

○   I think I should tithe, but my spouse is very strongly against giving tithe.

○   I need to know that if I tithe, more pastors will be employed and I will see a pastor more often

○   Other _____

○   I don't think anything would change what I do about tithing

How much do you agree with the following statements?

1 = strongly **disagree**
2 = disagree more than agree
3 = agree more than disagree
4 = strongly **agree**

To be a Seventh-day Adventist, it is *very important* to abstain from:

		1	2	3	4
B19. Alcohol (e.g. Beer, Wine, Spirits)	B19	①	②	③	④
B20. Coca Cola, Pepsi, Red Bull, etc	B20	①	②	③	④
B21. Eating meat	B21	①	②	③	④
B22. Tea and Coffee	B22	①	②	③	④
B23. Smoking	B23	①	②	③	④
B24. Illegal drugs	B24	①	②	③	④

B25. *My **gender**:*

Ⓕ   Female

Ⓜ   Male

B26. Do I have children that are of school age?

Ⓝ   No

Ⓨ   Yes – they attend an Adventist School

Ⓨ   Yes – they attend a Public School

Ⓨ   Yes – they are homeschooled

Ⓨ   Yes – other _____

B27. One or more of my **parents worked for the Seventh-day Adventist church** while I was growing up

(N)   **No**

(Y)   Yes

B28. I am a **student**:

(N)   No

(Y)   Yes➔ I study **Full Time**

(Y)   Yes➔ I study **Part Time**

B29. For purchases between $10 and $49, I would usually use [shade all that apply]

O   Cash

O   Debit Card

O   Credit Card

O   Check

O   Other: _____

B30. For purchases between $50 and $150, I would usually use [shade all that apply]

O   Cash

O   Debit Card

O   Credit Card

O   Check

O   Other: _____

B31. I have a personal budget

(Y)   Yes – I follow it very carefully

(Y)   Yes – I follow it usually

(Y)   Yes – but I do not follow it really

(N)   No

B32 (optional). The following question is **optional**: Rob & Steve, there are some things about tithe I would like to tell you that you have not really covered in your questionnaire:

_____

_____

> Just in case you are ever asked which version of the survey have done ...
>
> This is a Version 9-7B survey.
>
> Remember the picture: 🔔

The Back Page
(more information)

Who are Rob and Steve?

Associate Professor Dr. Robert K. McIver is the Head of the School of Ministry and
    Theology at Avondale College of Higher Education in Cooranbong NSW
    Australia.

Dr Stephen J. Currow is principal of Fulton College, Fiji.

Rob and Steve first starting researching tithe in 1999 when they were both lecturers
    together in the Faculty of Theology at Avondale College.

What we are doing

Some of the key leaders of the General Conference of Seventh-day Adventists (the
research is funded by the Future Plans Working Group) have asked Dr Rob McIver and Dr
Steve Currow to do some research into the motives for and patterns of tithing for several
conferences from around the World. Previous research in Australia indicate some trends that
could have very important implications for the Adventist church in the near future. We need
to find out whether Adventist Church members in other countries have similar giving patterns
and motives. To discover this we need to ask questions of as many people who are willing to
help us. This means we are asking you to answer the questions in this survey. You will see
that we have not only asked about tithe but a number of other things as well. The research
done by other people indicate that some of these may be related to patterns of giving. We
don't know if they are significant for Adventists in your country until we have asked you.
Many thanks for your willingness to help by answering these questions. We plan to report
our findings in a number of places, including Church publications and academic journals. We
will never do so in a form which will enable any one individual to be identified.

Special note re. ethics committee approval:

*As this research involves faculty of Avondale College, a research proposal has been
considered and approved by the Avondale College Human Research Ethics Committee. The
HREC asked that the following notice be included in the documents given to participants:*

Avondale College requires that all participants are informed that if they have any
complaint concerning the manner in which a research project is conducted it may be
given to the researcher [in this case – one of the members of the research group – Dr
Rob McIver, (02) 4980-2226 rob.mciver@hotmail.com], or if an independent person
is preferred, to the College's Human Research Ethics Committee Secretary, Avondale
College, PO Box 19, Cooranbong, NSW 2265, or phone (02) 4980 2121 or fax (02)
4980 2118.

Survey of Attitudes to Tithing and Other Church Matters

Would you help? We are seeking to understand more about why and how people tithe and give to the church.

Worship and mission are much more important than money in the priorities of a Church. Yet lack of funds reduces the church's ability to fulfil its purpose.

This research is very **important**.
It is completely **confidential**.
We need to hear from both those who tithe and those who do not.
We really would like to know what you think.

We can't do this without your help.

What is this survey about?
The General Conference of Seventh-day Adventists has asked Dr Rob McIver and Dr Steve Currow to do some research on tithe in selected Conferences around the world. It is important to the Church, and we seek your help in filling out this questionnaire. (There is more information about this survey on the back page.)

We won't know who you are, and will make no attempt to find out
We guarantee confidentiality. No individual will ever be identified. We can guarantee this because:
➢ Your survey will be one of several thousand that will be fed into a computer. We will only look at the overall pattern of results, not at any one return.
➢ The results of the survey will almost certainly be entered by somebody who does not know you, or the people in the Church you attend.
➢ We ask you not to put your name anywhere on this questionnaire.

Returning this questionnaire indicates your willingness to participate.

Many thanks,

Rob and Steve.

Version 9-7C ☺

Instructions: Please shade in the appropriate circle:
Like this: ●, not like this: ⊘ ⊗ ⊘; and cross out mistakes ✖ ② ③ ●

C1. *My **Age** Group:*

○ Under 15   ○ 50–59
○ 15–19   ○ 60–69
○ 20–29   ○ 70-79
○ 30–39   ○ Over 80
○ 40–49

C2 Today I am attending the church that I usually attend:

Ⓨ **Yes**
Ⓝ No

C3. **I am employed by the SDA church** or one of its institutions:

Ⓨ Yes
Ⓝ **No**

*My estimated **income** in US dollars. Answer per year (qu. C4) **or** per semi-monthly / bi-weekly (qu. C5)*

C4. *My estimated **income** per **YEAR** (before tax)*

○ Under $1,000   ○ $30,000–$39,999
○ $1,000–$1,999   ○ $40,000–$49,999
○ $2,000–$4,499   ○ $50,000–$74,999
○ $4,500–$6,999   ○ $75,000–$99,999
○ $7,000–$9,999   ○ $100,000-$125,000
○ $10,000–$19,999   ○ Over $125,000
○ $20,000–$29,999

Go to question C6

C5. *My estimated **income** per **SEMI-MONTHLY or BI-WEEKLY** (take-home pay)*

○ Under $40   ○ $1,250–$1,665
○ $40-$79   ○ $1,666-$2,079
○ $80-$189   ○ $2,080–$3,124
○ $190-$289   ○ $3,125–$4,149
○ $290-$419   ○ $4,150–$5,199
○ $420–$829   ○ More than $5,200
○ $830–$1,249

Tithe Survey: USA Ver 9-7C   Page: 15

C6.   In the last 12 months, as a percentage of my income, I estimate that I have given as tithe:

○   0%

○   <2%

○   2-4%

○   5-7%

○   8-9%

○   10%

○   11+%

C7.   In the last 12 months I have given **tithe** (shade all that apply):
To the Conference through:

○   the **tithe envelope** in my local church

○   **Adventist e-giving**

○   Directly to my **church treasurer**

○   Directly to the **local Conference**

○   Directly to the **Union Conference / NAD Division / General Conference**

C8:   The Seventh-day Adventist Church considers that tithes and offerings should be treated separately. Offerings are given *in addition to* tithe. The Church also suggests where tithes and offerings should be directed. But this question is about what you *actually* do with your tithes and offerings, *not* what you should be doing. Next to each of the list below, fill in:

the ⊚ circle for where you have given **offerings**;

the Ⓣ circle for where you have given **tithe**.

Shade all that apply (you may shade both ⊚ and Ⓣ if needed) and leave blank those that do not apply:

⊚ Ⓣ   to the **local** church **Budget/offering**

⊚ Ⓣ   to the **Church Building** Program

⊚ Ⓣ   to the local **SDA school / Education** offering

⊚ Ⓣ   to an **independent Adventist ministry** (e.g. Amazing Facts, It Is Written, Maranatha, Hope Chanel, etc.)

⊚ Ⓣ   to support a **youth worker or Bible worker** in our local church

⊚ Ⓣ   to supporting local pastors

⊚ Ⓣ   to **Adventist Community Services** or **ADRA**

⊚ Ⓣ   to local church based **appeals**

⊚ Ⓣ   to needs in **my country of origin or conference of origin**

⊚ Ⓣ   directly to overseas **mission field**

⊚ Ⓣ   to **Conference Advance**

⊚ Ⓣ   to a **non-SDA Christian ministry** (e.g. the Salvation Army, World Vision)

⊚ Ⓣ   to **non-SDA charity or non-profit** organisation (e.g. Red Cross, American Cancer Society, United Way, etc)

⊚ Ⓣ   Other _____

How much do you agree with the following statements?

1 = **strongly disagree**
2 = **disagree more than agree**
3 = **agree more than disagree**
4 = **strongly agree**

Shade in one number for each question:

		1 = strongly **disagree**	2 = disagree more than agree	3 = agree more than disagree	4 = strongly **agree**
I feel there is nothing wrong in giving tithe ...					
C9. to **special projects** (such as a new church building)	C9	①	②	③	④
C10. directly to an overseas **mission field**	C10	①	②	③	④
C11 to assist **volunteers** working in my local church	C11	①	②	③	④
C12. to the offering that supports the **local SDA school**	C12	①	②	③	④
C13. to help needy people through **Adventist Community Services** or **ADRA**	C13	①	②	③	④

C14. I try to return tithe:

O   Weekly
O   Semi-monthly / bi-weekly
O   Monthly
O   Quarterly
O   Yearly

C15. Sometimes I forget to return tithe

Ⓝ   No (I never forget, or only rarely) ➔ Go to question C17
Ⓨ   Yes ➔ Go to question C16

C16. Because I sometimes forget, I estimate that the number times **each year** I actually contribute tithe is about

O   1-3 times   O   18-24 times
O   4-6 times   O   25 –29 times
O   7-11 times   O   more than 30 times
O   12-17 times

Which of the following is true of you?
(1 = never; 2 = sometimes; 3 = often; 4 = always/ almost always)

		1 = never	2 = sometimes	3 = often	4 = almost always
Do you?:					
C17. Attend **Sabbath school**	C17	①	②	③	④
C18. **Open and close Sabbath**	C18	①	②	③	④
C19. Study the **Sabbath School Quarterly**	C19	①	②	③	④
C20. **Read** and reflect on the **Bible** each day	C20	①	②	③	④
C21. **Pray** often during the day	C21	①	②	③	④
C22. **Reflect on spiritual things** during the day	C22	①	②	③	④
C23. Attend **prayer meetings** or **small group meetings**	C23	①	②	③	④

C24. The number of times that I have heard a sermon on tithing or giving in the last 2 years:

⓪ 0 times   ③ 3 times
① 1 time   ④ 4 times
② 2 times   ⑤ 5/more than 5 times

C25. I have held office in my local church in the last 12 months:
Ⓨ Yes
Ⓝ No

C26. *Am I currently **married?***:
Ⓝ No
Ⓨ Yes: My partner attends the same congregation as I do
Ⓨ Yes: My partner does **not** attend the same congregation as I do, but does attend another Christian congregation
Ⓨ Yes: My partner does **not** attend the same congregation as I do, nor any other Christian congregation

C27. *I return tithe because it is something my parents taught me to do*

Ⓝ   No

Ⓨ   Yes

C28. *I **attend** an Adventist church*:

◯   Every week/most weeks

◯   2 to 3 times a month

◯   About once a month

◯   1 to 9 times per year

◯   Rarely/never

C29. *For purchases between $10 and $49, I would usually use [shade all that apply]*

◯   Cash

◯   Debit Card

◯   Credit Card

◯   Check

◯   Other: _____

C30. *For purchases between $50 and $150, I would usually use [shade all that apply]*

◯   Cash

◯   Debit Card

◯   Credit Card

◯   Check

◯   Other: _____

B31. I have a personal budget

Ⓨ   Yes – I follow it very carefully

Ⓨ   Yes – I follow it usually

Ⓨ   Yes – but I do not follow it really

Ⓝ   No

The following question is **optional**: C32. Rob & Steve, there are some things about tithe I would like to tell you that you have not really covered in your questionnaire:

_____

_____

Just in case you are ever asked which version of the surve
have done …

This is a Version 9-7C survey.
Remember the picture:

The Back Page
(more information)

Who are Rob and Steve?

Associate Professor Dr. Robert K. McIver is the Head of the School of Ministry and
   Theology at Avondale College of Higher Education in Cooranbong NSW
   Australia.

Dr Stephen J. Currow is principal of Fulton College, Fiji.

Rob and Steve first starting researching tithe in 1999 when they were both lecturers
   together in the Faculty of Theology at Avondale College.

What we are doing

*Some of the key leaders of the General Conference of Seventh-day Adventists (the
research is funded by the Future Plans Working Group) have asked Dr Rob McIver and Dr
Steve Currow to do some research into the motives for and patterns of tithing for several
conferences from around the World. Previous research in Australia indicate some trends that
could have very important implications for the Adventist church in the near future. We need
to find out whether Adventist Church members in other countries have similar giving patterns
and motives. To discover this we need to ask questions of as many people who are willing to
help us. This means we are asking you to answer the questions in this survey. You will see
that we have not only asked about tithe but a number of other things as well. The research
done by other people indicate that some of these may be related to patterns of giving. We
don't know if they are significant for Adventists in your country until we have asked you.
Many thanks for your willingness to help by answering these questions. We plan to report
our findings in a number of places, including Church publications and academic journals.
We will never do so in a form which will enable any one individual to be identified.*

Special note re. ethics committee approval:

*As this research involves faculty of Avondale College, a research proposal has been
considered and approved by the Avondale College Human Research Ethics Committee. The
HREC asked that the following notice be included in the documents given to participants:*

Avondale College requires that all participants are informed that if they have any
complaint concerning the manner in which a research project is conducted it may be
given to the researcher [in this case – one of the members of the research group – Dr
Rob McIver, (02) 4980-2226 rob.mciver@hotmail.com], or if an independent person
is preferred, to the College's Human Research Ethics Committee Secretary, Avondale
College, PO Box 19, Cooranbong, NSW 2265, or phone (02) 4980 2121 or fax (02)
4980 2118.

Appendix D: Report on Survey Demographics and Reported Tithing Behavior — Aggregated Data from Four Conferences representing Four Countries

Note on Sequencing of Tables: The following tables have been arranged in roughly the order by which they have been entered as variables in SPSS. The variable names are closely related to the questions found in Version 7.1 for Western Australia (see Appendix C.1). In this way, Da1 identifies an items related to demographics ("D") and the item is found in section A of the survey, and is item 1 ("a1"). Similarly, Da2 is item 2 in section A of Version 7.1 of the survey. Variations in total number of responses to a given question arise from several factors, such as the fact that not all respondents answered every question, and that not every question is asked in every version of the survey (especially those used in Brazil and the United States, where the three versions of the survey did ask some common questions, but where most questions were unique to that version, thus could be answered by only 1/3 of the participants in that country).

Country * Da1age My age-group Crosstabulation

		Da1age My age-group							Total
		20-29	30-39	40-49	50-59	60-69	70-79	≥ 80	
Country	Australia (WAC)	231	256	293	322	271	210	77	1660
	England (SEC)	66	119	216	278	178	103	95	1055
	Brazil (SPC)	353	496	440	344	198	119	23	1973
	USA (NCC)	216	338	483	698	748	503	384	3370
	Total	866	1209	1432	1642	1395	935	579	8058

Country * Da2aatten I attend an Adventist church Crosstabulation

		Da2aatten I attend an Adventist church					Total
		Rarely / never	1 to 9 times per year	About once a month	2 to 3 times a month	Every week / most weeks	
Country	Australia (WAC)	5	21	37	71	1487	1621
	England (SEC)	6	7	19	70	899	1001
	Brazil (SPC)	10	8	25	133	904	1080
	USA (NCC)	10	23	39	241	1907	2220
	Total	31	59	120	515	5197	5922

Country * Da3bapt I am a baptized member of the Seventh-day Adventist Church Crosstabulation

		Da3bapt I am a baptized member of the Seventh-day Adventist Church		Total
		No	Yes	
Country	Australia (WAC)	110	1532	1642
	England (SEC)	37	337	374
	Brazil (SPC)	40	449	489
	USA (NCC)	38	987	1025
	Total	225	3305	3530

Country * Da3bnumbe Number of years I have been a member of the SDA church Crosstabulation

		Da3bnumbe Number of years I have been a member of the SDA church								Total
		0-1	2-4	5-9	10-19	20-29	30-39	40-49	≥ 50	
Country	Australia (WAC)	30	53	118	292	295	250	260	217	1515
	England (SEC)	37	92	94	200	187	151	101	72	934
	USA (NCC)	31	59	61	102	132	174	186	359	1104
	Total	98	204	273	594	614	575	547	648	3553

Country * Da3bnumbe Number of years I have been a member of the SDA church Crosstabulation

	Da3bnumbe Number of years I have been a member of the SDA church					Total
	0-1	2-4	5-9	10-29	30+	
Brazil (SPC)	64	49	57	218	155	543

Country * Yearly Income in equivalent US$ Crosstabulation

		Yearly Income in equivalent US$						
		Under US$1,000	US$1,000-$1,999	US$2,000-$4,499	US$4,500-$6,999	US$7,000-$9,999	US$10,000-$19,999	US$20,000-$29,999
Country	Australia (WAC)	N/A	N/A	N/A	N/A	152	386	296
	England (SEC)	22	11	17	73	110	137	154
	Brazil (SPC)	130	64	142	242	246	400	206
	USA (NCC)	120	93	69	64	146	333	447
	Total	272	168	228	379	654	1256	1103

Country * Yearly Income in equivalent US$ Crosstabulation (Continued)

		US$30,000-$39,999	US$40,000-$49,999	US$50,000-$74,999	US$75,000-$99,999	US$100,000-$125,000	Over $125,000	Total
Country	Australia (WAC)	171	122	190	32	0	0	1349
	England (SEC)	67	91	51	6	4	0	743
	Brazil (SPC)	113	64	53	25	11	17	1713
	USA (NCC)	390	298	531	282	208	293	3274
	Total	741	575	825	345	223	310	7079

Da1age My age-group * Da2aatten I attend an Adventist church Crosstabulation

		Rarely / never	1 to 9 times per year	About once a month	2 to 3 times a month	Every week / most weeks	Total
Da1age My age-group	20-29	3	9	17	74	508	611
	30-39	7	13	16	99	737	872
	40-49	4	13	30	116	894	1057
	50-59	11	9	21	92	1085	1218
	60-69	2	5	17	87	922	1033
	70-79	3	6	14	33	652	708
	≥ 80	1	4	5	14	399	423
	Total	31	59	120	515	5197	5922

Da1age My age-group * Da3bapt I am a baptized member of the Seventh-day Adventist Church Crosstabulation

		No	Yes	Total
Da1age My age-group	20-29	61	330	391
	30-39	36	515	551
	40-49	43	590	633
	50-59	38	644	682
	60-69	31	597	628
	70-79	11	407	418
	≥ 80	5	222	227
	Total	225	3305	3530

Da1age My age-group * Da3bnumbe Number of years I have been a member of the SDA church Crosstabulation

		Da3bnumbe Number of years I have been a member of the SDA church								Total
		0-1	2-4	5-9	10-19	20-29	30-39	40-49	≥ 50	
Da1age My age-group	20-29	29	65	98	144	44	0	0	0	380
	30-39	35	52	71	211	155	62	1	1	588
	40-49	31	35	61	168	197	167	86	2	747
	50-59	37	45	42	133	179	158	192	75	861
	60-69	19	34	31	90	110	123	154	182	743
	70-79	10	12	21	46	59	49	85	213	495
	≥ 80	1	10	6	20	25	16	29	175	282
Total		162	253	330	812	769	575	547	648	4096

Country * a4employBrEnKeOzUs Crosstabulation

		a4employBrEnKeOzUs				Total
		Employed full time	Employed part time	Retired	Not currently employed	
Country	Australia (WAC)	416	285	492	193	1386
	England (SEC)	424	191	0	274	889
	Brazil (SPC)	186	287	0	97	570
	USA (NCC)	468	181	377	100	1126
	Total	1494	944	869	664	3971

Country * a4wageBrEnKeOzUs Self-employed or Wage-earner Crosstabulation

		a4wageBrEnKeOzUs Self-employed or Wage-earner				Total
		Self-employed	Wage/Salary earner paid monthly	Wage/Salary earner paid fortnightly/semi-monthly	Wage/Salary earner paid weekly	
Country	England (SEC)	78	465	16	79	638
	Brazil (SPC)	164	284	50	8	506
	USA (NCC)	148	125	412	31	716
	Total	390	874	478	118	1860

Country * 02 A7 If I work for SDA church Crosstabulation

		02 A7 If I work for SDA church		Total
		No - Does not work for SDA Church	Yes - Does work for SDA Church	
Country	Australia (WAC)	1362	130	1492
	England (SEC)	487	19	506
	Brazil (SPC)	471	83	554
	USA (NCC)	2589	326	2915
Total		4909	558	5467

Country * Da8educat Highest Level of Education Obtained Crosstabulation

Count

		Da8educat Highest Level of Education Obtained								Total
		Primary School	Year 10, High School	Year 12, High School	Trade Certificate	TAFE Certificate/Diploma/ Associate Degree	Bachelors Degree	Masters Degree	Doctoral Degree	
Country	Australia (WAC)	112	282	190	125	404	308	39	9	1469
	England (SEC)	34	99	91	153	257	191	97	10	932
	Brazil (SPC)	82	207	179	21	5	0	0	0	494
	USA (NCC)	0	0	271	142	199	288	128	88	1116
	Total	228	588	731	441	865	787	264	107	4011

Country * Da10gende What is your gender? Crosstabulation

		Da10gende What is your gender?		Total
		female	male	
Country	Australia (WAC)	889	653	1542
	England (SEC)	579	321	900
	USA (NCC)	594	465	1059
Total		2062	1439	3501

Country * Da11marr I am currently married Crosstabulation

Count

		Da11marr I am currently married		Total
		No - Not Married	Yes - Married	
Country	Australia (WAC)	413	1217	1630
	England (SEC)	315	497	812
	USA (NCC)	410	627	1037
Total		1138	2341	3479

Country * Da11aprtn Does your partner attend the same congregation as you do?
Crosstabulation

| | | Da11aprtn Does your partner attend the same congregation as you do? | | | Total |
		Not married	no - Partner Does not attend the same Congregation	Yes - Partner Does attend same congregation	
Country	Australia (WAC)	415	196	969	1580
	England (SEC)	315	115	382	812
	USA (NCC)	410	85	542	1037
	Total	1140	396	1893	3429

Country * Qa13paren One or both of my parents was/were/are Seventh-day Adventists
Crosstabulation

| | | Qa13paren One or both of my parents was/were/are Seventh-day Adventists | | Total |
		No	Yes	
Country	Australia (WAC)	521	1085	1606
	England (SEC)	301	582	883
	Total	822	1667	2489

Country * Qa14worke One or more of my parents worked for the Seventh-day Adventist church while I was growing up Crosstabulation

| | | Qa14worke One or more of my parents worked for the Seventh-day Adventist church while I was growing up | | Total |
		No	Yes	
Country	Australia (WAC)	1295	253	1548
	England (SEC)	700	167	867
	USA (NCC)	893	217	1110
	Total	2888	637	3525

Country * 01 Tithe given as percent of income Crosstabulation

| | | 01 Tithe given as percent of income | | | | | | | Total |
		0%	<2%	2-4%	5-7%	8-9%	10%	11+%	
Country	Australia (WAC)	127	90	75	84	84	938	81	1479
	England (SEC)	103	93	73	72	67	425	91	924
	Brazil (SPC)	220	0	142	140	443	877	0	1822
	USA (NCC)	190	200	186	256	161	1800	451	3244
	Total	640	383	476	552	755	4040	623	7469

Country * b46 I try to return tithe Crosstabulation

		b46 I try to return tithe					Total
		Weekly	Semi-Monthly / bi-weekly / fortnightly	Monthly	Quarterly	Yearly	
Country	Australia (WAC)	395	745	69	147	175	1531
	England (SEC)	211	34	610	39	16	910
	Brazil (SPC)	116	122	1452	43	7	1740
	USA (NCC)	210	521	1126	258	122	2237
Total		932	1422	3257	487	320	6418

Country * b47a Sometimes I forget to tithe Crosstabulation

		b47a Sometimes I forget to tithe		Total
		No	Yes	
Country	Australia (WAC)	1007	508	1515
	England (SEC)	496	130	626
	Brazil (SPC)	803	595	1398
	USA (NCC)	2081	846	2927
Total		4387	2079	6466

Country * b47b Number of times contribute tithe each year Crosstabulation

		b47b Number of times contribute tithe each year							Total
		1-3 times	4-6 times	7-11 times	12-17 times	18-24 times	25-29 times	≥ 30 times	
Country	Australia (WAC)	122	80	62	44	50	31	94	483
	England (SEC)	123	68	84	45	16	9	49	394
	Brazil (SPC)	182	138	174	251	2	0	0	747
	USA (NCC)	232	144	223	289	110	73	167	1238
Total		659	430	543	629	178	113	310	2862

Country * d01 No of sermons on tithing or giving in last 12 months Crosstabulation

		d01 No of sermons on tithing or giving in last 12 months						Total
		0 times	1 time	2 times	3 times	4 times	≥ 5 times	
Country	Australia (WAC)	343	464	366	126	99	81	1479
	England (SEC)	238	166	138	91	158	77	868
	USA (NCC)	181	230	267	123	82	168	1051
Total		762	860	771	340	339	326	3398

Da1age My age-group * 01 Tithe given as percent of income Crosstabulation

| | | 01 Tithe given as percent of income | | | | | | | Total |
		0%	<2%	2-4%	5-7%	8-9%	10%	11+%	
Da1age My age-group	20-29	128	68	85	63	104	338	20	806
	30-39	145	79	97	90	145	530	45	1131
	40-49	136	71	94	136	162	660	87	1346
	50-59	116	77	101	112	147	829	142	1524
	60-69	71	53	60	93	119	758	141	1295
	70-79	37	29	28	40	61	548	103	846
	≥ 80	7	6	11	18	17	377	85	521
Total		640	383	476	552	755	4040	623	7469

Da1age My age-group * b46 I try to return tithe Crosstabulation

| | | b46 I try to return tithe | | | | | Total |
		Weekly	Semi-Monthly / bi-weekly / fortnightly	Monthly	Quarterly	Yearly	
Da1age My age-group	20-29	106	168	355	53	42	724
	30-39	145	225	539	51	56	1016
	40-49	160	268	587	87	57	1159
	50-59	215	295	628	102	73	1313
	60-69	165	265	527	79	51	1087
	70-79	90	151	355	72	28	696
	≥ 80	51	50	266	43	13	423
Total		932	1422	3257	487	320	6418

Da1age My age-group * b47a Sometimes I forget to tithe Crosstabulation

| | | b47a Sometimes I forget to tithe | | Total |
		No	Yes	
Da1age My age-group	20-29	348	360	708
	30-39	555	421	976
	40-49	739	399	1138
	50-59	935	386	1321
	60-69	839	285	1124
	70-79	581	156	737
	≥ 80	390	72	462
Total		4387	2079	6466

Da1age My age-group * b47b Number of times contribute tithe each year Crosstabulation

		b47b Number of times contribute tithe each year							Total
		1-3 times	4-6 times	7-11 times	12-17 times	18-24 times	25-29 times	≥ 30 times	
Da1age My age-group	20-29	120	87	92	63	24	13	42	441
	30-39	154	76	113	95	33	14	47	532
	40-49	130	87	102	113	36	17	49	534
	50-59	116	86	92	121	39	26	67	547
	60-69	74	54	85	94	26	31	63	427
	70-79	48	29	43	69	12	8	27	236
	≥ 80	17	11	16	74	8	4	15	145
Total		659	430	543	629	178	113	310	2862

Da1age My age-group * d01 No of sermons on tithing or giving in last 12 months Crosstabulation

		d01 No of sermons on tithing or giving in last 12 months						Total
		0 times	1 time	2 times	3 times	4 times	≥ 5 times	
Da1age My age-group	20-29	76	83	86	37	26	32	340
	30-39	71	121	108	50	44	52	446
	40-49	129	156	136	54	78	60	613
	50-59	169	184	168	84	88	65	758
	60-69	146	166	135	66	58	61	632
	70-79	103	94	90	32	28	41	388
	≥ 80	68	56	48	17	17	15	221
Total		762	860	771	340	339	326	3398

Da1age My age-group * 01 Tithe given as percent of income Crosstabulation

		01 Tithe given as percent of income							Total
		0%	<2%	2-4%	5-7%	8-9%	10%	11+%	
Da1age My age-group	20-29	128	68	85	63	104	338	20	806
	30-39	145	79	97	90	145	530	45	1131
	40-49	136	71	94	136	162	660	87	1346
	50-59	116	77	101	112	147	829	142	1524
	60-69	71	53	60	93	119	758	141	1295
	70-79	37	29	28	40	61	548	103	846
	≥ 80	7	6	11	18	17	377	85	521
Total		640	383	476	552	755	4040	623	7469

Da1age My age-group * Tither Crosstabulation

		Tither			Total
		No tithe	1-8% tithe	9-10% tithe	
Da1age My age-group	20-29	129	216	458	803
	30-39	144	266	711	1121
	40-49	136	299	894	1329
	50-59	118	290	1093	1501
	60-69	72	205	989	1266
	70-79	37	97	685	819
	≥ 80	7	33	467	507
Total		643	1406	5297	7346

Da1age My age-group * b47a Sometimes I forget to tithe Crosstabulation

		b47a Sometimes I forget to tithe		Total
		No	Yes	
Da1age My age-group	20-29	348	360	708
	30-39	555	421	976
	40-49	739	399	1138
	50-59	935	386	1321
	60-69	839	285	1124
	70-79	581	156	737
	≥ 80	390	72	462
Total		4387	2079	6466

Da1age My age-group * b47b Number of times contribute tithe each year Crosstabulation

		b47b Number of times contribute tithe each year							Total
		1-3 times	4-6 times	7-11 times	12-17 times	18-24 times	25-29 times	≥ 30 times	
Da1age My age-group	20-29	120	87	92	63	24	13	42	441
	30-39	154	76	113	95	33	14	47	532
	40-49	130	87	102	113	36	17	49	534
	50-59	116	86	92	121	39	26	67	547
	60-69	74	54	85	94	26	31	63	427
	70-79	48	29	43	69	12	8	27	236
	≥ 80	17	11	16	74	8	4	15	145
Total		659	430	543	629	178	113	310	2862

Age band * 01 Tithe given as percent of income Crosstabulation

		01 Tithe given as percent of income							Total
		0%	<2%	2-4%	5-7%	8-9%	10%	11+%	
Age band	20-39	273	147	182	154	249	869	65	1939
	40-59	252	148	196	248	309	1490	229	2872
	≥ 60	109	83	91	139	182	1358	256	2218
Total		634	378	469	541	740	3717	550	7029

Age band * Tither Crosstabulation

		Tither			Total
		No tithe	1-8% tithe	9-10% tithe	
Age band	20-39	273	483	1170	1926
	40-59	254	590	1988	2832
	≥ 60	110	312	1740	2162
Total		637	1385	4898	6920

Age band * b47a Sometimes I forget to tithe Crosstabulation

		b47a Sometimes I forget to tithe		Total
		No	Yes	
Age band	20-39	904	782	1686
	40-59	1676	785	2461
	≥ 60	1472	446	1918
Total		4052	2013	6065

Age band * b47b Number of times contribute tithe each year Crosstabulation

		b47b Number of times contribute tithe each year							Total
		1-3 times	4-6 times	7-11 times	12-17 times	18-24 times	25-29 times	≥ 30 times	
Age band	20-39	274	164	205	158	57	27	89	974
	40-59	246	173	194	234	75	44	116	1082
	≥ 60	124	86	131	170	39	39	94	683
Total		644	423	530	562	171	110	299	2739

b46 I try to return tithe * Da1age My age-group Crosstabulation

		Da1age My age-group							Total
		20-29	30-39	40-49	50-59	60-69	70-79	≥ 80	
b46 I try to return tithe	Weekly	106	145	160	215	165	90	51	932
	Semi-Monthly / bi-weekly / fortnightly	168	225	268	295	265	151	50	1422
	Monthly	355	539	587	628	527	355	266	3257
	Quarterly	53	51	87	102	79	72	43	487
	Yearly	42	56	57	73	51	28	13	320
Total		724	1016	1159	1313	1087	696	423	6418

b46 I try to return tithe * b47a Sometimes I forget to tithe Crosstabulation

| | | b47a Sometimes I forget to tithe | | Total |
		No	Yes	
b46 I try to return tithe	Weekly	538	246	784
	Semi-Monthly / bi-weekly / fortnightly	919	396	1315
	Monthly	1887	803	2690
	Quarterly	176	232	408
	Yearly	168	120	288
	Total	3688	1797	5485

b46 I try to return tithe * b47b Number of times contribute tithe each year Crosstabulation

| | | b47b Number of times contribute tithe each year | | | | | | | Total |
		1-3 times	4-6 times	7-11 times	12-17 times	18-24 times	25-29 times	≥ 30 times	
b46 I try to return tithe	Weekly	85	50	58	31	14	23	103	364
	Semi-Monthly / bi-weekly / fortnightly	74	58	63	81	79	41	87	483
	Monthly	255	180	301	357	41	21	35	1190
	Quarterly	45	54	40	37	10	1	8	195
	Yearly	77	21	10	9	3	0	12	132
	Total	536	363	472	515	147	86	245	2364

Appendix E: Report on Survey Demographics and Reported Tithing Behavior — By Conference

E.1 Northern California Conference, United States

Country * D Version Crosstabulation

		D Version			Total
		9.7A	9.7B	9.7C	
Country	USA (NCC)	1107	1176	1139	3422
	Total	1107	1176	1139	3422

Da1age My age-group * a2aatte I attend an Adventist Church ... Crosstabulation

		a2aatte I attend an Adventist Church ...					Total
		Rarely/Never/ Less than once a month	1 to 9 times a year	About once a month	2 to 3 times a month	Always / Most weeks	
Da1age My age-group	20-29	2	2	4	22	99	129
	30-39	3	8	4	34	170	219
	40-49	1	5	12	49	260	327
	50-59	4	3	6	58	394	465
	60-69	0	1	10	50	430	491
	70-79	0	1	0	18	314	333
	≥ 80	0	3	3	10	240	256
	Total	10	23	39	241	1907	2220

Da1age My age-group * Da3bnumbe Number of years I have been a member of the SDA church Crosstabulation

		Da3bnumbe Number of years I have been a member of the SDA church								Total
		0-1	2-4	5-9	10-19	20-29	30-39	40-49	≥ 50	
Da1age My age-group	20-29	5	5	12	18	22	0	0	0	62
	30-39	4	11	11	17	30	41	0	1	115
	40-49	3	11	8	13	32	45	54	1	167
	50-59	10	14	13	17	19	35	65	55	228
	60-69	6	10	9	21	20	37	39	97	239
	70-79	3	6	6	11	7	9	21	105	168
	≥ 80	0	2	2	5	2	7	7	100	125
	Total	31	59	61	102	132	174	186	359	1104

Da1age My age-group * a4wageBrEnKeOzUs Self-employed or Wage-earner Crosstabulation

		a4wageBrEnKeOzUs Self-employed or Wage-earner				Total
		Self-employed	Wage/Salary earner paid monthly	Wage/Salary earner paid fortnightly/semi-monthly	Wage/Salary earner paid weekly	
Da1age My age-group	20-29	4	4	41	5	54
	30-39	14	14	64	3	95
	40-49	29	25	86	6	146
	50-59	48	33	112	12	205
	60-69	36	27	83	5	151
	70-79	14	14	25	0	53
	≥ 80	3	8	1	0	12
Total		148	125	412	31	716

Da1age My age-group * 01 Tithe given as percent of income Crosstabulation

		01 Tithe given as percent of income							Total
		0%	<2%	2-4%	5-7%	8-9%	10%	11+%	
Da1age My age-group	20-29	26	20	20	23	12	95	15	211
	30-39	34	39	20	37	14	155	25	324
	40-49	34	35	41	59	33	207	58	467
	50-59	43	46	50	54	38	353	93	677
	60-69	28	38	31	52	39	432	105	725
	70-79	19	17	16	23	17	296	86	474
	≥ 80	6	5	8	8	8	262	69	366
Total		190	200	186	256	161	1800	451	3244

Da1age My age-group * Tither Crosstabulation

		Tither			Total
		No tithe	1-8% tithe	9-10% tithe	
Da1age My age-group	20-29	27	63	115	205
	30-39	33	96	183	312
	40-49	34	133	279	446
	50-59	44	150	451	645
Total		191	637	2250	3078

Da1age My age-group * b47a Sometimes I forget to tithe Crosstabulation

| | | b47a Sometimes I forget to tithe | | Total |
		No	Yes	
Da1age My age-group	20-29	88	100	188
	30-39	173	121	294
	40-49	268	155	423
	50-59	427	196	623
	60-69	496	150	646
	70-79	348	77	425
	≥ 80	281	47	328
Total		2081	846	2927

Da1age My age-group * b47b Number of times contribute tithe each year Crosstabulation

| | | b47b Number of times contribute tithe each year | | | | | | | Total |
		1-3 times	4-6 times	7-11 times	12-17 times	18-24 times	25-29 times	≥ 30 times	
Da1age My age-group	20-29	34	27	23	22	11	5	11	133
	30-39	42	20	27	23	21	10	25	168
	40-49	37	26	37	40	21	10	27	198
	50-59	44	29	49	44	24	20	42	252
	60-69	37	23	54	55	19	23	42	253
	70-79	26	11	23	44	9	2	12	127
	≥ 80	12	8	10	61	5	3	8	107
Total		232	144	223	289	110	73	167	1238

Age-group (Simplified) * 01 Tithe given as percent of income Crosstabulation

| | | 01 Tithe given as percent of income | | | | | | | Total |
		0%	<2%	2-4%	5-7%	8-9%	10%	11+%	
Age-group	20-39	60	59	40	61	26	251	40	537
	40-59	77	81	92	113	71	561	151	1146
	≥ 60	47	55	48	75	56	734	191	1206
Total		184	195	180	249	153	1546	382	2889

Age-group (Simplified) * Tither (Simplified) Crosstabulation

| | | Tither | | | Total |
		No tithe	1-8% tithe	9-10% tithe	
Age-group	20-39	60	160	299	519
	40-59	78	284	731	1093
	≥ 60	47	177	906	1130
Total		185	621	1936	2742

Age band * b47a Sometimes I forget to tithe Crosstabulation

| | | b47a Sometimes I forget to tithe | | Total |
		No	Yes	
Age-group	20-39	262	222	484
	40-59	697	351	1048
	≥ 60	851	227	1078
Total		1810	800	2610

Age band * b47b Number of times contribute tithe each year Crosstabulation

| | | b47b Number of times contribute tithe each year | | | | | | | Total |
		1-3 times	4-6 times	7-11 times	12-17 times	18-24 times	25-29 times	≥ 30 times	
Age-group	20-39	76	48	50	45	32	15	36	302
	40-59	81	55	86	84	45	31	69	451
	≥ 60	63	34	77	102	28	25	54	383
Total		220	137	213	231	105	71	159	1136

b46 I try to return tithe * Da1age My age-group Crosstabulation

| | | Da1age My age-group | | | | | | | Total |
		20-29	30-39	40-49	50-59	60-69	70-79	≥ 80	
b46 I try to return tithe	Weekly	15	21	26	56	54	27	11	210
	Semi-Monthly / bi-weekly / fortnightly	52	74	97	127	134	33	4	521
	Monthly	41	77	140	208	255	213	192	1126
	Quarterly	13	22	32	57	52	47	35	258
	Yearly	10	18	22	30	22	9	11	122
Total		131	212	317	478	517	329	253	2237

b46 I try to return tithe * b47a Sometimes I forget to tithe Crosstabulation

| | | b47a Sometimes I forget to tithe | | Total |
		No	Yes	
b46 I try to return tithe	Weekly	140	55	195
	Semi-Monthly / bi-weekly / fortnightly	364	129	493
	Monthly	814	243	1057
	Quarterly	70	147	217
	Yearly	52	50	102
Total		1440	624	2064

b46 I try to return tithe * b47b Number of times contribute tithe each year Crosstabulation

		b47b Number of times contribute tithe each year							Total
		1-3 times	4-6 times	7-11 times	12-17 times	18-24 times	25-29 times	≥ 30 times	
b46 I try to return tithe	Weekly	26	9	11	7	5	10	37	105
	Semi-Monthly / bi-weekly / fortnightly	20	20	25	41	35	18	50	209
	Monthly	51	35	98	120	31	18	22	375
	Quarterly	19	16	16	19	7	1	3	81
	Yearly	32	11	7	3	2	0	2	57
Total		148	91	157	190	80	47	114	827

E.2 São Paulo Conference, Brazil

Country * D Version Crosstabulation

| | | D Version | | | Total |
		9.6A	9.6B	9.6C	
Country	Brazil (SPC)	838	633	685	2156

Da1age My age-group * a2aatte I attend an Adventist Church ... Crosstabulation

| | | a2aatte I attend an Adventist Church ... | | | | | Total |
		Rarely/Never/Less than once a month	1 to 9 times a year	About once a month	2 to 3 times a month	Always / Most weeks	
Da1age My age-group	20-29	0	2	5	34	151	192
	30-39	1	2	1	41	238	283
	40-49	2	2	6	28	195	233
	50-59	4	0	4	8	154	170
	60-69	1	1	2	16	84	104
	70-79	1	1	7	6	68	83
	≥ 80	1	0	0	0	14	15
Total		10	8	25	133	904	1080

Da1age My age-group * Da3bnumbe Number of years I have been a member of the SDA church Crosstabulation

| | | Da3bnumbe Number of years I have been a member of the SDA church | | | | | Total |
		0-1	2-4	5-9	10-19	20-29	
Da1age My age-group	20-29	10	10	11	41	1	73
	30-39	22	18	18	58	31	147
	40-49	14	4	8	43	51	120
	50-59	8	5	8	34	22	77
	60-69	6	6	7	27	27	73
	70-79	4	5	5	12	18	44
	≥ 80	0	1	0	3	5	9
Total		64	49	57	218	155	543

Da1age My age-group * a4wageBrEnKeOzUs Self-employed or Wage-earner Crosstabulation

		a4wageBrEnKeOzUs Self-employed or Wage-earner				Total
		Self-employed	Wage/Salary earner paid monthly	Wage/Salary earner paid fortnightly/ semi-monthly	Wage/Salary earner paid weekly	
Da1age My age-group	20-29	15	44	12	0	71
	30-39	41	83	14	1	139
	40-49	45	59	14	4	122
	50-59	27	33	5	2	67
	60-69	18	40	2	1	61
	70-79	16	23	2	0	41
	≥ 80	2	2	1	0	5
Total		164	284	50	8	506

Da1age My age-group * Yearly Income in equivalent US$ Crosstabulation

		Yearly Income in equivalent US$					
		Under US$1,000	US$1,000-$1,999	US$2,000-$4,499	US$4,500-$6,999	US$7,000-$9,999	US$10,000-$19,999
Da1age My age-group	20-29	27	10	29	67	54	97
	30-39	25	15	18	53	86	110
	40-49	23	9	26	46	51	79
	50-59	25	18	22	35	29	55
	60-69	18	11	21	25	13	36
	70-79	9	1	23	11	11	17
	≥ 80	3	0	3	5	2	6
Total		130	64	142	242	246	400

Da1age My age-group * Yearly Income in equivalent US$ Crosstabulation Continued

		$20,000-$29,999	$30,000-$39,999	$40,000-$49,999	$50,000-$74,999	$75,000-$99,999	$100,000-$125,000	≥ 125,000	Total
Da1age My age-group	20-29	17	12	4	2	0	0	0	319
	30-39	60	35	21	17	3	2	6	451
	40-49	61	31	15	18	7	3	8	377
	50-59	40	17	11	13	9	3	2	279
	60-69	15	12	9	3	2	0	1	166
	70-79	12	6	4	0	4	3	0	101
	≥ 80	1	0	0	0	0	0	0	20
Total		206	113	64	53	25	11	17	1713

Da1age My age-group * 01 Tithe given as percent of income Crosstabulation

		01 Tithe given as percent of income					Total
		0%	2-4%	5-7%	8-9%	10%	
Da1age My age-group	20-29	55	36	25	71	147	334
	30-39	68	42	22	112	218	462
	40-49	45	30	44	96	201	416
	50-59	24	18	23	75	170	310
	60-69	22	9	15	51	76	173
	70-79	6	6	8	32	53	105
	≥ 80	0	1	3	6	12	22
Total		220	142	140	443	877	1822

Da1age My age-group * Tither Crosstabulation

		Tither			Total
		No tithe	1-8% tithe	9-10% tithe	
Da1age My age-group	20-29	55	61	218	334
	30-39	68	64	330	462
	40-49	45	74	297	416
	50-59	24	41	245	310
	60-69	22	24	127	173
	70-79	6	14	85	105
	≥ 80	0	4	18	22
Total		220	282	1320	1822

Da1age My age-group * b47a Sometimes I forget to tithe Crosstabulation

		b47a Sometimes I forget to tithe		Total
		No	Yes	
Da1age My age-group	20-29	154	120	274
	30-39	196	167	363
	40-49	188	128	316
	50-59	141	82	223
	60-69	71	57	128
	70-79	41	31	72
	≥ 80	12	10	22
Total		803	595	1398

Da1age My age-group * b47b Number of times contribute tithe each year Crosstabulation

		b47b Number of times contribute tithe each year					Total
		1-3 times	4-6 times	7-11 times	12-17 times	18-24 times	
Da1age My age-group	20-29	39	33	40	32	0	144
	30-39	63	35	51	53	1	203
	40-49	37	30	38	59	0	164
	50-59	25	21	21	60	1	128
	60-69	12	12	12	25	0	61
	70-79	5	7	9	17	0	38
	≥ 80	1	0	3	5	0	9
Total		182	138	174	251	2	747

Age band * 01 Tithe given as percent of income Crosstabulation

		01 Tithe given as percent of income					Total
		0%	2-4%	5-7%	8-9%	10%	
Age-band	20-39	123	78	47	183	365	796
	40-59	69	48	67	171	371	726
	≥ 60	28	15	23	83	129	278
Total		220	141	137	437	865	1800

Age band * Tither Crosstabulation

		Tither			Total
		No tithe	1-8% tithe	9-10% tithe	
Age-group	20-39	123	125	548	796
	40-59	69	115	542	726
	≥ 60	28	38	212	278
Total		220	278	1302	1800

Age band * b47a Sometimes I forget to tithe Crosstabulation

		b47a Sometimes I forget to tithe		Total
		No	Yes	
Age-group	20-39	350	287	637
	40-59	329	210	539
	≥ 60	112	88	200
Total		791	585	1376

Age band * b47b Number of times contribute tithe each year Crosstabulation

| | | b47b Number of times contribute tithe each year | | | | | Total |
		1-3 times	4-6 times	7-11 times	12-17 times	18-24 times	
Age-group	20-39	102	68	91	85	1	347
	40-59	62	51	59	119	1	292
	≥ 60	17	19	21	42	0	99
Total		181	138	171	246	2	738

b46 I try to return tithe * Da1age My age-group Crosstabulation

| | | Da1age My age-group | | | | | | | Total |
		20-29	30-39	40-49	50-59	60-69	70-79	≥ 80	
b46 I try to return tithe	Weekly	17	24	34	28	8	4	1	116
	Semi-Monthly / bi-weekly / fortnightly	16	34	37	25	5	3	2	122
	Monthly	289	391	305	232	136	80	19	1452
	Quarterly	5	6	16	5	9	2	0	43
	Yearly	0	4	0	1	1	1	0	7
Total		327	459	392	291	159	90	22	1740

b46 I try to return tithe * b47a Sometimes I forget to tithe Crosstabulation

| | | b47a Sometimes I forget to tithe | | Total |
		No	Yes	
b46 I try to return tithe	Weekly	57	40	97
	Semi-Monthly / bi-weekly / fortnightly	50	56	106
	Monthly	713	529	1242
	Quarterly	21	9	30
	Yearly	6	1	7
Total		847	635	1482

b46 I try to return tithe * b47b Number of times contribute tithe each year Crosstabulation

| | | b47b Number of times contribute tithe each year | | | | | Total |
		1-3 times	4-6 times	7-11 times	12-17 times	18-24 times	
b46 I try to return tithe	Weekly	12	13	16	18	0	59
	Semi-Monthly / bi-weekly / fortnightly	16	14	13	18	1	62
	Monthly	156	117	157	219	1	650
	Quarterly	6	8	3	10	0	27
	Yearly	1	1	2	2	0	6
Total		191	153	191	267	2	804

E.3 South England Conference, United Kingdom

Country * D Version Crosstabulation

		D Version		Total
		9.1A	9.4B	
Country	England (SEC)	672	472	1144

Da1age My age-group * a2aatte I attend an Adventist Church ... Crosstabulation

		a2aatte I attend an Adventist Church ...					Total
		Rarely/ Never/ Less than once a month	1 to 9 times a year	About once a month	2 to 3 times a month	Always / Most weeks	
Da1age My age-group	20-29	1	0	3	5	51	60
	30-39	1	1	1	8	105	116
	40-49	1	1	4	22	181	209
	50-59	1	2	4	13	247	267
	60-69	1	1	1	15	156	174
	70-79	1	1	4	3	85	94
	≥ 80	0	1	2	4	74	81
Total		6	7	19	70	899	1001

Da1age My age-group * Da3bnumbe Number of years I have been a member of the SDA church Crosstabulation

		Da3bnumbe Number of years I have been a member of the SDA church								Total
		0-1	2-4	5-9	10-19	20-29	30-39	40-49	≥ 50	
Da1age My age-group	20-29	7	23	18	4	0	0	0	0	52
	30-39	6	18	27	29	16	0	0	0	96
	40-49	7	15	28	74	33	38	0	0	195
	50-59	13	19	10	48	77	49	43	0	259
	60-69	2	10	5	24	35	45	25	22	168
	70-79	1	1	4	11	15	13	20	22	87
	≥ 80	1	6	2	10	11	6	13	28	77
Total		37	92	94	200	187	151	101	72	934

Da1age My age-group * a4wageBrEnKeOzUs Self-employed or Wage-earner Crosstabulation

		a4wageBrEnKeOzUs Self-employed or Wage-earner				Total
		Self-employed	Wage/Salary earner paid monthly	Wage/Salary earner paid fortnightly/semi-monthly	Wage/Salary earner paid weekly	
Da1age My age-group	20-29	1	3	1	5	10
	30-39	7	51	2	18	78
	40-49	15	119	5	21	160
	50-59	27	156	3	21	207
	60-69	16	108	3	9	136
	70-79	7	23	2	3	35
	≥ 80	5	5	0	2	12
Total		78	465	16	79	638

Da1age My age-group * Yearly Income in equivalent US$ Crosstabulation

		Yearly Income in equivalent US$					
		Under US$1,000	US$1,000-$1,999	US$2,000-$4,499	US$4,500-$6,999	US$7,000-$9,999	US$10,000-$19,999
Da1age My age-group	20-29	5	1	1	4	4	0
	30-39	6	4	1	16	19	16
	40-49	3	1	1	24	21	30
	50-59	2	1	3	9	22	39
	60-69	1	1	0	7	16	27
	70-79	2	2	9	5	14	10
	≥ 80	3	1	2	8	14	15
Total		22	11	17	73	110	137

Da1age My age-group * Yearly Income in equivalent US$ Crosstabulation (Continued)

		$20,000-$29,999	$30,000-$39,999	$40,000-$49,999	$50,000-$74,999	$75,000-$99,999	$100,000-$125,000	Total
Da1age My age-group	20-29	1	0	0	1	0	0	17
	30-39	14	5	3	2	0	0	86
	40-49	30	14	25	8	0	1	158
	50-59	45	31	37	22	2	1	214
	60-69	35	13	21	13	2	0	136
	70-79	17	4	2	4	0	1	70
	≥ 80	12	0	3	1	2	1	62
Total		154	67	91	51	6	4	743

Da1age My age-group * 01 Tithe given as percent of income Crosstabulation

		01 Tithe given as percent of income							Total
		0%	<2%	2-4%	5-7%	8-9%	10%	11+%	
Da1age My age-group	20-29	13	7	6	3	3	12	2	46
	30-39	17	19	12	16	3	41	3	111
	40-49	28	24	14	15	17	81	17	196
	50-59	28	23	20	16	18	120	29	254
	60-69	10	12	14	11	17	77	20	161
	70-79	6	7	5	5	7	47	8	85
	≥ 80	1	1	2	6	2	47	12	71
Total		103	93	73	72	67	425	91	924

Da1age My age-group * Tither Crosstabulation

		Tither			Total
		No tithe	1-8% tithe	9-10% tithe	
Da1age My age-group	20-29	13	16	17	46
	30-39	17	47	47	111
	40-49	28	53	115	196
	50-59	28	59	167	254
	60-69	10	37	114	161
	70-79	6	17	62	85
	≥ 80	1	9	61	71
Total		103	238	583	924

Da1age My age-group * b47a Sometimes I forget to tithe Crosstabulation

		b47a Sometimes I forget to tithe		Total
		No	Yes	
Da1age My age-group	20-29	14	9	23
	30-39	44	36	80
	40-49	102	21	123
	50-59	150	27	177
	60-69	91	21	112
	70-79	49	11	60
	≥ 80	46	5	51
Total		496	130	626

Da1age My age-group * b47b Number of times contribute tithe each year Crosstabulation

		1-3 times	4-6 times	7-11 times	12-17 times	18-24 times	25-29 times	≥ 30 times	Total
Da1age My age-group	20-29	12	7	7	1	1	3	6	37
	30-39	24	7	22	8	0	0	6	67
	40-49	34	17	12	8	6	3	10	90
	50-59	28	22	17	9	4	1	10	91
	60-69	15	8	14	9	1	1	9	57
	70-79	8	4	9	5	3	1	4	34
	≥ 80	2	3	3	5	1	0	4	18
Total		123	68	84	45	16	9	49	394

Age-group * 01 Tithe given as percent of income Crosstabulation

		0%	<2%	2-4%	5-7%	8-9%	10%	11+%	Total
Age-group	20-39	30	26	18	19	6	53	5	157
	40-59	56	47	34	31	35	201	46	450
	≥ 60	17	20	21	22	26	171	40	317
Total		103	93	73	72	67	425	91	924

Age-group * Tither Crosstabulation

		Tither			Total
		No tithe	1-8% tithe	9-10% tithe	
Age-group	20-39	30	63	64	157
	40-59	56	112	282	450
	≥ 60	17	63	237	317
Total		103	238	583	924

Age-group * b47a Sometimes I forget to tithe Crosstabulation

		b47a Sometimes I forget to tithe		Total
		No	Yes	
Age-group	20-39	58	45	103
	40-59	252	48	300
	≥ 60	186	37	223
Total		496	130	626

Age-group * b47b Number of times contribute tithe each year Crosstabulation

		b47b Number of times contribute tithe each year							Total
		1-3 times	4-6 times	7-11 times	12-17 times	18-24 times	25-29 times	≥ 30 times	
Age-group	20-39	36	14	29	9	1	3	12	104
	40-59	62	39	29	17	10	4	20	181
	≥ 60	25	15	26	19	5	2	17	109
Total		123	68	84	45	16	9	49	394

b46 I try to return tithe * Da1age My age-group Crosstabulation

		Da1age My age-group							Total
		20-29	30-39	40-49	50-59	60-69	70-79	≥ 80	
b46 I try to return tithe	Weekly	21	33	32	47	27	24	27	211
	Semi-Monthly / bi-weekly / fortnightly	2	4	9	7	4	4	4	34
	Monthly	18	61	130	179	120	54	48	610
	Quarterly	5	4	8	9	4	7	2	39
	Yearly	3	7	1	2	3	0	0	16
Total		49	109	180	244	158	89	81	910

b46 I try to return tithe * b47a Sometimes I forget to tithe Crosstabulation

		b47a Sometimes I forget to tithe		Total
		No	Yes	
b46 I try to return tithe	Weekly	99	38	137
	Semi-Monthly / bi-weekly / fortnightly	14	5	19
	Monthly	372	65	437
	Quarterly	18	7	25
	Yearly	6	5	11
Total		509	120	629

b46 I try to return tithe * b47b Number of times contribute tithe each year Crosstabulation

		b47b Number of times contribute tithe each year							Total
		1-3 times	4-6 times	7-11 times	12-17 times	18-24 times	25-29 times	≥ 30 times	
b46 I try to return tithe	Weekly	33	13	14	5	7	5	26	103
	Semi-Monthly / bi-weekly / fortnightly	6	1	3	0	1	1	4	16
	Monthly	59	40	65	40	7	3	12	226
	Quarterly	3	9	4	1	0	0	1	18
	Yearly	7	2	1	1	0	0	2	13
Total		108	65	87	47	15	9	45	376

E.4 Western Australia Conference, Australia

Country * D Version Crosstabulation

		D Version	Total
		7.1	
Country	Australia (WAC)	1209	1209

Da1age My age-group * a2aatte I attend an Adventist Church ... Crosstabulation

		Rarely/ Never/Less than once a month	1 to 9 times a year	About once a month	2 to 3 times a month	Always / Most weeks	Total
Da1age My age-group	20-29	0	3	10	170	3	186
	30-39	1	1	14	161	7	185
	40-49	0	4	13	180	6	203
	50-59	1	3	11	223	4	243
	60-69	0	2	5	186	2	195
	70-79	0	2	5	132	2	141
	≥ 80	0	0	0	29	0	29
Total		2	15	58	1081	24	1182

Da1age My age-group * Da3bnumbe Number of years I have been a member of the SDA church Crosstabulation

		Da3bnumbe Number of years I have been a member of the SDA church								Total
		0-1	2-4	5-9	10-19	20-29	30-39	40-49	≥ 50	
Da1age My age-group	20-29	4	21	44	66	20	0	0	0	155
	30-39	2	3	12	70	62	17	1	0	167
	40-49	5	2	12	29	57	60	22	0	187
	50-59	5	5	9	25	41	59	68	13	225
	60-69	4	5	8	13	22	30	62	50	194
	70-79	1	0	5	6	15	16	30	65	138
	≥ 80	0	1	2	1	6	1	3	16	30
Total		21	37	92	210	223	183	186	144	1096

Da1age My age-group * a4employBrEnKeOzUs Crosstabulation

		a4employBrEnKeOzUs				Total
		Employed full time	Employed part time	Retired	Not currently employed	
Da1age My age-group	20-29	64	48	1	44	157
	30-39	60	47	3	42	152
	40-49	80	45	5	28	158
	50-59	80	53	32	25	190
	60-69	25	19	129	6	179
	70-79	1	0	141	3	145
	≥ 80	0	0	31	1	32
Total		310	212	342	149	1013

Da1age My age-group * Da4wage Wage/salary earner or Self-employed Crosstabulation

		Da4wage Wage/salary earner or Self-employed			Total
		Not Employed	Wage/Salary Earner	Self-employed	
Da1age My age-group	20-29	46	82	15	143
	30-39	45	79	29	153
	40-49	32	108	38	178
	50-59	56	108	48	212
	60-69	122	28	29	179
	70-79	127	2	9	138
	≥ 80	29	0	1	30
Total		457	407	169	1033

Da1age My age-group * Yearly Income in equivalent US$ Crosstabulation

		Yearly Income in equivalent US$							Total
		≤ $9,999	$10,000-$19,999	$20,000-$29,999	$30,000-$39,999	$40,000-$49,999	$50,000-$74,999	≥ $75,000	
Da1age My age-group	20-29	18	33	40	26	9	12	2	140
	30-39	10	30	29	27	17	31	5	149
	40-49	14	33	34	24	23	38	9	175
	50-59	17	35	50	40	23	37	3	205
	60-69	29	62	44	8	8	15	2	168
	70-79	13	67	25	8	2	5	1	121
	≥ 80	6	12	3	0	1	0	0	22
Total		107	272	225	133	83	138	22	980

Da1age My age-group * 01 Tithe given as percent of income Crosstabulation

| | | 01 Tithe given as percent of income | | | | | | | Total |
		0%	<2%	2-4%	5-7%	8-9%	10%	11+%	
Da1age My age-group	20-29	29	32	20	9	14	69	2	175
	30-39	18	17	17	12	12	81	12	169
	40-49	21	8	7	13	12	124	5	190
	50-59	16	6	10	16	11	139	16	214
	60-69	6	3	6	11	9	122	14	171
	70-79	3	4	1	1	4	108	7	128
	≥ 80	0	0	0	1	1	18	2	22
Total		93	70	61	63	63	661	58	1069

Da1age My age-group * Tither Crosstabulation

| | | Tither | | | Total |
		No tithe	1-8% tithe	9-10% tithe	
Da1age My age-group	20-29	29	61	86	176
	30-39	18	46	107	171
	40-49	21	28	143	192
	50-59	17	32	174	223
	60-69	6	20	155	181
	70-79	3	6	124	133
	≥ 80	0	1	25	26
Total		94	194	814	1102

Da1age My age-group * b47a Sometimes I forget to tithe Crosstabulation

| | | b47a Sometimes I forget to tithe | | Total |
		No	Yes	
Da1age My age-group	20-29	71	110	181
	30-39	99	74	173
	40-49	125	72	197
	50-59	167	60	227
	60-69	132	46	178
	70-79	102	29	131
	≥ 80	16	8	24
Total		712	399	1111

Da1age My age-group * b47b Number of times contribute tithe each year Crosstabulation

		b47b Number of times contribute tithe each year							Total
		1-3 times	4-6 times	7-11 times	12-17 times	18-24 times	25-29 times	≥ 30 times	
Da1age My age-group	20-29	29	18	19	5	10	4	22	107
	30-39	17	11	10	8	11	4	9	70
	40-49	18	8	14	5	6	3	9	63
	50-59	16	7	2	7	8	5	11	56
	60-69	7	10	5	5	6	5	7	45
	70-79	7	5	2	3	0	3	8	28
	≥ 80	0	0	0	3	2	1	2	8
Total		94	59	52	36	43	25	68	377

Age-group * 01 Tithe given as percent of income Crosstabulation

		01 Tithe given as percent of income							Total
		0%	<2%	2-4%	5-7%	8-9%	10%	11+%	
Age-group	20-39	47	49	37	21	26	150	14	344
	40-59	37	14	17	29	23	263	21	404
	≥ 60	9	7	7	12	13	230	21	299
Total		93	70	61	62	62	643	56	1047

Age-group * Tither Crosstabulation

		Tither			Total
		No tithe	1-8% tithe	9-10% tithe	
Age-group	20-39	47	107	193	347
	40-59	38	60	317	415
	≥ 60	9	26	279	314
Total		94	193	789	1076

Age-group * b47a Sometimes I forget to tithe Crosstabulation

		b47a Sometimes I forget to tithe		Total
		No	Yes	
Age-group	20-39	170	184	354
	40-59	292	132	424
	≥ 60	234	75	309
Total		696	391	1087

Age-group * b47b Number of times contribute tithe each year Crosstabulation

		b47b Number of times contribute tithe each year							Total
		1-3 times	4-6 times	7-11 times	12-17 times	18-24 times	25-29 times	≥ 30 times	
Age-group	20-39	46	29	29	13	21	8	31	177
	40-59	34	15	16	12	14	8	20	119
	≥ 60	14	15	7	8	6	8	15	73
Total		94	59	52	33	41	24	66	369

b46 I try to return tithe * Da1age My age-group Crosstabulation

		Da1age My age-group							Total
		20-29	30-39	40-49	50-59	60-69	70-79	≥ 80	
b46 I try to return tithe	Weekly	41	49	48	65	52	29	7	291
	Semi-Monthly / bi-weekly / fortnightly	77	80	88	98	90	74	15	522
	Monthly	6	8	7	9	12	4	4	50
	Quarterly	27	15	21	26	12	13	0	114
	Yearly	23	20	27	34	20	12	2	138
Total		174	172	191	232	186	132	28	1115

b46 I try to return tithe * b47a Sometimes I forget to tithe Crosstabulation

		b47a Sometimes I forget to tithe		Total
		No	Yes	
b46 I try to return tithe	Weekly	186	92	278
	Semi-Monthly / bi-weekly / fortnightly	333	162	495
	Monthly	40	10	50
	Quarterly	51	59	110
	Yearly	83	49	132
Total		693	372	1065

b46 I try to return tithe * b47b Number of times contribute tithe each year Crosstabulation

		b47b Number of times contribute tithe each year							Total
		1-3 times	4-6 times	7-11 times	12-17 times	18-24 times	25-29 times	≥ 30 times	
b46 I try to return tithe	Weekly	13	15	14	4	2	8	32	88
	Semi-Monthly / bi-weekly / fortnightly	25	21	20	17	35	17	22	157
	Monthly	0	0	2	4	2	0	1	9
	Quarterly	16	16	15	6	3	0	3	59
	Yearly	29	3	0	3	1	0	7	43
Total		83	55	51	34	43	25	65	356

Appendix F: Report on on Selected Items fromScales Measuring Beliefs, Motives and Attitudes (Four Countries)

Motive M1: A Biblical Requirement

Country * m1b22 The Bible is clear that I should give 10% of my income as tithe Crosstabulation

		Strongly Disagree	Disagree More Than Agree	Agree More Than Disagree	Strongly Agree	Total
Country	Australia (WAC)	52	41	196	1317	1606
	England (SEC)	48	14	59	825	946
	Brazil (SPC)	46	12	28	628	714
	USA (NCC)	40	37	99	880	1058
	Total	186	104	382	3650	4324

Motive M2: God Will Bless

Country * m2b10 God will protect me from future harm if I return tithe Crosstabulation

		m2b10 God will protect me from future harm if I return tithe				Total
		Strongly Disagree	Disagree More Than Agree	Agree More Than Disagree	Strongly Agree	
Country	Australia (WAC)	561	389	329	301	1580
	England (SEC)	233	136	188	290	847
	Brazil (SPC)	218	108	146	284	756
	USA (NCC)	300	185	305	243	1033
	Total	1312	818	968	1118	4216

Motive M3: Church as Family

Country * m3c01 My local church feels like my extended family Crosstabulation

		m3c01 My local church feels like my extended family				Total
		Strongly Disagree	Disagree More Than Agree	Agree More Than Disagree	Strongly Agree	
Country	Australia (WAC)	57	145	581	830	1613
	England (SEC)	48	91	298	503	940
	Brazil (SPC)	43	64	162	441	710
	USA (NCC)	32	83	360	577	1052
	Total	180	383	1401	2351	4315

Motive M4: Gratitude

Country * m4b11 I show my gratitude to God by returning tithe Crosstabulation

		m4b11 I show my gratitude to God by returning tithe				
		Strongly Disagree	Disagree More Than Agree	Agree More Than Disagree	Strongly Agree	Total
Country	Australia (WAC)	69	68	317	1156	1610
	England (SEC)	59	35	112	696	902
	Brazil (SPC)	47	27	46	604	724
	USA (NCC)	46	51	162	799	1058
	Total	221	181	637	3255	4294

Motive M5: Pay Your Way

Country * m5b25 I need to contribute my tithe and offerings so the church can continue its work Crosstabulation

		m5b25 I need to contribute my tithe and offerings so the church can continue its work				Total
		Strongly Disagree	Disagree More Than Agree	Agree More Than Disagree	Strongly Agree	
Country	Australia (WAC)	44	101	502	958	1605
	England (SEC)	45	17	124	735	921
	Brazil (SPC)	35	15	53	609	712
	USA (NCC)	36	49	205	760	1050
	Total	160	182	884	3062	4288

Belief B1: Bible is Rule of Faith

Country * b1b33The Bible provides detailed guidance for my life Crosstabulation

		b1b33The Bible provides detailed guidance for my life				
		Strongly Disagree	Disagree More Than Agree	Agree More Than Disagree	Strongly Agree	Total
Country	Australia (WAC)	39	48	324	1194	1605
	England (SEC)	33	12	82	790	917
	Brazil (SPC)	35	7	33	638	713
	USA (NCC)	19	26	163	856	1064
	Total	126	93	602	3478	4299

Belief B3: Belief in Global Mission of SDA Church

Country * b3c16 I believe the SDA church has a mission to the whole world Crosstabulation

		b3c16/c02 I believe the SDA church has a mission to the whole world				
		Strongly Disagree	Disagree More Than Agree	Agree More Than Disagree	Strongly Agree	Total
Country	Australia (WAC)	26	24	210	1339	1599
	England (SEC)	28	10	103	816	957
	Brazil (SPC)	25	4	39	626	694
	USA (NCC)	22	16	131	892	1061
	Total	101	54	483	3673	4311

Belief B4: Strategically Valuable to Pool Tithe

Country * b4b13 If not pooled bigger churches would have too much money and the smaller churches not enough Crosstabulation

		b4b13 If not pooled bigger churches would have too much money and the smaller churches not enough				
		Strongly Disagree	Disagree More Than Agree	Agree More Than Disagree	Strongly Agree	Total
Country	Australia (WAC)	109	160	489	832	1590
	England (SEC)	121	91	241	347	800
	Brazil (SPC)	104	85	128	390	707
	USA (NCC)	100	147	341	402	990
	Total	434	483	1199	1971	4087

Belief B5: Church Not Needy

Country * b5c17 The Adventist Church has enough money to operate without my tithe Crosstabulation

		b5c17 The Adventist Church has enough money to operate without my tithe				Total
		Strongly Disagree	Disagree More Than Agree	Agree More Than Disagree	Strongly Agree	
Country	Australia (WAC)	897	373	233	85	1588
	England (SEC)	410	247	161	92	910
	Brazil (SPC)	497	67	55	64	683
	USA (NCC)	440	316	191	96	1043
	Total	2244	1003	640	337	4224

Attitude A1: Confidence in SDA Church Admin

Country * a1c12 I trust the handling and allocation of funds by the conference, union and division leaders Crosstabulation

		a1c12 I trust the handling and allocation of funds by the conference, union and division leaders				Total
		Strongly Disagree	Disagree More Than Agree	Agree More Than Disagree	Strongly Agree	
Country	Australia (WAC)	78	175	617	726	1596
	England (SEC)	67	117	343	396	923
	Brazil (SPC)	32	90	187	400	709
	USA (NCC)	69	144	413	423	1049
	Total	246	526	1560	1945	4277

Attitude A3: Comfort as SDA

Country * a3c05 I enjoy being an Adventist Crosstabulation

		a3c05 I enjoy being an Adventist				Total
		Strongly Disagree	Disagree More Than Agree	Agree More Than Disagree	Strongly Agree	
Country	Australia (WAC)	28	46	307	1225	1606
	England (SEC)	26	29	156	745	956
	Brazil (SPC)	32	8	43	626	709
	USA (NCC)	16	33	195	806	1050
	Total	102	116	701	3402	4321

Attitude A4: Attitude to Local Pastor

Country * a4c06 Overall, my church pastor is doing a good job Crosstabulation

| | | a4c06 Overall, my church pastor is doing a good job | | | | |
		Strongly Disagree	Disagree More Than Agree	Agree More Than Disagree	Strongly Agree	Total
Country	Australia (WAC)	64	112	489	921	1586
	England (SEC)	36	54	266	579	935
	Brazil (SPC)	28	40	160	480	708
	USA (NCC)	36	47	263	691	1037
	Total	164	253	1178	2671	4266

Attitude A5: God in Control of my Life

Country * a5c20 God is in control of everything in my life Crosstabulation

| | | a5c20 God is in control of everything in my life | | | | |
		Strongly Disagree	Disagree More Than Agree	Agree More Than Disagree	Strongly Agree	Total
Country	Australia (WAC)	28	71	435	1061	1595
	England (SEC)	27	15	78	827	947
	Brazil (SPC)	31	6	60	598	695
	USA (NCC)	21	47	248	743	1059
	Total	107	139	821	3229	4296

Attitude A6: OK to Divert Tithe

Country * a6b34 I feel there is nothing wrong in giving tithe to special projects (such as a new church building) Crosstabulation

| | | a6b34 I feel there is nothing wrong in giving tithe to special projects (such as a new church building) | | | | |
		Strongly Disagree	Disagree More Than Agree	Agree More Than Disagree	Strongly Agree	Total
Country	Australia (WAC)	648	198	284	429	1559
	England (SEC)	186	87	176	455	904
	Brazil (SPC)	153	35	64	262	514
	USA (NCC)	384	139	173	331	1027
	Total	1371	459	697	1477	4004

Country * a6b35 I feel there is nothing wrong in giving tithe directly to the mission field Crosstabulation

| | | a6b35 I feel there is nothing wrong in giving tithe directly to the mission field | | | | Total |
		Strongly Disagree	Disagree More Than Agree	Agree More Than Disagree	Strongly Agree	
Country	Australia (WAC)	572	197	337	447	1553
	England (SEC)	160	118	207	374	859
	Brazil (SPC)	122	45	80	202	449
	USA (NCC)	327	152	217	319	1015
Total		1181	512	841	1342	3876

Country * a6b36 I feel there is nothing wrong in giving tithe to assist student missionaries working in my local church Crosstabulation

| | | a6b36 I feel there is nothing wrong in giving tithe to assist student missionaries working in my local church | | | | Total |
		Strongly Disagree	Disagree More Than Agree	Agree More Than Disagree	Strongly Agree	
Country	Australia (WAC)	568	227	355	396	1546
	England (SEC)	178	104	216	351	849
	Brazil (SPC)	152	45	76	174	447
	USA (NCC)	343	170	229	251	993
Total		1241	546	876	1172	3835

Country * a6b37 I feel there is nothing wrong in giving tithe to the offering that supports the local SDA school Crosstabulation

| | | a6b37 I feel there is nothing wrong in giving tithe to the offering that supports the local SDA school | | | | Total |
		Strongly Disagree	Disagree More Than Agree	Agree More Than Disagree	Strongly Agree	
Country	Australia (WAC)	656	232	294	365	1547
	England (SEC)	170	102	215	370	857
	Brazil (SPC)	185	52	71	136	444
	USA (NCC)	366	133	214	283	996
Total		1377	519	794	1154	3844

Country * a6b40 I feel there is nothing wrong in giving tithe to help needy people through the Red Cross or the Salvation Army Crosstabulation

| | | a6b40 I feel there is nothing wrong in giving tithe to help needy people through the Red Cross or the Salvation Army | | | | |
		Strongly Disagree	Disagree More Than Agree	Agree More Than Disagree	Strongly Agree	Total
Country	Australia (WAC)	748	241	245	313	1547
	England (SEC)	213	128	188	320	849
	Brazil (SPC)	170	45	70	155	440
	Total	1131	414	503	788	2836

Adventist Package P1A: No Alcohol, Smoking, Drugs

Country * p1c31 To be a Seventh-day Adventist, it is very important to abstain from alcohol Crosstabulation

| | | p1c31 To be a Seventh-day Adventist, it is very important to abstain from alcohol | | | | Total |
		Strongly Disagree	Disagree More Than Agree	Agree More Than Disagree	Strongly Agree	
Country	Australia (WAC)	98	81	177	1210	1566
	England (SEC)	60	23	103	776	962
	Brazil (SPC)	72	12	32	388	504
	USA (NCC)	88	78	178	748	1092
	Total	318	194	490	3122	4124

Country * p1c34 To be a Seventh-day Adventist, it is very important to abstain from illegal drugs Crosstabulation

| | | p1c34 To be a Seventh-day Adventist, it is very important to abstain from illegal drugs | | | | Total |
		Strongly Disagree	Disagree More Than Agree	Agree More Than Disagree	Strongly Agree	
Country	Australia (WAC)	100	17	59	1388	1564
	England (SEC)	70	7	23	858	958
	Brazil (SPC)	58	5	12	384	459
	USA (NCC)	87	30	91	886	1094
	Total	315	59	185	3516	4075

Country * p1c36 To be a Seventh-day Adventist, it is very important to abstain from smoking Crosstabulation

| | | p1c36 To be a Seventh-day Adventist, it is very important to abstain from smoking | | | | Total |
		Strongly Disagree	Disagree More Than Agree	Agree More Than Disagree	Strongly Agree	
Country	Australia (WAC)	108	59	116	1292	1575
	England (SEC)	68	14	44	823	949
	Brazil (SPC)	56	9	11	368	444
	USA (NCC)	192	205	234	459	1090
	Total	424	287	405	2942	4058

Adventist Package P1B: No Meat, Coffee, Pepsi

Country * p1c32 To be a Seventh-day Adventist, it is very important to abstain from Coca-Cola and Pepsi Crosstabulation

| | | p1c32 To be a Seventh-day Adventist, it is very important to abstain from Coca-Cola and Pepsi | | | | Total |
		Strongly Disagree	Disagree More Than Agree	Agree More Than Disagree	Strongly Agree	
Country	Australia (WAC)	235	323	391	606	1555
	England (SEC)	94	118	223	503	938
	Brazil (SPC)	54	41	93	259	447
	USA (NCC)	129	126	216	621	1092
	Total	512	608	923	1989	4032

Country * p1c35 To be a Seventh-day Adventist, it is very important to abstain from tea and coffee Crosstabulation

| | | p1c35 To be a Seventh-day Adventist, it is very important to abstain from tea and coffee | | | | Total |
		Strongly Disagree	Disagree More Than Agree	Agree More Than Disagree	Strongly Agree	
Country	Australia (WAC)	293	385	429	459	1566
	England (SEC)	129	145	236	418	928
	Brazil (SPC)	52	53	86	263	454
	USA (NCC)	254	278	285	266	1083
	Total	728	861	1036	1406	4031

Country * p1c37 To be a Seventh-day Adventist, it is very important to abstain from eating meat Crosstabulation

| | | p1c37 To be a Seventh-day Adventist, it is very important to abstain from eating meat | | | | Total |
		Strongly Disagree	Disagree More Than Agree	Agree More Than Disagree	Strongly Agree	
Country	Australia (WAC)	333	394	470	372	1569
	England (SEC)	217	239	274	193	923
	Brazil (SPC)	71	87	120	178	456
	USA (NCC)	210	236	335	303	1084
	Total	831	956	1199	1046	4032

Adventist Package P2: Personal Piety

Country * p2c38 Do you attend Sabbath school Crosstabulation

| | | p2c38 Do you attend Sabbath school | | | | Total |
		Never	Sometimes	Often	Almost always	
Country	Australia (WAC)	141	186	171	1090	1588
	England (SEC)	54	156	170	585	965
	Brazil (SPC)	57	96	86	287	527
	USA (NCC)	77	200	155	634	1066
	Total	329	638	582	2596	4146

Country * p2c39 Do you open and close Sabbath Crosstabulation

| | | p2c39 Do you open and close Sabbath | | | | Total |
		Never	Sometimes	Often	Almost always	
Country	Australia (WAC)	265	491	383	435	1575
	England (SEC)	81	281	229	315	906
	Brazil (SPC)	95	147	128	122	494
	USA (NCC)	135	262	205	375	977
	Total	576	1181	945	1247	3952

Country * p2c40 Do you study the Sabbath-School quarterly Crosstabulation

| | | p2c40 Do you study the Sabbath-School quarterly | | | | Total |
		Never	Sometimes	Often	Almost always	
Country	Australia (WAC)	285	412	361	526	1584
	England (SEC)	104	289	204	324	921
	Brazil (SPC)	56	112	143	192	504
	USA (NCC)	244	344	149	294	1031
	Total	689	1157	857	1336	4040

Country * p2c41 Do you pray often during the day Crosstabulation

		p2c41 Do you pray often during the day				Total
		Never	Sometimes	Often	Almost always	
Country	Australia (WAC)	35	253	544	760	1592
	England (SEC)	19	172	276	474	941
	Brazil (SPC)	17	132	153	207	509
	USA (NCC)	11	123	243	697	1074
	Total	82	680	1216	2138	4116

Country * p2c43 Do you attend prayer meetings Crosstabulation

		p2c43 Do you attend prayer meetings				Total
		Never	Sometimes	Often	Almost always	
Country	Australia (WAC)	555	459	256	288	1558
	England (SEC)	223	395	146	177	941
	USA (NCC)	316	332	145	250	1043
	Total	1094	1186	547	715	3542